KEEPING AMERICA SANE

CORNELL STUDIES IN THE HISTORY OF PSYCHIATRY

Edited by Sander L. Gilman and George J. Makari

KEEPING AMERICA SANE

PSYCHIATRY AND EUGENICS
IN THE UNITED STATES
AND CANADA, 1880–1940

IAN ROBERT DOWBIGGIN

CORNELL UNIVERSITY PRESS

ITHACA AND LONDON

Copyright © 1997 by Cornell University

All rights reserved. Except for brief quotations in a review, this book, or parts thereof, must not be reproduced in any form without permission in writing from the publisher. For information, address Cornell University Press, Sage House, 512 East State Street, Ithaca, New York 14850.

First published 1997 by Cornell University Press.

Printed in the United States of America.

Cornell University Press strives to utilize environmentally responsible suppliers and materials to the fullest extent possible in the publishing of its books. Such materials include vegetable-based, low-VOC inks, and acid-free papers that are also either recycled, totally chlorine-free, or partly composed of nonwood fibers.

Library of Congress Cataloging-in-Publication Data

Dowbiggin, Ian Robert, 1952–
    Keeping America sane : psychiatry and eugenics in the United
States and Canada, 1880–1940 / Ian Robert Dowbiggin.
        p.   cm. — (Cornell studies in the history of psychiatry)
    Includes index.
    ISBN 0-8014-3356-8 (alk. paper). — ISBN 0-8014-8398-0 (pbk. : alk. paper)
        1. Mental illness—Prevention—Government policy—United States.   2. Eugenics—
United States.   3. Mental illness—Prevention—Government policy—Canada.
4. Eugenics—Canada.   I. Title.   II. Series.
RA790.5.D69   1997
616.89'00973—dc21   97-3425

Cloth printing   10 9 8 7 6 5 4 3 2 1

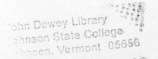

CONTENTS

PREFACE

ew health care issues today are more controversial than the growth of reproductive and genetic technologies. In vitro fertilization, sperm banks, gene-splicing, genetic screening and counseling—while some demand access to these technologies and services, others fear that their use will adversely affect matters ranging from job prospects, immigration policy, and health care rationing, to the freedom to bear children. Many of the alarmed openly express their fear that breakthroughs in genetic and reproductive technologies signal a return of the eugenics movement that swept much of the globe in the early twentieth century.

The term *eugenics* is derived from the Greek word meaning "wellborn." Charles Darwin's cousin Francis Galton, who coined the term in 1883, defined eugenics as "the study of the agencies under social control that may improve or impair the racial qualities of future generations, either physically or mentally."[1] Following Galton's lead, eugenicists began arguing that measures such as involuntary sterilization, marriage laws, immigration restriction, and the segregation of the mentally hand-

1. Francis Galton, *Inquiries into Human Faculty and Its Development* (New York: Dutton, 1907), p. 17 n.

icapped were necessary to prevent the inheritance of pathological traits. Obviously someone was listening. By 1940, thirty American states had at one time or another passed sterilization laws for the mentally ill. The U.S. federal government enacted immigration laws that sharply reduced the influx of aliens from southern and eastern Europe. In Canada, Parliament passed analogous though somewhat less draconian immigration legislation, and sterilization laws were introduced in two provinces. In both countries, politicians also spent large amounts of money building custodial institutions for the mentally ill. Physicians in general and psychiatrists in particular played pivotal roles in the history of these eugenic policies.

The specter of eugenics also haunts the controversy sparked by the publication of Charles Murray and Richard J. Herrnstein's *The Bell Curve: Intelligence and Class Structure in American Life* (1994). *The Bell Curve* argues that among blacks, whites, Asians, and other groups there are significant statistical differences in intelligence that cannot be erased by government measures designed to equalize social, economic, and educational opportunities. Reaction to Murray and Herrnstein's thesis dramatizes the fact that lurking behind many objections to *The Bell Curve* is the allegation that its thesis, eugenics, and much of the current interest in genetics can be directly linked to the genocidal atrocities of the Nazi Third Reich.[2] Indeed, in the 1930s the Nazi state, citing U.S. sterilization legislation as precedent, launched involuntary sterilization and euthanasia programs that targeted handicapped men, women, and children. Although exact data are not available, the most reliable estimate is that during the Third Reich some 375,000 persons were sterilized and roughly 80,000 were euthanized (including 5,000 children). According to one historian, these eugenic policies were actually "the first chapter" of

2. As one scholar has written, some critics try to discredit *The Bell Curve* by "conjur[ing] up fearful memories of Nazi eugenics run wild." Richard A. Soloway, *Demography and Degeneration: Eugenics and the Declining Birthrate in Twentieth-Century Britain*, 2d ed. (Chapel Hill: University of North Carolina Press, 1995), p. xii.

3. Henry Friedlander, *The Origins of Nazi Genocide: From Euthanasia to the Final Solution* (Chapel Hill: University of North Carolina Press, 1995), pp. xii, 30, 61, 85. See also Stefan Kühl, *The Nazi Connection: Eugenics, American Racism, and German National Socialism* (New York: Oxford University Press, 1994). For accounts of the role of German physicians in the history of eugenics, see Michael Kater, *Doctors under Hitler* (Chapel Hill: University of North Carolina Press, 1989); Robert Proctor, *Racial Hygiene: Medicine under the Nazis* (Cambridge: Harvard University Press, 1988); and Paul Weindling, *Health, Race, and German Politics between National Unification and Nazism, 1870–1945* (Cambridge: Cambridge University Press, 1989). See also Kristie Macrakis, "Coming to Terms with Medicine and Eugenics in Germany: An Essay Review," *Journal of the History of Medicine and Allied Sciences* 46 (1991): 97–109; and Robert Gellately, "Medicine and Collaboration under Hitler," *Canadian Journal of History* 26 (1991): 479–85.

the Holocaust.[3] Little wonder, then, that deep feelings are inflamed when anything remotely resembling eugenics is proposed today.[4]

With so much of the criticism of eugenics hinging on the use of examples from the past, it is all the more important to separate historical fact from fiction. Such is my aim in this book, an inquiry into the role of U.S. and Canadian psychiatrists in the eugenics movement. The project's origins date back to the winter of 1989/90 when I was introduced to the correspondence and personal papers of G. Alder Blumer. From 1899 to 1921, Blumer was the head psychiatrist of the Butler Hospital of Providence, Rhode Island, one of the best-known mental hospitals on either side of the Atlantic Ocean. While reading these materials I came to two chief conclusions: first, that Blumer had once been a convinced eugenicist; and second, that his papers constituted one of the most important unpublished sources for the history of Anglo-American psychiatry, offering an intriguing glimpse into the mental processes of an influential U.S. psychiatrist. As a historian of psychiatry I hoped that my work in the Butler archives would be the first step toward answering questions that scholars have hitherto overlooked: Why and to what extent did psychiatrists actually endorse eugenics? What caused so many psychiatrists to admire eugenics? How responsible were they for eugenic laws? When did psychiatric support for eugenics begin and when—if ever—did it end? These questions led me well beyond the Blumer papers, to analyze the lives and careers of such prominent psychiatrists as Charles Kirk Clarke, Thomas Salmon, Clare Hincks, Helen MacMurchy, and William Partlow. These people figure prominently because their impressions of and attitudes toward eugenics typified those of many psychiatrists. By examining their views of eugenics and those of other psychiatrists, I hope not only to document the integral history of eugenics and psychiatry but to shed some light on the present-day public debate over genetics and human reproduction. It is for the reader to decide if these hopes have been realized.

Briefly, in this book I argue, in contrast to many accounts of the history of eugenics which stress the decisive power of racial, class, and gender prejudice, that psychiatrists were drawn to eugenics largely for profes-

4. For samples of the debate over eugenics, see Cecily Ross, "Birth of a Notion," *Next City*, summer 1996; 28–32, 55–56; "Eugenics Movement Revival?" *Montreal Gazette*, 31 December 1995; David L. Wheeler, "The Biology of Crime: Protesters Disrupt Meeting on Possible Genetic Basis of Criminal Behavior," *Chronicle of Higher Education*, 6 October 1995, A10–A11; Varda Burstyn, "Breeding Discontent," *Saturday Night*, June 1993, 15–17, 62–67; "Cures from the Womb," *Newsweek*, 22 February 1993, 49–53; Ian Dowbiggin, "Improving the Human Breed," *Toronto Star*, 16 November 1992, and Richard John Neuhaus, "The Return of Eugenics," *Commentary*, April 1988, 15–26.

sional reasons. In the early twentieth century the two leading features of psychiatrists' professional lives were medical practice in public asylums and service in public health organizations. Eugenics addressed both these dimensions of psychiatry in profoundly meaningful ways. It explained why psychiatrists had such pronounced difficulties trying to cure their institutional patients. It also legitimated psychiatrists' involvement in the community outside the mental hospital, a crucial consideration at a time when psychiatric practice was so dissatisfying inside the asylum. These two influential factors combined to help script one of the dimmest chapters in the history of modern psychiatry. But an examination of this same chapter also undermines the conventional theory that all eugenicists were protonazis, a stereotype that has characterized so much popular thinking about the issue. This conclusion is not meant to exonerate psychiatrists; for their contributions to eugenics are a matter of record. It simply situates them squarely in the one context that ultimately meant the most to them: their jobs as physicians to the mentally ill.

What follows is a story about men and women who, though fired with an incandescent zeal to help those less fortunate than themselves, made what in hindsight were morally and scientifically dubious decisions. It is a story of human fallibility, of human beings who, when faced with the daunting challenge of caring for emotionally and mentally disabled people, resorted to extreme theories and practices. Most of these men and women were convinced they were absolutely right, even when they might have known better. But condemning these same psychiatrists for paths not taken ignores the historical environment in which they lived and worked. They were psychiatrists who found themselves living in an age of rapid and unnerving change, a time filled with both promise and acute uncertainty. It was the age of "progressivism," which stretched roughly from the 1890s to the New Deal of the 1930s, years when Americans and Canadians were inspired by the dream of reform. Eugenics emerged during this period as a quintessentially progressive reform. The issues of reproduction, heredity, public health, and racial anthropology gripped the educated public's imagination, and the word *eugenics* seemed to be on the lips of countless prominent Americans. Although there is no denying the impact psychiatrists themselves had on the growth of eugenics, it would be ahistorical to expect the psychiatric profession to have been immune to this influence. Because it stressed the hereditary roots of patterns in dependence and deviance, eugenics had an obvious resonance for psychiatrists laboring in state institutions for the mentally handicapped.

Psychiatrists were also physicians in a hurry to catch up with the seeming march of science, often driven to impotent anxiety when it appeared they were simply treading water. They felt pressure from governments and other physicians to reform and modernize their medical specialty. To their dismay they discovered that to politicians and state officials, psychiatric reform really meant cost cutting and bureaucratic ukases. Above all, they were painfully conscious of their professional vulnerability; though in fact they stood on the verge of what might be called psychiatry's "golden age." After the Second World War, psychiatrists largely broke away from the state hospital, formerly their habitual site of practice, and emerged as a corps of medical experts respected and generously rewarded for their knowledge about a wide range of conditions governing the emotional health of Americans. But most psychiatrists in the decades leading up to the Second World War could only see this future dimly. In the meantime, many took the path of least resistance and followed fashionable trends in public health policy which helped to obscure psychiatry's shortcomings, penalizing innocent men, women, and children in the process.

The seminal question is not why more eugenicist psychiatrists did not see the errors of their ways. The bigger question is why *any* psychiatrists resisted the eugenic message in the first place. Most historians of eugenics have been preoccupied with the task of distinguishing eugenicists from noneugenicists. The trouble is that on close inspection there was virtually no psychiatrist who did not at one time express an opinion favorable toward eugenics. Assuming that psychiatrists were not terribly different from most other groups of public-spirited people, I hope to demonstrate that, given the historical climate surrounding the rise of eugenics, the more edifying task is to try to determine the different *shades* of eugenicism in early twentieth-century Canada and the United States.

Thus, in the history of eugenics, there were precious few heroes among psychiatrists. Yet, at the same time, there were few certifiable villains. In this book I describe how and to what extent a group united by training, credentials, and occupation became closely associated with a cause their profession might prefer to forget. This group boasted none of the luminaries who led Anglo-American eugenics, figures such as Karl Pearson, Francis Galton, Charles Davenport, Madison Grant, Leonard Darwin, and Harry Hamilton Laughlin. Instead, this effort to shed new light on the history of eugenics is part of a recent scholarly trend that has shifted attention away from the headline-grabbing leaders of the eugenics movement and toward the comparatively anonymous rank and file.[5] The aim

5. For an example of a prosopographical approach to the history of eugenics that similarly seeks "to go beyond the small circle of individuals studied in the major works [on eugenics]

is not to discredit earlier histories of eugenics. Rather, it is to complement them by documenting how one elite professional group responded to the theories of the movement's leaders and deployed the eugenic message both for its own purposes and purportedly in the interests of its clientele. By examining the history of a professional community and its adoption of a particular form of discourse and practice, not only can we see how a biomedical theory like eugenics was translated into policy; we can also identify likely reasons why certain professionals tended to think in distinctive patterns and along common lines at specific times in history.

In focusing on psychiatrists I have adopted a somewhat elastic definition of "psychiatry" itself. By psychiatrists I mean physicians engaged in the study, management, or treatment of mentally and emotionally disabled people. This definition includes public mental health officers, medically trained state hospital physicians, private practice therapists and clinicians, general hospital practitioners, laboratory researchers, and superintendents of institutions for the mentally retarded. In addition, I discuss Canadian as well as U.S. psychiatrists for two reasons: one, the advantages of a comparative frame of reference; and two, because they belonged to a single professional organization—the American Psychiatric Association. Canadian and U.S. psychiatrists thought of themselves as constituting a united medical community that transcended political borders. This common organizational affiliation reflected their many similarities of interest, theory, and practice.[6]

The research for this book would not have been possible without the invaluable and courteous assistance of numerous librarians, archivists, and scholars. They include Ann Beardsley, Robert J. Westlake, and Linda Walton of the Butler Hospital; Diane Thomas of the Clarke Institute; Jack Griffin, Cyril Greenland, and Betty Jo Moore of the Griffin-Greenland Archives on the History of Canadian Psychiatry; William Baxter, Susan Heffner, and Spencerita Bellinger of the American Psychiatric Association Archives; William R. Day, Arian D. Ravanbakhsh, Gerard Shorb, and Anne Slakey of the Alan Mason Chesney Medical Archives at the John Hopkins University; Paul Bunten of the Oskar Diethelm Library at the New York Hospital–Cornell Medical Center;

thus far," see Barry Alan Mehler, "A History of the American Eugenics Society, 1921–1940" (Ph.D. diss., University of Illinois at Urbana-Champaign, 1988), p. 178.
6. For an account that makes a similar point about the "Continental" rather than "imperial" nature of the twentieth-century Canadian eugenics and mental hygiene movements, see Kathleen Janet McConnachie, "Science and Ideology: The Mental Hygiene and Eugenics Movements in the Inter-War Years, 1919–1939" (Ph.D. diss., University of Toronto, 1987), p. 8.

Ginny Kopachevsky of the Robertson Library's Inter-Library Loan Department at the University of Prince Edward Island; and the staff at the McGill University Medical Sciences Library, the Dalhousie University Medical School Library, the Ontario Provincial Archives, the Public Archives of Canada, the British Museum, and the National Archives in Washington. Special thanks go to Edward M. Brown for first drawing my attention to the historical records at the Butler Hospital, as well as Gerald N. Grob for unselfishly lending me his research notes on the history of U.S. psychiatry. Thanks also to the members of the Triangle Workshop in the History of Science, Medicine, and Technology at Duke University/University of North Carolina who in 1992 provided me with an opportunity to talk about my early research. Others kind enough to share with me their thoughts on various aspects of the history of eugenics and related topics were Mark Adams, Garland Allen, Phil Brown, Theodore M. Brown, John Burnham, Gilbert Germain, Jonathan Gottshall, Sung Lee, Lindsay Linkletter, the late William McLoughlin, Barry Mehler, Mark Micale, George Mora, Nicole Neatby, James T. Patterson, Hans Pols, Joan Richards, David Rochefort, and Donald Brian Smith. Much of the travel and research costs for this book were covered by the Social Sciences and Humanities Research Council of Canada and the University of Prince Edward Island Senate Committee on Research. I thank both agencies for their generous support. Parts of this book appeared previously in altered form in: " 'An Exodus of Enthusiasm': G. Alder Blumer, Eugenics, and U.S. Psychiatry, 1890–1920," *Medical History* 36 (1992): 379–402 (Copyright The Trustee, The Wellcome Trust, reproduced with permission); " 'Midnight Clerks and Daily Drudges': Hospital Psychiatry in New York State, 1890–1905," *Journal of the History of Medicine and Allied Sciences* 47 (1992): 130–52; and " 'Keeping This Young Country Sane': C. K. Clarke, Immigration Restriction, and Canadian Psychiatry, 1890–1925," *Canadian Historical Review* 76 (1995): 598–627. I am grateful to these publications for their referees' comments and their permission to reproduce copyrighted material.

Above all, it is my wife, Christine, and our children, Beth and Christopher, who deserve special credit. By putting up with my lengthy absences from home and indulging my reclusive moods they made it possible for me to get my work done. It is to them that I dedicate this book.

IAN ROBERT DOWBIGGIN

Charlottetown, Prince Edward Island

ABBREVIATIONS

AES   American Eugenics Society
AFMH   American Foundation for Mental Hygiene Collection, Archives of Psy-
            chiatry, Oskar Diethelm Library, New York Hospital–Cornell Medical
            Center, New York
AJI   *American Journal of Insanity*
AJP   *American Journal of Psychiatry*
AMCMA   Adolf Meyer Papers, Alan Mason Chesney Medical Archives, Johns
            Hopkins Medical Institutions, Baltimore
AMPA   American Medico-Psychological Association
AMSAII   Association of Medical Superintendents of American Institutions for
            the Insane
APA   American Psychiatric Association Archives, Washington
ARK   Annual Report of the Medical Superintendent of the Asylum for the
            Insane, Kingston, Ontario
ART   Annual Report of the Medical Superintendent of the Asylum for the
            Insane, Toronto
BAR   *Annual Report* of the Trustees and Superintendent of the Butler Hos-
            pital for the Insane
BOHI   *Bulletin of the Ontario Hospitals for the Insane*
BP   G. Alder Blumer Papers, Isaac Ray Historical Library, Butler Hospital,
            Providence, Rhode Island
BPR   Butler Hospital Patient Records, Providence, Rhode Island

CKCA	C. K. Clarke Archives, C. B. Farrar Library, Clarke Institute of Psychiatry, Toronto
CJMH	*Canadian Journal of Mental Hygiene*
CNCMH	Canadian National Committee for Mental Hygiene
ERO	Eugenics Records Office
ESC	Eugenics Society of Canada
IRL	Immigration Restriction League
JAMA	*Journal of the American Medical Association*
NCMH	National Committee for Mental Hygiene
NCW	National Council of Women
NYSLA	Annual Report of the Managers of the State Lunatic Asylum at Utica, New York
PAC	Public Archives of Canada
PACFM	Provincial Association for the Care of the Feeble-Minded
PAMPA	*Proceedings of the American Medico-Psychological Association*
PAO	Public Archives of Ontario
PHS	Public Health Service
QSMHC	Griffin-Greenland Archives on the History of Canadian Psychiatry, Queen Street Mental Health Centre, Toronto
TGH	Toronto General Hospital
WAW	William A. White Papers, RG 418, Records of St. Elizabeths Hospital, National Archives, Washington

KEEPING AMERICA SANE

INTRODUCTION

I n November 1877 a twenty-year old named George Alder Blumer disembarked at the port of New Orleans, touching U.S. soil for the first time. Blumer—who used the first name Alder—was on the verge of a distinguished medical career, one that would see him emerge as a key figure in early twentieth-century psychiatry. His first major professional success would come in 1886 when he landed the post of head psychiatrist at the Utica Asylum, an internationally famous mental hospital. In 1899 he accepted the same position at the equally prestigious Butler Hospital for the Insane in Providence, Rhode Island. Over the next twenty-two years he served as the president of the American Medico-Psychological Association (the forerunner of the present-day American Psychiatric Association) and took an active part in both the Rhode Island and national committees for mental hygiene, organizations that spearheaded the twentieth-century campaign to prevent mental illness. From 1886 to 1894 he was also editor-in-chief of the *American Journal of Insanity* (which in 1921 became the *American Journal of Psychiatry*), the foremost psychiatric journal in English-speaking North America. Blumer used his position at the journal and his amicable relations with subsequent editors to introduce readers to developments in European psychiatry, thereby exerting an influence on the history of ideas in North American psychiatry. His efforts to import European theories earned him international respect and admiration. His own theories about the treatment of psychiatric patients gained him the deserved reputation of one committed to the humane care of the mentally ill. He also radiated a toleration and eclecticism that made him one of the most genuinely liked figures in U.S. psychiatry. These qualities led a journalist to say, in 1912, "I am sure Blumer that you are the most famous alienist and the most talked about student of psychiatry in this country."[1] Undoubtedly there was a generous dose of hyperbole in this comment; it does, however, indicate that Blumer enjoyed a formidable reputation that stretched well beyond the boundaries of the medical profession.

When Blumer retired in 1921 psychiatry barely resembled what it had been in 1880. Psychiatrists were experimenting with psychoanalysis, eugenics, child guidance, outpatient clinics, intelligence testing, industrial psychology, and preventive mental health. But even as psychiatrists began exploring these different approaches to mental health there was still a great deal of affection in professional circles for doctors who, like Blumer, had overseen the awkward transition between nineteenth- and twentieth-century mental medicine. Although early twentieth-century physicians such as Adolf Meyer, William A. White, Smith Ely Jelliffe, and Clarence Hincks received most of the headlines, Blumer belonged to another group who tried to navigate between the competing imperatives of new and old psychiatry. In the face of pressures to strike out in alluring but uncertain directions he refused to jettison the past entirely. Throughout his career he warned against the temptation to adopt fashionable trends that meant sacrificing what physicians had learned laboriously and incrementally over a century of psychiatric practice.[2] In this respect Blumer stands out less as a harbinger of future currents than an articulate spokesman for the typical concerns and attitudes of early twentieth-century Anglo-American psychiatrists. These very attitudes are the basis for an understanding of the motives behind U.S. and Canadian psychiatrists' support for eugenics in the twentieth century.

1. G. E. Dunham to Blumer, 17 March 1912, BP, box 32.
2. G. Alder Blumer, "The Progress and Promise of Psychiatry in America," ca. 1898, BP, box 40.

I

Blumer's career might never have unfolded, were it not for a decisive event in 1877. Born 25 May 1857 in Sunderland, England, he began medical studies at the University of Edinburgh. This step had made eminent sense given that he came from a family of physicians, among them his father and two brothers.[3] But Blumer, obviously restless and rebellious, dropped out of medical school in 1876. One year later he impetuously decided that Texas was the place for his raw talents. He abruptly booked passage on a steamer, leaving family and friends behind.

What exactly Blumer hoped to accomplish in the Lone Star State is uncertain, but what is clear is that he was an adventurous and self-confident young man willing to acccept the daunting challenges of seeking his fortune in an unfamiliar land. There was also another quality in Blumer which impressed people. It was not his physical stature; for he was of medium height with a large head, which overemphasized his slender frame. What impressed others were manners and bearing that betokened a superior, old-world education and a sensitivity to the arts and classical literature. As one psychiatrist wrote, he was "a gentleman of the old school whose urbanity and charm made an indelible impression upon those who were associated with him."[4] In later years colleagues and friends would repeatedly praise him for his command of spoken English, his polished prose, and his fine sense of humor.[5] These qualities graced and enlivened the pages of the *American Journal of Insanity* (*AJI*) between the mid-1880s and 1940. They also made him a genial companion and a wonderful after-dinner speaker much in demand at professional and social gatherings.

It was probably these qualities that convinced Dr. George Cupples, a San Antonio physician and president of the Texas State Medical Society, that frontier Texas was not the place for Blumer. The two men met crossing the Gulf of Mexico on the way to Galveston in 1877. Fully aware of Blumer's skills and intelligence, Cupples used all his powers of persuasion to talk Blumer into resuming his medical education. This he did by entering the University of Pennsylvania in 1878 and graduating with

3. The family medical ties did not end there; a cousin, Dr. George Blumer, later became clinical professor of medicine at the Yale Medical School.
4. "Obituary," *AJP* 96 (1940): 1469.
5. As the president of Brown University wrote Blumer, "No man in Rhode Island wields a more graceful pen than yourself." W. H. P. Faunce to Blumer, 23 November 1929, BP, box 35.

his M.D. in 1879. As he later reminisced, "It was at the Pennsylvania Hospital for the Insane . . . that I got my inspiration for the specialty which I embraced."[6]

In an age when there was no formal, medical school training for psychiatry, physicians gravitated toward mental medicine for a variety of reasons; one being intrinsic fascination with the study of the mind and its functions. Another was a compelling urge to help those unfortunate enough to suffer from mental illness. In Blumer's case, he also had the privilege of being taught medicine by one of the most esteemed U.S. psychiatrists of the nineteenth century, Thomas Story Kirkbride (1809–83). From 1840 to 1883, Kirkbride was the head psychiatrist at the Pennsylvania Hospital for the Insane, where Blumer did clinical training in the late 1870s. Kirkbride believed adamantly that confinement in a mental hospital was the best remedy for mental illness.[7] Blumer's similarly unshakeable confidence in later years in the virtues of hospitalization suggests that Kirkbride exerted a strong influence over the impressionable yet bright younger man.

Another reason physicians became psychiatrists was the lure of a relatively secure livelihood. As late as 1880 private medical practice offered few advantages and plenty of drawbacks. One great disadvantage was the formidable difficulty of earning a living, a stiff challenge in view of the fact that many Americans—particularly those outside urban centres—preferred to rely on home remedies or the services of itinerant, unorthodox healers. Competition from other physicians was also stiff, thanks to a galaxy of widely different medical schools that flooded the market with an oversupply of doctors. Another difficulty for licensed doctors was collecting their fees. Perhaps no other activity frustrated them more than this. Patients were rarely affluent, and their poverty had a persistent way of dragging their doctors down to their own socioeconomic level.[8]

Nor did certified physicians in nineteenth-century America have effective therapies to offer their patients. Throughout the first half of that century, medical treatment was still dominated by theories and techniques

6. Blumer to Owen Copp, 14 January 1911, BP, box 31.
7. On Kirkbride and his career, see Nancy Tomes, *A Generous Confidence: Thomas Story Kirkbride and the Art of Asylum-Keeping, 1840–1883* (Cambridge: Cambridge University Press, 1984). For Blumer's observations on Kirkbride, see G. Alder Blumer, "A Half-Century of American Medico-Psychological Literature," *AJI* 51 (1895): 40–50.
8. As one doctor wrote in 1882, "The truth is, when a doctor dies, his family is usually left poor and helpless, unless he has acquired money otherwise than by practice." Daniel W. Cathell, *The Physician Himself and What He Should Add to the Strictly Scientific* (Baltimore, 1882), p. 188. Cited in Edward Shorter, *Bedside Manners: The Troubled History of Doctors and Patients* (New York: Simon and Schuster, 1985), p. 52.

from classical antiquity. Therapeutics mainly consisted of a dreary routine of bleeding, blistering, purging, sweating, and vomiting, aptly dubbed "heroic" therapy. Many antebellum U.S. patients actually preferred a therapeutic regimen that produced demonstrable physiological effects because of the apparent proof that the administered drugs were working. But the debilitation and suffering accompanying such treatments led physicians around midcentury to adopt a more moderate and skeptical approach.[9] Some went even further, calling into question organized medicine's entire arsenal of drugs.[10] This professional skepticism, the culmination of the centuries-long futile struggle of organized medicine to cure disease, ultimately persuaded the medicine-consuming public as well.

By contrast, nineteenth-century psychiatry—commonly known as "alienism" or asylum medicine—looked good. Psychiatry had been one of the first specialties to branch off from general medicine in the early nineteenth century, and it grew increasingly dissimilar to the rest of medicine as the century progressed. This state of affairs stemmed from the salient fact that nineteenth-century psychiatry was almost entirely a specialty limited to the practice of medicine in asylums.[11] Indeed, psychiatry's beginnings were firmly rooted in the origins of the modern asylum itself.[12] In the decades before the Civil War, philanthropic and reform-minded men and women such as Dorothea Dix, Horace Mann, and Thomas Eddy campaigned to draw attention to the inadequacies of U.S. facilities and therapies for the mentally ill. These people, often members of dissenting Christian churches, argued that the mentally ill had been

9. On the relations between physicians and patients, see Charles E. Rosenberg, "The Therapeutic Revolution: Medicine, Meaning, and Social Change in Nineteenth-Century America," in *The Therapeutic Revolution: Essays in the Social History of American Medicine*, ed. Morris J. Vogel and Charles E. Rosenberg (Philadelphia: University of Pennsylvania Press, 1979), pp. 3–25. See also John Harley Warner, *The Therapeutic Perspective: Medical Practice, Knowledge, and Identity in America, 1820–1885* (Cambridge: Harvard University Press, 1986); Kenneth M. Ludmerer, *Learning to Heal: The Development of American Medical Education* (New York: Basic Books, 1985), pp. 3–46; Charles E. Rosenberg, *The Care of Strangers: The Rise of America's Hospital System* (New York: Basic Books, 1987), pp. 69–93; and Shorter, *Bedside Manners*.
10. William G. Rothstein, *American Physicians in the Nineteenth Century: From Sects to Science* (Baltimore: Johns Hopkins University Press, 1972), p. 178. For example, at midcentury Dr. Oliver Wendell Holmes remarked that "if the whole *materia medica*, as now used, could be sunk to the bottom of the sea, it would be all the better for mankind—and all the worse for the fishes." Cited in Ronald L. Numbers, "The Fall and Rise of the American Medical Profession," in *Sickness and Health in America: Readings in the History of Medicine and Public Health*, ed. Judith Walzer Leavitt and Ronald L. Numbers (Madison: University of Wisconsin Press, 1985), pp. 185–96, 187.
11. Gerald N. Grob, *The Mad Among Us: A History of the Care of America's Mentally Ill* (New York: Free Press, 1994), p. 55.
12. For an interpretation of the origins of the asylum which stresses its political and social context, see David J. Rothman, *The Discovery of the Asylum: Social Order and Disorder in the New Republic* (Boston: Little, Brown, 1971).

grossly mistreated by doctors who—insofar as they ministered to the insane at all—reputedly abused their patients with heroic therapy. Reformers insisted that such forms of treatment reflected both a prejudice against and an insensitiveness toward the mentally ill. These attitudes, they contended, were embodied in the jails, almshouses, and workhouses in which the insane were often housed. They cited case after case of mentally deranged homeless persons who either "wander[ed] from place to place without food and without decent apparel" or were living in chains, filth, and squalor.[13] The solution they espoused was to remove the mentally ill from these and similar conditions and hospitalize them in new, clean, and orderly institutions, appropriately enough called "asylums." There the mentally ill would enjoy fresh air, nutritious food, and a disciplined atmosphere that would literally soothe their nerves.

This new therapeutic approach owed a great deal to the "moral treatment" pioneered by European psychiatrists, principally the Paris-based Philippe Pinel (1745–1826). Around the turn of the nineteenth century Pinel had argued that corporal punishment and medicine's customary somatic remedies were largely useless in the treatment of insanity. Instead he recommended employing kindness, reason, and discipline to enable the patient to mobilize his or her intelligence and emotions in the struggle against obsessional and delusional thinking. For moral treatment to work, physicians thought they needed control over their patients' lives, and they believed this was only possible through confinement in an asylum away from families, friends, and every-day distractions. Thus moral treatment was thought to be inseparable from the asylum itself. Underlying the introduction of the asylum as a social institution, then, was the notion that hospitalization was *the* most effective therapy for mental illness.[14]

Philanthropists, religious organizations, and state legislatures responded to the lunacy reform movement by providing the funds to build both private and public asylums. By 1840 three states had their own public facilities. In the next decade eight new public asylums began operations, and in the 1850s sixteen state, one federal, and four municipal institutions were opened. Though cost cutting frequently characterized

13. *Report of a Committee of the Connecticut State Medical Society, respecting an Asylum for the Insane* (Hartford, 1821). Cited in Grob, *Mad among Us*, p. 33. See also ibid., p. 44.
14. For Pinel and his role in the origins of psychiatry and moral treatment, see Dora B. Weiner, *The Citizen-Patient in Revolutionary and Imperial Paris* (Baltimore: Johns Hopkins University Press, 1993), pp. 247–77. See also Jan Goldstein, *Console and Classify: The French Psychiatric Profession in the Nineteenth Century* (Cambridge: Cambridge University Press, 1987), pp. 67–119; and Ian Dowbiggin, *Inheriting Madness: Professionalization and Psychiatric Knowledge in Nineteenth-Century France* (Berkeley: University of California Press, 1991), esp. pp. 11–53.

the planning, building, and management of these public asylums—primarily because they were viewed as places for the pauper insane—the motive behind their construction was the same as that behind the erection of private asylums: to rescue the mentally ill from the neglect and abuse they allegedly suffered. Thus the origins of the asylum were little different from those of new, early nineteenth-century schools and prisons. Fear and intolerance were mixed liberally with benevolence, humanitarianism, and an optimistic faith in the efficacy of institutions to reform human nature.[15]

From the beginning, physicians figured prominently in the U.S. asylum reform movement. They quite easily convinced their lay colleagues that the management of asylums ought to lie in medical hands.[16] Despite the prevalence of popular healing movements, the U.S. had a well-developed public predisposition to trust "regular" physicians. After all, orthodox physicians controlled most medical schools and hospitals and thus enjoyed greater social prominence than their "sectarian" competitors. The professed willingness to use more benign and less debilitating therapies solidified the profession's trustworthiness in the eyes of citizens.[17]

Moral treatment fit nicely into the shift of medical attitudes toward therapy. Doctors championed it primarily because it represented a dramatic departure from earlier and presumably more barbaric therapies. Asylum moral treatment appeared to lack the punitive and invasive elements of traditional therapeutics. It is not surprising, then, that doctors eventually were entrusted with the management of the new asylums: their medical theories, stressing therapeutic moderation and de-emphasizing harsh remedies, were highly consistent with popular views about asylum treatment and its "moral" foundations.

As physicians quickly staked out their role in the new asylums, they lost very little time in organizing as an occupational group. In 1844 they formed the Association of Medical Superintendents of American Institutions for the Insane (AMSAII), the forerunner of the American Med-

---

15. Grob, *Mad among Us*, pp. 31–49. For an interpretation that stresses the punitive aspects of the asylum's origins in the United States, see Rothman, *Discovery of the Asylum*.

16. For an account that stresses the tactics employed by psychiatrists to assume leadership of U.S. asylums, see Andrew Scull, "The Discovery of the Asylum Revisited: Lunacy Reform in the New American Republic," in *Madhouses, Mad-Doctors, and Madmen: The Social History of Psychiatry in the Victorian Era*, ed. Andrew Scull (Philadelphia: University of Pennsylvania Press, 1981), pp. 144–65. See also Andrew Scull, *Social Order/Mental Disorder: Anglo-American Psychiatry in Historical Perspective* (Berkeley: University of California Press, 1989), pp. 31–53, 95–117.

17. Rosenberg, *Care of Strangers*, pp. 15–93.

ico-Psychological Association (AMPA) and American Psychiatric Association (APA). The AMSAII's early members sensed that asylum medicine offered them an unprecedented opportunity to create model communities that featured the order, charity, health, and deference to authority apparently lacking in the raucous and turbulent antebellum era. They consequently imagined themselves as moral leaders as well as stewards of the sick and infirm.[18] That the AMSAII predated the American Medical Association by three years and consistently refused to merge with it speak volumes about the sudden rise to prominence of these medical superintendents of asylums and their status relative to the rest of organized medicine. Psychiatrists perceived that their unique professional identity would be jeopardized by uniting with physicians whom they believed were their professional inferiors.

By choosing psychiatry as a career, physicians had to accept a rather cloistered existence alongside patients whose behavioral traits were often erratic. But if a physician could acquire one of the coveted positions as medical superintendent of an asylum, the reward would be a steady salary, room and board, and considerable prestige. Sometimes places where people who disturbed the peace were institutionalized, asylums were also facilities where families could send ailing relatives for treatment at private or state expense. As the correspondence between medical superintendents and nineteenth-century families repeatedly shows, there were many men and women who were exceedingly grateful that there were publicly funded institutions which received emotionally and behaviorally disturbed family members and dispensed benevolent care under the supervision of a trained physician. The medical superintendents' availability to reassure relatives that hospitalization was the best course of action and to ease the process brought them gratitude and respect as long as public confidence in the asylum grew; as it did, so did the community's "generous confidence in those to whose care their friends have been entrusted," in the words of Thomas Kirkbride.[19]

Thus, by the 1860s, psychiatry was a prestigious and remunerative branch of medicine. Asylums dotted the countryside, proof of psychiatry's institutional power and social status. Psychiatrists enjoyed a control over their patients and occupational conditions which other physicians

18. On the original cohort of U.S. asylum psychiatrists and the social conditions surrounding their lives as physicians, see Constance M. McGovern, *Masters of Madness: Social Origins of the American Psychiatric Profession* (Hanover, N.H.: University Press of New England, 1985), pp. 44–61.

19. Tomes, *Generous Confidence*, p. 130. Kirkbride was a notable exception to the theory that physicians turned to asylum employment because of economic insecurity; see ibid., p. 70.

could only envy. They had their own professional organization and their own journal which published a growing body of medical literature on the causes, pathology, and treatment of insanity. Governments and the public relied on them for expert information and policy recommendations. In short, psychiatry was a mid-nineteenth-century American success story.[20]

By the time Blumer had finished medical school in 1879, however, psychiatry had reached a critical juncture. He may or may not have known it, but the country's "generous confidence" in psychiatrists was in decline. The profession of asylum medicine had never been easy at the best of times, but after the Civil War it became even more arduous, leading one psychiatrist to compare it in 1869 with "living over a volcano."[21] As more and more families trusted institutionalization as a treatment for mental illness, the patient population of asylums rose, and with it rose the number of violent or chronically ill patients. Medical superintendents watched with dismay as more and more infirm, syphilitic, aged, and alcoholic patients were admitted to their institutions. This state of affairs not only reduced the number of patients physicians could discharge as cured but adversely affected the atmosphere in the asylum itself. Violent patients, harder to deal with and control, sometimes attacked their doctors. Fatalities among physicians, though not numerous, did occur—reminders that beneath everyday life in the asylum lurked real danger.

Another thing that was beginning to disturb psychiatrists by the late 1870s was the mounting criticism directed against them by charity reformers, state officials, ex-patients, and other physicians, especially from the emerging specialty of neurology. Charity reformers were public-spirited men and women whose ranks had grown in the 1860s as more and more official attention shifted to the problems of dependence and indigence. Earlier in the nineteenth century, charity had been practiced on a largely voluntary basis. After midcentury the belief had spread that governments ought to assume the responsibility for administering and funding forms of public assistance to the disadvantaged. State governments had responded by creating boards of charities that quickly began to treat the asylum as simply one institution in a much larger network of public welfare facilities which included prisons, almshouses, and orphanages. As central control over public asylums from state capitols

20. Grob, *Mad among Us*, pp. 76–77.
21. Charles Nichols to Dorothea Dix, 4 July 1869, Dorothea Dix Papers, Houghton Library, Harvard University. Cited in Tomes, *Generous Confidence*, p. 277.

tightened, medical superintendents were increasingly held accountable for costs and administration. Psychiatrists deeply resented this intensifying supervision of their work and correctly saw it as a reflection of an escalating public and official skepticism about their ability to treat the mentally ill.

The complaints of ex-patients had also added to the woes of psychiatrists. With the opening of the first modern asylums, patient grievances had quickly become a part of a psychiatrist's life, but after the Civil War more and more patients took their complaints to lawyers and the press. Ironically, the popularity of asylums as places to put inconvenient relatives eventually led to psychiatry's fall in prestige; for men and women who had been institutionalized because of borderline mental states sometimes protested their incarceration. Perhaps the most famous case of alleged unfair confinement in the United States was that of Elizabeth Packard. In 1860 her husband and a state asylum psychiatrist arranged to have her institutionalized under a law that allowed husbands to do just that without the usual formalities. After a three-year stay, Packard was released. She then proceeded to lobby several states to safeguard the rights of all patients in commitment procedures. Her campaign carried over into the 1870s and helped to foster the largely inaccurate perception that psychiatrists wielded arbitrary powers of confinement. Just as seriously, Packard's efforts drew uncomfortable attention to the genuinely deteriorating conditions within asylums.

Exacerbating this problem was the fact that the post–Civil War press seemed all too happy to publish scandalous stories about asylum life, regardless of their veracity. A favorite topic of the press—particularly the newer newspapers practicing "yellow journalism"—was insanity trials during which patients and ex-patients alleged a variety of abuses, including illegal commitment and physical punishment. Just as newspapers appeared to welcome this form of sensationalist reporting, so too lawyers seemed to be on the lookout for these kinds of cases to represent. In short, asylums and their medical superintendents found themselves caught up in the post–Civil War tendency to find fault with urban institutions, professional motives, and political authority.[22] Psychiatrists and their institutional staffs felt the sting of criticism sharply and often took it personally.

On yet another front the allure and reputation of psychiatry was fading by 1880. Neurology, a new medical specialty beginning in the 1860s, soon trained its sights on the practice of asylum medicine. Neurologists

22. Tomes, *Generous Confidence*, p. 261.

singled out what they claimed were psychiatrists' therapeutic failures and ignorance of medical science. Neurology had emerged thanks primarily to two influences: developments in European medical science stressing the rigorous clinical investigation of how mental and nervous disease could be linked to the structure and functions of the nervous system, and the Civil War experiences of physicians who treated wounds involving damage to nervous tissue. Physicians interested in these subjects had established themselves by the 1870s in private practice in the major urban areas of the East. They publicized their expertise both in plainly neurological conditions such as paralysis, chorea, and locomotor ataxia and in more borderline states such as dyspepsia, anxiety, insomnia, mild depression, and general malaise. It was chiefly their success in recruiting patients with the latter symptoms that sustained neurology's rise; for it often meant that neurologists treated patients with money and social rank. In this they stood in stark contrast to psychiatrists, who dealt mostly with institutionalized patients, often paupers afflicted with symptoms resistant to medical intervention.

Styling themselves as physicians familiar with the most recent scientific medicine of Europe—and disdainful of psychiatrists' seeming obsession with asylum management, administration, and treatment—neurologists attacked medical superintendents increasingly vociferously in the late 1870s. Little short of professional war broke out between neurology and psychiatry, a conflict centered in New York State. Edward C. Spitzka, a noted and acerbic neurologist, and William A. Hammond, the surgeon general in the Union Army during the Civil War, were the most vocal critics among the neurologists.[23] If psychiatrists were to have anything to do with the treatment of insanity in the future, neurologists were convinced it would have to be under their supervision. That would mean psychiatrists deferring to neurologists within the asylum, psychiatry's bailiwick. Neurologists were even skeptical of the value of psychiatric hospitalization itself and often repeated the standard charge that institutionalization of mental patients was "in many instances . . . not only unnecessary but positively injurious," in Hammond's words. From the neurologists' point of view, asylums were valuable primarily for supplying physicians with plenty of clinical material to study.[24]

23. See, e.g., Edward C. Spitzka, "Reform in the Scientific Study of Psychiatry," *Journal of Nervous and Mental Disease* 5 (1878): 201–29. Cited in Grob, *Mad among Us*, p. 133.
24. W. A. Hammond, "The Non-Asylum Treatment of the Insane," Medical Society of the State of New York, *Transactions* (1879): 280–97. Cited in Gerald N. Grob, *Mental Illness and American Society, 1875–1940* (Princeton: Princeton University Press, 1983), p. 53. For more on the conflict between U.S. psychiatrists and neurologists, see Bonnie Blustein, *Preserve Your*

Neurologists' withering criticism of asylum psychiatry combined with that of lay reformers to prod the New York State Senate into striking a committee to look into allegations of psychiatric ignorance, neglect, and abuse. A prime target of these allegations was the Utica State Asylum headed by John Gray, but in taking on Gray, state investigators had their hands full. He was nationally notorious because of his well-publicized involvement as an expert witness in the trial of Charles Guiteau, who had assassinated President James Garfield in 1881. Head psychiatrist of the Utica Asylum since 1854, Gray had also been editor of the *AJI* since 1855. He frequently used the journal to publicize his own views and discredit those he opposed. His editorial policy made him few friends, but his reputation throughout the European and Anglo-American psychiatric communities had never been seriously damaged.[25] A devout Christian, he was also an opinionated, scheming, and censorious public figure who feuded with lawyers, officials, colleagues at the AMSAII, and members of his own medical staff.[26]

Despite his quarrelsome nature, Gray did have good qualities. He encouraged his assistant physicians at Utica to learn more about mental illness by freeing them from their duties at the hospital so they could travel to the best medical schools in Europe for postgraduate study. He was also a fierce defender of pathological research in psychiatry and made sure that this kind of investigation was carried out at Utica and published in the *AJI*. These virtues, however, did not stem the attacks on him, the his asylum, and New York State's entire system of mental health care.[27] In 1880–81 a three-person committee held hearings that collected testimony from psychiatrists, attendants, trustees, neurologists, and state officials. Neurologists denounced Gray and his staff for their censorship of patient correspondence and their reliance on mechanical restraints, such as the notorious "Utica crib," a wooden, covered-bed apparatus for confining aggressive patients. The neurologists also recommended that locked doors and barred windows be minimized and that future asylums

Love of Science: The Life of William A. Hammond, American Neurologist (Cambridge: Cambridge University Press, 1991); F. G. Gosling, *Before Freud: Neurasthenia and the American Community, 1870–1910* (Urbana: University of Illinois Press, 1987); and John A. Pitts, "The Association of Medical Superintendents of American Institutions for the Insane, 1844–1892: A Case Study of Specialism in American Medicine" (Ph.D. diss., University of Pennsylvania, 1978), pp. 150–86.

25. Ellen Dwyer, *Homes for the Mad: Life inside Two Nineteenth-Century Asylums* (New Brunswick, N.J.: Rutgers University Press, 1987), pp. 67–71.

26. Charles E. Rosenberg, *The Trial of the Assassin Guiteau: Psychiatry and Law in the Gilded Age* (Chicago: University of Chicago Press, 1968), p. 73.

27. For the history of legislative investigations into New York State asylums, see Dwyer, *Homes for the Mad*, pp. 193–208.

be erected on a smaller scale. Some of Gray's enemies appeared at the hearings, accusing him of using asylum funds for his own benefit and deliberately covering up evidence of patient abuse.

Gray escaped the 1880–81 hearings largely unscathed, but in 1884 his enemies got another chance. Early that year, shortly after admission, a Utica patient fought with three attendants, who proceeded to break his jaw and seven of his ribs, one of which punctured his lungs, the probable cause of his death. The three attendants were discharged from asylum service and indicted for murder. A public outcry led to another legislative investigation into conditions at Utica. Newspapers across New York State had a field day, running headlines such as "Dr. Gray's Butchers" and "The Utica Crime" while chortling that this time the "suave, politic, influential Gray" would not evade justice. The upshot was a two-month-long hearing and the publication of the lengthy investigative proceedings.[28]

Although much of the furor was about patient abuse, censorship of patient correspondence, the training and pay of attendants, and the relations between male doctors and female patients, what was really at stake was state control of asylums, particularly Gray's. With the perception spreading that Utica was Gray's miniature fiefdom, politicians quickly realized that political benefits might accrue from attacking the state mental health system. So, as the investigation progressed in early 1884, politicians called for strict business management and accountability of the state's mental hospitals and the end of the system by which asylum boards, the State Board of Charities, and the commissioner in lunacy informally oversaw the administration of mental institutions.

Although sympathetic to Utica's opponents, the committee that drew up the final report failed to make any radical recommendations beyond those that earlier investigators had urged: reduced reliance on restraint, more pay for assistant physicians, better supervision of attendants, and the hiring of female doctors to serve the special needs of women patients. Probably sensing that sensationalist attacks on asylum specific scandals would get them nowhere, critics of Gray and his so-called asylum ring instead devoted most of their energies to the campaign for a centralized and expanded mental health care system directly accountable to state officials. That would entail the elimination of care of the insane at the county level and the ultimate shift of all insane patients to state-run institutions. To asylum doctors and their boards, this change posed the danger of fiscal control over their hospitals exerted from Albany. An era

28. Dwyer, *Homes for the Mad*, p. 202.

in asylum history in New York State was coming to an end, just as it had recently in Pennsylvania and would in many other states.[29] No longer would asylums enjoy their pre–Civil War autonomy. State psychiatrists' freedom to manage their asylums would gradually erode as they became more and more accountable to state bureaucrats and politicians. This development had profound psychological and intellectual consequences for Blumer's generation of psychiatrists.

The end of this era of asylum psychiatry roughly coincided with the death of Gray himself in 1886. On the evening of Gray's return in 1882 from testifying at the Guiteau trial, a local masseur, who was most likely insane at the moment, entered Gray's office and shot him in the face. The wound did not kill Gray, who lived for another four years, but his health was permanently affected. When he passed away in 1886 there were few in psychiatry who missed the symbolism: his death closed a chapter in asylum medicine. The path was now open to a younger generation of psychiatrists, one that would be closely associated with G. Alder Blumer and his colleagues in New York State mental health care.

II

The origins of Canadian psychiatry resembled the early history of U.S. psychiatry. The first Canadian asylum for the insane was opened in Saint John, New Brunswick, in 1836, to be replaced twelve years later with a permanent facility. What made the Saint John Asylum noteworthy was that it housed only insane people, marking a departure in the institutional treatment of the mentally ill in Canada. Finally those disordered in mind were recognized as needing their own kind of supervision in their own kind of institution, separate from paupers, criminals, and alcoholics.

In neighboring Nova Scotia it was not until 1844 that serious consideration was given to the idea of a separate asylum for lunatics, but even then little action was taken despite the impassioned plea of U.S. reformer Dorothea Dix in 1850. The Act for Founding a Lunatic Asylum did finally pass the Nova Scotia Assembly in 1852, but reformers had to wait until January 1859 before a new asylum would admit its first patients.[30]

---

29. On Pennsylvania mental health care politics, see Tomes, *Generous Confidence*, pp. 306–310.

30. Daniel Francis, "The Development of the Lunatic Asylum in the Maritime Provinces," in *Medicine in Canadian Society: Historical Perspectives*, ed. S. E. D. Shortt (Montreal: McGill-Queen's University Press, 1981), pp. 93–114.

In Lower Canada (a region roughly corresponding to present-day Quebec), care of the insane in the early nineteenth century was an equally haphazard and informal affair.[31] The mentally ill were housed—if indeed they were institutionalized at all—in special *loges*, or cells, in buildings on the grounds of general hospitals. Their custodians were members of the female religious orders, Quebec being a heavily Catholic and over-whelmingly French-speaking colony. But in the early decades of the century some physicians and public officials began criticizing the conditions of the *loges*, saying that they were not the proper places for applying consistent rules of medical therapy. Reformers suggested building a hospital solely dedicated to the treatment of the mentally ill. In 1831 the doctors got their way when the insane were excluded from treatment in general hospitals. But from 1831 to 1839 there was *no* institutional provision made for Quebec's mentally ill, and after 1839 only temporary quarters were made available in the Montreal prison. In 1845, Quebec finally received its first bonafide asylum, the Beauport. When over-crowding quickly became a problem, the "incurables" were dispatched to the hospital at Longue Pointe (renamed St. Jean de Dieu in 1852), which was operated by the Catholic Sisters of Charity. Many reformers begrudgingly admired the selflessness of the nuns at Longue Pointe, but they contended that medical and moral treatment of the patients were almost nonexistent.

Conditions at these Quebec asylums, by most accounts deplorable, were loudly publicized in the 1880s when the well-known British psychiatrist Daniel Hack Tuke visited North American mental hospitals. Calling what he witnessed at Beauport and Longue Pointe a "chamber of horrors," Tuke's report persuaded the Montreal Medico-Chirurgical Society, and ultimately the Quebec government, to reform and reorganize the asylums by providing for greater government control and supervision of their operations.[32] But faced with Catholic, Francophone resistance reformers concluded that the only way materially to improve the treatment of Quebec's mentally ill was to build a modern, medically run asylum. The result was the Verdun Protestant Hospital outside Montreal, opened in 1890. Although the provincial government did not want to assume full financial and administrative responsibility for the new hos-

31. See Peter Keating, *La science du mal: L'institution de la psychiatrie au Québec, 1800–1914* (Montreal: Boréal, 1993), esp. chaps. 2 and 3.
32. D. H. Tuke, *The Insane in the United States and Canada* (London: H. K. Lewis, 1885), p. 193. Cited in Maude Abbott, *The History of Medicine in the Province of Quebec* (Toronto: Macmillan, 1931), p. 76.

pital, it did pay the salary of the medical superintendent and agree to pay for all Protestant public patients.[33]

In Upper Canada (roughly equivalent to Ontario), legislation providing relief for the indigent insane was first passed in 1832. Not until seven years later did the legislative assembly authorize the construction of a new, central institution in Toronto to house the mentally ill of the colony, so that it would no longer be necessary in Upper Canada to keep the insane in the common jails. But as in Jacksonian America, lunacy reform in Upper Canada was neither solely a response to populist demand for the construction of asylums nor the outcome of a widespread campaign driven exclusively by humanitiarian concerns for the welfare of the dependent mentally ill. Upper Canada in the 1830s was a tiny and insular community wracked by political dissent that would explode in the 1837 Rebellion. Its political and social leaders were also worried about what appeared to be the growing menace of crime, pauperism, drunkeness, and immigration. Lunacy reform in the shape of a new asylum was just one of the institutional solutions Upper Canadians devised to address their "anxiety and fear about the swelling ranks of the urban poor and ultimately about the state of the Upper Canadian social order itself," as Thomas Brown has pointed out.[34]

In 1850 the Toronto Asylum was finally built. But the coming of the new asylum with its five hundred patients did little in the long run to solve the problem of housing those of the mentally ill who relied on public charity. When it became apparent that the new asylum could not absorb all the patients being legally processed for institutionalization, the government began opening branch asylums. By 1881 the province of Ontario was responsible for the upkeep of 2,652 mentally disturbed persons. As one historian has written, Ontario's

extensive system of imposing institutions consumed 16.4% of the provincial budget, an amount that stabilized at more than 19% in the late 1880s. Such a figure, in 1893, for example, was almost twice the combined provincial expenditure on penal institutions, general hospitals, houses of refuge, and orphanages. The asylum, in effect, held pride of place in the provincial welfare system. It was both a symbol of state benevolence and official affir-

33. T. J. W. Burgess, "The Care of the Insane in Quebec," in *The Institutional Care of the Insane in the United States and Canada*, ed. Henry Hurd, 4 vols. (Baltimore: Johns Hopkins University Press, 1916–17), 4: 237–331, 309.
34. Thomas E. Brown, "The Origins of the Asylum in Upper Canada, 1830–1839," *Canadian Bulletin of Medical History* 1 (1984): 27–58, 32, 38.

mation that to medicine had been delegated the task of defining the limits of normal thought and behavior.[35]

Thus, paralleling developments south of the border, Ontario had by the final third of the nineteenth century established an expensive mental health care system that provincial officials believed was necessary to meet the needs of the insane, their families, and the civil authorities responsible for law and order. At the center of this costly system was the asylum and the physicians who staffed it. They were expected to ensure that their charges received the best level of care; they were also accountable to the provincial government for what was spent on treatment, maintenance, and salaries. From the perspective of a medical profession still struggling to eliminate competition from practitioners it regarded as quacks, this occupational arrangement offered great opportunities to show what educated, enlightened, and humane doctors could do to cure mental disease. But as in New York State, these opportunities cut two ways. By the end of the century psychiatrists were beginning to realize that service in the provincial mental health care system could also turn them into virtual bureaucrats. No Canadian psychiatrist's career embodied this predicament more than C. K. Clarke's.

Charles Kirk Clarke—or "C.K." as his friends called him—was born in Elora, Ontario, on 16 February 1857 (the same year as Blumer). By his death in 1924, Clarke, after whom the Clarke Institute of Psychiatry in Toronto is named, was arguably the most famous psychiatrist Canada had produced. He belonged to one of Ontario's most respected political families, ironic given his later hatred of politicians' influence over mental health care policy. He was the only son of Colonel Charles C. Clarke, a prominent member of the provincial Liberal Party. At the age of fifteen Clarke lost his two middle fingers in a hunting accident, but this injury did not keep him from winning the Canadian doubles tennis championship nor from playing violin in the Toronto Symphony Orchestra in later years.[36]

Thanks in large measure to the fact that two of his sisters married

35. S. E. D. Shortt, *Victorian Lunacy: Richard M. Bucke and the Practice of Late Nineteenth-Century Psychiatry* (Cambridge: Cambridge University Press, 1986), p. 26. See also Cheryl Krasnick Warsh, *Moments of Unreason: The Practice of Canadian Psychiatry and the Homewood Retreat, 1883–1923* (Montreal: McGill-Queen's University Press, 1989).

36. The only monograph on Clarke and his career in psychiatry is Cyril Greenland, *Charles Kirk Clarke: A Pioneer of Canadian Psychiatry* (Toronto: Clarke Institute of Psychiatry, 1966). See also Ian Dowbiggin, "'Keeping This Young Country Sane': C. K. Clarke, Immigration Restriction, and Canadian Psychiatry, 1890–1925," *Canadian Historical Review* 76 (1995): 598–627.

A young C. K. Clarke. Courtesy of the Archives of Canadian Psychiatry and Mental Health Services.

psychiatrists, one the son of Joseph Workman (1805–94), medical superintendent of the Toronto Asylum, Clarke landed his first job in psychiatry in 1874 as an assistant under Workman. Clarke's relationship to Workman meant he and Thomas Burgess (1849–1926), the Verdun Asylum's first medical superintendent, had much in common. Burgess was Workman's godson, underscoring the familial bonds that helped to knit the small Canadian psychiatric community together in the latter part of the century.[37]

In retrospect Clarke's career has the appearance of a spectacular ascent. His first appointment as a medical superintendent was at the Rockwood Asylum in Kingston in 1885, roughly when Blumer would begin his own career as a head psychiatrist at Utica. In 1905, Clarke became medical superintendent of the Toronto Asylum, and in 1908 he was appointed dean of the Faculty of Medicine and professor of psychiatry at the University of Toronto. In 1911 he left the Toronto Asylum to become su-

37. C. G. Stogdill, "Joseph Workman, M.D., 1805–1894," *Canadian Medical Association Journal* 95 (1966): 917–23. See also T. J. W. Burgess, "Dr. Joseph Workman," in Hurd, *Institutional Care of the Insane*, 4:599–600.

perintendent of the Toronto General Hospital. At this stage most physicians would have been satisfied; but not Clarke. In 1909 he had already opened Canada's first outpatient psychiatric clinic, which he closed in 1913 and reopened in 1914. Then in 1918 he became the first medical director of the Canadian National Committee for Mental Hygiene (CNCMH), the forerunner of the Canadian Mental Health Association and counterpart to the U.S. National Committee for Mental Hygiene (NCMH). In this capacity he influenced policies that governed hospitals and schools across Canada by urging the use of intelligence testing, child guidance, vocational schooling, improved medical inspection of immigrants, better medical education for psychiatrists, and the reform of provincial mental hospitals.

Nonetheless, Clarke died a bitter man, with as many enemies as friends. He believed implacably that only trained physicians should determine how the mentally ill were treated. Like John Gray, Clarke from time to time showed an avuncular affection for younger doctors who shared his enthusiasm for psychiatry but whose own views often diverged substantially from his. Just as Gray was to befriend and promote the young G. Alder Blumer, so Clarke—though no lover of Freudian psychology—collaborated with the difficult Welshman and Freudian proselytizer Ernest Jones at a time (1908–13) when Jones had few allies and when psychoanalysis was in its infancy. This and other examples notwithstanding, Clarke could be acerbic and combative, especially when crossed or simply when others failed to share his fervor for reform. Unfortunately for the stubborn Clarke, this happened frequently throughout his career. It is a sad commentary on a career dedicated to what he imagined were the best interests of the mentally ill in Canada that during the First World War the Ontario government refused to allow him to visit provincial hospitals for the insane.[38]

The careers of Clarke and Thomas Burgess point up an important distinction between Canadian and U.S. political culture. In Canada the ties between psychiatry and government tended to be firmer than in the United States. In the United States, private and corporate mental hospitals dotted the map, especially in the Northeast. But Canada's population was much smaller and more dispersed, so the only realistic option for the vast majority of Canadian psychiatrists was to practice medicine as public servants and government employees. This feature of Canadian psychiatry also stemmed from the national preference for government

38. C. B. Farrar, "I Remember C. K. Clarke," *AJP* 114 (1957): 4.

responsibility for social welfare and from the indistinct boundary separating Canadian public and private life.[39] Historically Canadians have resorted to statist, corporatist approaches to social welfare, whereas U.S. citizens have preferred limited government involvement in welfare and health care. U.S. individualism has helped to sustain a faith in voluntary, private charity and philanthropy as an alternative to government control. With a Tory orientation rather than the "classically liberal-Whig" U.S. orientation, Canadians have been far more receptive than Americans to the allocation of public resources for group needs.[40] This tradition began in the late nineteenth century when Canada started the awkward transition from a country dominated by an economy of lumbering, mining, fishing, and farming to a nation characterized by growing industries and cities. As the old Canada of farm and village began disappearing, Canadians, like Americans, began voicing alarm over social ills, as the image of the typical frontier Canadian as a self-reliant master of his or her own fate began to be replaced by a model that depicted society as an organism of interdependent individuals in need of assistance, discipline, and control administered by elite professionals. By the end of the nineteenth century many Canadians were viewing the state as a potentially benevolent agency that ought to take an unprecedentedly active role in the management of deviance, charity, rehabilitation, education, child welfare, and public health.[41] Clarke and other Canadian psychiatrists were among those who urged the provinces and Ottawa to assume greater legislative and fiscal responsibility for mental health. It was their troubled attempt to forge a working alliance with the state that predisposed them to countenance extreme solutions to the problems of public health.

This difference between the United States and Canada notwithstanding, Clarke and Blumer were alike in one important respect: both belonged to a generation of physicians who entered asylum life in the late nineteenth century, intent on recapturing the original spirit of the first generation of psychiatrists and restoring the asylum-based moral treatment their forerunners had pioneered. But they also sought to integrate into asylum medicine new technologies of physical diagnosis and some of the innovative discoveries of late nineteenth-century medical science in such fields as bacteriology, surgery, and pathological anatomy. Clarke

39. Warsh, *Moments of Unreason*, p. 4.
40. Seymour Martin Lipset, *Continental Divide: The Values and Institutions of the United States and Canada* (New York: Routledge, 1990), pp. 136–51.
41. Neil Sutherland, *Children in English-Canadian Society: Framing the Twentieth-Century Consensus* (Toronto: University of Toronto Press, 1976).

and Blumer's generation conceded that the recent history of the asylum had not been particularly glorious, given the rising rates of chronic illness among patients, the accusations of patient abuse, the allegations of financial improprieties, and the charges of therapeutic incompetence and scientific ignorance. But they believed in the soundness of much of what had animated psychiatrists since the birth of the asylum. They agreed that a mental hospital was the best place for treating mental disease and consequently that it was in the patient's best interests to accept hospitalization. They were certain that predictions of the asylum's demise were premature; indeed they looked forward to the opportunity to revitalize it, mixing the best of new and old psychiatry for the benefit of the mentally ill.

By the mid-1880s, then, the future looked bright for both Blumer and Clarke as they began potentially impressive careers in psychiatry. The death and retirement of Gray and others of the old guard opened up new possibilities for the practice of asylum medicine along with new employment opportunities. But if Blumer, Clarke, and their generation expected easy going, a rude surprise awaited them. They soon discovered that the task of reconciling reform with psychiatry's traditions was ill suited to the times. They found themselves in an era of falling revenues, growing governmental control of social welfare services, and diminishing psychiatric power to determine mental hospital policy, management, and treatment. Restrictions on psychiatric autonomy were hardly novel, but the popular and official climate of the late nineteenth century engendered a taste for quick and often arbitrary solutions based on public impatience with social and institutional conditions. This mood was incompatible with the approach favored by hospital psychiatrists like Blumer and Clarke, who knew all too well that asylum treatment could not work wonders overnight or with everyone. They believed they should be free to improve conditions in their asylums in their own ways and at their own pace. In a supposed time of reform, they discovered to their chagrin that circumstances forced on them new and sometimes all too familiar masters who ended up destroying many of the dreams psychiatrists had entertained about the future of institutional psychiatry. By the early twentieth century the mental hospital was no longer a place of therapeutic optimism. Some psychiatrists left the asylum to pursue psychoanalysis or preventive mental health care, fields that looked exciting and promising at the time. For those still at work in the mental hospitals there was little hope and much frustration as the century progressed, a condition reflected in the sporadic recourse to desperate techniques such as lobotomies, electrotherapy, focal infection therapy, malarial shock, and insulin coma treatments.[42] The difficulties of hospital psychiatry also, as it happened, inculcated a taste for the fashionable theory of eugenics. As an approach to the problem of mental illness, eugenics suited the pessimism, disappointments, and flagging hopes of hospital psychiatry.

42. See Elliot S. Valenstein, *Great and Desperate Cures: The Rise and Decline of Psychosurgery and Other Radical Treatments for Mental Illness* (New York: Basic Books, 1986); and Jack D. Pressman, "Uncertain Promise: Psychosurgery and the Development of Scientific Psychiatry in America, 1933 to 1955" (Ph.D. diss., University of Pennsylvania, 1986). See also Jack D. Pressman, "Sufficient Promise: John F. Fulton and the Origins of Psychosurgery," *Bulletin of the History of Medicine* 62 (1988): 1–22. For focal infection theory, see Andrew Scull, "Desperate Remedies: A Gothic Tale of Madness and Modern Medicine," *Psychological Medicine* 17 (1987): 561–77.

1/

AN EXODUS OF ENTHUSIASM: PSYCHIATRY IN CANADA AND THE UNITED STATES, 1880–1920

he mid-1880s were watershed years in the lives and careers of Blumer and Clarke and in the history of U.S.-Canadian psychiatry. Clarke's appointment as medical superintendent of the Rockwood Asylum in 1885 and Blumer's as medical superintendent of the Utica Asylum in 1886 carried with them considerable prestige and were the envy of many U.S. and Canadian assistant asylum physicians working long hours at low pay with little job security. Both men dedicated themselves to reforming their asylums in ways they believed would serve the needs of their patients; yet they encountered obstacles that they had hoped would vanish as the wider cause of asylum reform gained momentum and converts. These largely political obstacles were evoking bitter feelings as the century drew to a close. Physicians were beginning to believe that the future in state asylum psychiatry would see psychiatrists reduced to the status of powerless and vulnerable civil servants. The fear that their professional dreams would never be realized if they stayed in public psychiatry eventually prompted both Clarke and Blumer to venture into new endeavors, but the struggle to survive—and ultimately escape—state psychiatry would affect their personalities and ideas in subtle ways, leaving them responsive to new and sometimes ill-advised theories about the nature and treatment of mental illness. Their intellectual and emotional reactions to the evolution of hospital psychiatry, though far from identical, refracted the frustrations, unhappiness, and demoralization of many psychiatrists as they uneasily prepared themselves for the new century.

I

There were two stages to Clarke's career: the first, 1874 to 1911, in the provincial asylum system; and the second, when he cut his ties to the provincial service and threw his energies into preventive psychiatry, from 1911 until his death in 1924. His first eight years in the provincial service culminated in a stint as an assistant physician at the Hamilton Asylum from 1880 to 1882. His stay at Hamilton "was like a horrible dream," Clarke confessed. He had taken the job in the first place because of his first wife's illness. The cost of her treatment had forced him to postpone plans to set himself up in private practice.[1]

That he had made such plans says a great deal about Clarke's early impressions of the provincial mental health care system. In his first job at the Toronto Asylum, his career had overlapped briefly with that of Joseph Workman, the medical superintendent, perhaps Canada's greatest nineteenth-century psychiatrist. Clarke was later to call Workman "the greatest man I have ever known," and he plainly learned from him some indelible lessons. As Clarke revealed, Workman retired in 1875 because he was "angered at the political game being carried on by Mr. [J. W.] Langmuir (Inspector of Asylums) who tried to act the lay dictator."[2] In 1881, Workman made his own views public when he attacked the prevailing practice of political appointments to asylum staffs.[3] "Much government is in all departments of life a fundamental evil," Workman said, and Clarke wholeheartedly agreed.[4] Swayed by the personal grudges of an old man near retirement, Clarke drew the conclusion—one that was to stay with him for the rest of his life—that politicians and bureaucrats

1. For biographical details about Clarke, see Cyril Greenland, *Charles Kirk Clarke: A Pioneer of Canadian Psychiatry* (Toronto: Clarke Institute of Psychiatry, 1966), p. 9; see also Cyril Greenland, "The Origins of the Toronto Psychiatric Hospital," in "TPH: History and Memories of the Toronto Psychiatric Hospital," ed. Edward Shorter, QSMHC, Unpublished MSS., 1993, pp. 28–90.
2. Greenland, *Charles Kirk Clarke*, pp. 8–9.
3. For similar complaints, see the comments of Thomas Burgess in *Dominion Medical Monthly* 29 (1907): 136.
4. C. G. Stogdill, "Joseph Workman, M.D., 1805–1894: Alienist and Medical Teacher," *Canadian Medical Association Journal* 95 (1966): 917–23, 921.

should always defer to psychiatrists in the formulation and implementation of mental health care policy.

As Clarke began his psychiatric career, such was not the case. Medical superintendents, their assistant physicians, and their staff were answerable to the inspector of prisons and public charities, who in turn was accountable to the provincial secretary, the provincial government minister in charge of the asylum system. In other words, a medical superintendent was essentially a public-salaried civil servant locked into a hierarchical network dominated by elected politicians. Medical superintendents were increasingly expected to account for more details of finances and patient treatment, which inevitably led to more record keeping and absorbed more and more of a medical superintendent's time. Officials insisted all this was intended to ensure that patients were neither neglected nor abused, but it was also clear that governments were intent on reining in the growing cost of funding the asylum system. Ontario psychiatrists, including Clarke, denied there was any "extravagance" in provincial spending on asylums.[5] To them the whole problem could be distilled into one axiom: governments invariably behaved in ways detrimental to the effective treatment of the insane.[6] Clarke thus realized what the future held for him as a provincial psychiatrist: he would always be at the mercy of officials who took their orders from politicians.

Financial compensation was the other reason for Clarke to entertain the idea of going into private practice. By the end of the century the salary as well as the perquisites and allowances of a provincial psychiatrist were no longer terribly generous. In 1894 an Ontario medical superintendent made only half of what a psychiatrist made in the New York State system.[7] The provincial government was continually seeking to reduce the fringe benefits medical superintendents enjoyed, such as free room and board. Already, by the mid-1880s, making a living as an Ontario asylum psychiatrist was looking less and less attractive.

Yet Clarke did not leave the public service after the Hamilton Asylum job. Instead, he accepted the offer of his brother-in-law William Metcalf to join him as an assistant physician at the Rockwood Asylum in Kingston. Not only were Metcalf and Clarke related through marriage; they

5. "Annual Report of the Medical Superintendent of the Asylum for the Insane, Kingston, 1894" (hereafter cited as ARK), app. to *Annual Report of the Inspector of Prisons and Public Charities upon the Lunatic and Idiot Asylums of the Province of Ontario* (Toronto: Queen's Printer, 1895), p. 72.
6. S. E. D. Shortt, *Victorian Lunacy: Richard M. Bucke and the Practice of Late Nineteenth-Century Psychiatry* (Cambridge: Cambridge University Press, 1986), pp. 36–42.
7. Shortt, *Victorian Lunacy*, pp. 35–36.

thought alike about how to provide humane treatment for their patients. Their collaboration was brief, however. On 13 August 1885 a patient named Patrick Maloney attacked Metcalf with a knife, dealing him a mortal blow. Luckily Clarke, who was present when the patient assaulted Metcalf, was a physically powerful man and was not wounded when Maloney turned on him. Aid arrived in time to subdue Maloney and save Clarke. Metcalf died shortly thereafter.[8]

After Metcalf's death Clarke was offered the position of medical superintendent at Kingston. He accepted, despite the fact that only the day before Metcalf's murder he had handed in his written resignation from government service. He agreed to stay on in Kingston "in order," he said, "to protect several hundred defenceless creatures from a political hireling who might be pitchforked into the position." He added: "I love psychiatry, but I hate politics: I felt that much could be accomplished if the politicians could be fought off with any degree of success."[9] Many who knew Clarke confirmed that he deeply empathized with the mentally ill and actually enjoyed their company.[10] But it is telling that he scrapped his plans for private practice once he was offered the post of medical superintendent. Obviously, three years working at Rockwood had not changed his mind about politics and politicians. He believed it was his duty to use his new position of relative power to safeguard the interests of the insane. But it is also indicative of Clarke's keen personal ambition that he only decided to pursue a career as an asylum psychiatrist, irrevocably turning his back on private practice, once he was appointed Rockwood's medical superintendent.

Clarke plunged into his new duties at Kingston, intent on reforming the asylum from top to bottom. Canadian psychiatrists shared the views of their late nineteenth-century U.S. counterparts about the need to transform asylums from custodial institutions into hospitals dedicated to the scientific treatment and diagnosis of mental diseases. They were becoming increasingly anxious about the way contemporaneous discoveries in biologic science were widening the gap between psychiatry and the rest of medicine. Psychiatrists worried that as other branches of medicine proved more adept at curing ailments, the public would expect more out of mental medicine than the therapeutic pessimism of Workman's generation.

8. See "Fatal Assault on Dr. Metcalf," *AJI* 42 (1885): 259–64.
9. Greenland, *Charles Kirk Clarke*, p. 10.
10. See, e.g., C. M. Hincks, "Prospecting for Mental Health: The Autobiography of Clare Hincks," QSMHC, Unpublished MSS., 1962, p. 28.

Psychiatrists were reminded of these disquieting circumstances by the well-known U.S. neurologist S. Weir Mitchell. In 1894, Mitchell was invited to give the keynote address on the fiftieth anniversary of the American Medico-Psychological Association. He at first declined the invitation knowing full well that as a neurologist he would have to say something critical of psychiatry. But the AMPA pressed him and Mitchell eventually agreed to attend. When he spoke he took psychiatry severely to task for remaining isolated from the rest of medicine. He also cited neurologists' other standard complaints about asylum psychiatry. Yet, curiously, the AMPA reaction was far from hostile. Clarke himself admitted that "it required a good deal of forbearance to endure" Mitchell's speech, if only because "in some of the institutions of Ontario, we had done so many of the things that he said ought to be done." Still, he conceded, "there was a great deal of truth in what was said."[11]

Indeed Clarke had already been vigorously championing "the hospital idea," the notion that a psychiatric asylum should cease being a receptacle for hopeless and destitute welfare cases and start being an institution oriented toward the cure of the mentally ill.[12] He dearly wished to throw off psychiatry's growing reputation as a group of professionals entrusted with the custody of incurable and violent patients. The list of his reforms at Kingston was quite impressive. For example, over Workman's objections, he continued the policy against restraints, introduced in 1883 under Metcalf, even though it could be blamed in part for Metcalf's death.[13] Clarke was also a firm believer in formal training for nurses and attendants in mental hospitals; for he knew all too well what abuses stemmed from poorly trained and underpaid staff. To Clarke goes the credit for establishing in 1888 the first Canadian course in psychiatry for student nurses. He was instrumental in introducing occupational therapy to offset the abolition of restraint. One of his favorite projects was a brush-making factory staffed by patients. He hoped that profits from the patients' labor could be used to improve the asylum's financial position and he was gratified that such programs kept patients occupied instead of sitting about all day. But no sooner was his factory up and running in 1886 than

11. S. Weir Mitchell, "Address before the Fiftieth Annual Meeting of the American Medico-Psychological Association . . . 1894," *PAMPA* 1 (1894): 101–21. See also Walter Channing, "Some Remarks on the Address Delivered . . . by S. Weir Mitchell . . . 1894," *AJI* 51 (1894): 171–81; and H. A. Tomlinson letter in *Journal of Nervous and Mental Diseases* 21 (1894): 512–15. Cited in Gerald N. Grob, *Mental Illness and American Society, 1875–1940* (Princeton: Princeton University Press, 1983), pp. 61–62. For Clarke's comments, see ARK, 1894, p. 72.
12. ARK, 1891, p. 75; 1893, pp. 67–68.
13. C. K. Clarke, "The Care of the Insane in Canada," *AJI* 50 (1894): 381–85, 381.

politicians, organized labor, and brush-making manufacturers complained to the inspector of asylums about price undercutting and unfair competition, and he ordered Clarke to shut down his workshops.

Undaunted, Clarke shifted to other forms of activity, including a school for female patients.[14] Another step in the right direction, he believed, would be the establishment of a provincial institute equipped with laboratories and gifted pathologists who could then pursue studies in physiology, biochemistry, and psychology.[15] But Clarke's energy began to dissipate as the 1890s wore on. One thing he wanted changed was the official name of the Rockwood Asylum. He thought changing the word *asylum* to "hospital" would do much to remove the stigma from mental illness, mental institutions, and the mentally ill.[16] But the government never followed his advice while he was at Kingston. During his stay the institution continued to be known formally as the Kingston Asylum for the Insane, its name serving as a constant reminder that, officially at least, it was something less than a regular hospital.

Like other institutional psychiatrists of his day, Clarke was also growing uneasy about the mixing of the mentally ill and the criminally insane. The problem was particularly nettlesome to him because the proximity of the Kingston Provincial Penitentiary meant that insane convicts whose sentences had expired were often transferred to Rockwood.[17] The presence of the criminally insane in asylums lowered the status of psychiatry and reinforced the popular image of the psychiatrist as a jailer who managed violent inmates. Naturally, Clarke wanted his wards free of violent patients, and when the government did nothing, he became increasingly frustrated and dispirited.

Nor was Clarke pleased with another element of his patient population in the 1890s. By the last years of that decade the admission of incurable patients far outstripped the admission of curable ones. Clarke was not far wrong when he wrote that this situation was due to "the old story of careless relatives, who take advantage of the warrant system, to get rid of the feeble dements who need a little care and nursing, not detention in a hospital for the insane."[18] In practice it was not too difficult to get

14. "Many of the people of this district are illiterate," he wrote, "and the patients are delighted at the prospect of being taught to read and write." ARK, 1891, p. 75.
15. ARK, 1894, p. 72; 1897, p. 96.
16. ARK, 1893, p. 67.
17. ARK, 1896, p. 118. Clarke wrote in 1899 that the criminal mentally ill were "degenerates [who] not only use language of the most shocking character, and disseminate the most degrading ideas, but they make repeated attempts at homicide without the least provocation." ARK, 1899, p. 103.
18. ARK, 1897, p. 93.

two physicians to sign a written certificate and commit a family member as long as the patient showed a psychological break with reality or was dangerous to self or others. Families often took the initiative and arranged interviews with regular physicians to get the necessary signatures.[19] Instances of this behavior by Canadian families increased until asylum psychiatrists had to spend much of their time ministering to people for whom there was little prospect of cure.

Clarke and his psychiatric colleagues found professional life equally difficult outside their hospitals. During the nineteenth century throughout the Western world magistrates in criminal cases increasingly solicited the advice of physicians regarding the responsibility of defendants. But identifying the fine distinctions between sanity and insanity was at best an imprecise art. When psychiatrists testified in favor of nonresponsibility in sensational and highly publicized trials like the Guiteau case, they rarely escaped public opprobrium. They also faced opposition from members of the legal profession who resented what seemed like medical interference in purely judicial matters. But disapproval did not stop psychiatrists from campaigning for recognition of their status as expert witnesses. Whenever they helped convince a judge and jury that a defendant was insane they congratulated themselves on having saved a lunatic from the gallows.

Clarke himself gained national notoriety when he appeared as a witness for the defense in a sensational Quebec trial of 1895. On the night of 1 March, Valentine Shortis, a recent immigrant from an affluent Irish family, shot and killed two men and seriously wounded a third, all without any apparent motive or emotion. Clarke's diagnosis and testimony that Shortis was "an imbecile" who suffered from "homicidal mania" did not help Shortis much: he was found guilty of murder and condemned to die. Shortis was saved from hanging when the governor-general refused to sign the death warrant and commuted his sentence to life imprisonment. The Montreal French-speaking press attacked Clarke's personal integrity and acumen for defending the English-speaking Shortis.[20] It is

19. Jacalyn Duffin, *Langstaff: A Nineteenth-Century Medical Life* (Toronto: University of Toronto Press, 1993), pp. 126–44.
20. This decision was highly unpopular among French-speaking Quebeckers because they wanted Shortis to share the fate of Louis Riel, the "Metis" rebel whose uprising in Manitoba ten years earlier had ended in his execution at the hands of the Canadian government. Clarke agreed that Riel, whom he labeled an "insane paranoiac," should not have been hanged. Cyril Greenland, "*L'affaire Shortis* and the Valleyfield Murders," *Canadian Psychiatric Association Journal* 7 (1962): 261–71. See also Martin L. Friedland, "The Case of Valentine Shortis: A Study of Crime and Politics in Canada" (Ph.D. diss., University of Toronto Faculty of Law, 1985); and Irwin N. Perr, "The Trial of Louis Riel: A Study in Canadian Psychiatry," *Journal of Forensic Sciences* 37 (1992): 845–52.

little wonder, then, that Clarke and other psychiatrists thought that serving as expert witnesses was a thankless task.

Clarke also felt this way because of instances of direct political pressure on psychiatric witnesses. For example, he alleged in 1897 that the provincial government "in its recent crusades took up the subject of expert evidence in murder trials and quietly intimated that the general public wished to hang insane murderers and as the 'general public' means 'votes,' the edict went forth that Superintendents should be muzzled." What this meant for psychiatrists active in legal medicine became obvious to Clarke when he was ordered by the provincial attorney general to render his opinion in a trial involving a child murderer. After examining the defendant Clarke testified that he was mentally retarded. When he went to collect his fees and traveling expenses he "was politely told that the government has issued an order that they were not to be paid and the result is that I have had to foot the whole bill myself." Clarke drew the "worse than disheartening" conclusion that "a petty persecution is being waged against faithful officials [like myself] not because they are distrusted but because such persecution is popular with an ignorant but powerful class of voters."[21] To Clarke, then, political interference in legal medicine was another instance of the way politicians dependent on votes kept psychiatrists from doing their jobs as they saw fit. This was a complaint he would repeatedly voice throughout the balance of his career, particularly with regard to the issue of immigration restriction.

Thus by the turn of the century Clarke's attitude toward the practice of psychiatry in asylums and courts of law had grown bitter and pessimistic. The seemingly incessant political interference disheartened him and made him feel older than he was. He was in fact so tired of political meddling that he had begun looking for employment outside the Ontario mental health care system. "If we could only get rid of the curse of politics," he wrote Blumer in 1905, "the future would be far more hopeful."[22]

Just as things looked darkest, however, they took a decided turn for the better. Much to his surprise and joy the new Conservative provincial government offered him the post of medical superintendent of the Toronto Asylum, the institution where he had begun his psychiatric career. Clarke's suddenly improved disposition is clear in a letter to Blumer shortly after he had accepted the Toronto appointment. "I go to Toronto," Clarke confided,

21. C. K. Clarke to G. Alder Blumer, 16 February 1897, BP, box 29.
22. Clarke to Blumer, 16 February 1897, BP, box 29; 11 September 1905, BP, box 30.

unhampered by political conditions, with a free hand to do as I please in the way of making reforms, changes and additions, and as an adviser to the Government in inaugurating a new era in asylum affairs. Behind the scenes there looms up a $2,000,000 General Hospital, with Psychopathic branch; it will be largely in regard to this [that] my services will be called on, that is of course "entre nous."

I have a sad task at the old Asylum, as chaos reigns there. Of course I shall benefit financially, professionally, and almost every other way, and I think there is enough energy left to stir things up as thoroughly as should have been done long ago. This coming from a hostile government is a great compliment, and great promise for better things, as the old government would never have made the slightest advance, as they were hopelessly wedded to their one fad of economy. Rockwood is really the only half up to date institution in the whole outfit, and unless they are content to let me play Nero, and fiddle Toronto to destruction, the case up there will be pretty hopeless.[23]

Clarke's "new era in asylum affairs" included his advice to tear down the old Toronto Asylum, which had stood for sixty years, and replace it with a psychiatric institute. The idea of such an institute was quite new in medicine, although the theory behind it was as old as psychiatry itself. More and more psychiatrists had come to be convinced that if physicians were going to be more effective at curing emotional disorders, they would have to devote themselves primarily to the treatment of recent or acute cases. Psychiatrists had always insisted that the chances for a cure improved the sooner a patient was brought to the attention of a physician and committed to an asylum. But asylums filled with hopeless cases could only serve as public charity facilities for the chronically ill. What was needed, psychiatrists now believed, was a special institution, affiliated with a university medical school and a general hospital, where genuinely remedial medical care could be practiced. Clarke added that the costs of renovating the Toronto Asylum were so high that the government might as well build an entirely new institution.[24] He hoped that with a psychiatric institute he would be able to say good-bye to the disheartening and dissatisfying experience of asylum medicine and function instead as a

23. Clarke to Blumer, 11 September 1905, BP, box 30.
24. "Annual Report of the Medical Superintendent of the Asylum for the Insane, Toronto, 1906" (hereafter cited as ART), app. to the *Annual Report of the Inspector of Prisons and Public Charities upon the Lunatic and Idiot Asylums of the Province of Ontario* (Toronto: King's Printer, 1907), pp. 4–6.

The Toronto Asylum, ca. 1910. Courtesy of the Archives of Canadian Psychiatry and Mental Health Services.

modern and scientific physician employing the most up-to-date techniques for the diagnosis and treatment of curable patients.

Clarke's campaign for a provincial psychiatric institute went well at first. In 1907 the provincial government sent him and two other physicians to Europe to study the Continent's major psychiatric clinics. What they saw pleased them immensely, especially the Munich clinic run by the German psychiatrist Emil Kraepelin (1856–1926), who was then widely considered the reigning authority in clinical psychiatry. Kraepelin's hugely influential *Textbook of Psychiatry* was published in eight editions from 1883 to 1915, growing from 384 pages to 3,000 pages in four volumes. Kraepelin's Munich clinic with its facilities for treatment, clinical study, and pathological research was just what Clarke had in mind.[25]

Clarke returned from Europe hopeful that the provincial government was ready to go ahead, but despite an announcement in 1908 of its intention to erect such an institute, it later changed its mind.[26] Clarke

25. For Clarke's impressions, see his "Notes on Some of the Psychiatric Clinics and Asylums of Germany," *AJI* 65 (1908): 357–76.
26. R. Andrew Paskauskas, "Ernest Jones: A Critical Study of His Scientific Development, 1896–1913" (Ph.D. diss., University of Toronto, 1985), pp. 191–94. See also Greenland, "Toronto Psychiatric Hospital."

C. K. Clarke, 1907. Courtesy of the Archives of Canadian Psychiatry and Mental Health Services.

blamed primarily his colleagues in Ontario asylum psychiatry for this change in plans, and for the rest of his life he rarely missed an opportunity to heap abuse on them. In 1911 he wrote peevishly that opposition to the psychiatric institute plan could be traced to his fellow psychiatrists, who thought a facility along the Munich lines would "destroy the usefulness of the present Hospitals for the Insane by drawing from them the interesting patients and interfering with the scientific enthusiasm of the staffs."[27] In 1923, a year before his death, he was more uncharitable, calling his erstwhile "brethren" in provincial psychiatry "a group of little Canadians, who feared that their personal glory might be dimmed."[28] Indeed Clarke's colleagues may well have resented the threat of his projected new institute siphoning off the most curable patients and reducing their institutions to mere holding tanks for chronically ill inmates. Funneling the most hopeful cases into one hospital could only have reinforced the bad reputation asylums had already acquired.[29]

27. ART, 1911, p. 100.
28. C. K. Clarke, "The Fourth Maudsley Lecture," *Journal of Mental Science* 69 (1923): 279–95, 284.
29. Thomas E. Brown, " 'Living with God's Afflicted': A History of the Provincial Lunatic Asylum at Toronto, 1830–1911" (Ph.D. diss., Queen's University, 1980), p. 370.

Clarke's dreams for a grand reform of the Ontario asylum system were temporarily in ruins. It is a measure of the esteem he enjoyed within general medicine that he was able to resign his post at the Toronto Asylum in 1911 to become superintendent of the Toronto General Hospital. Together with his 1908 appointments as dean of the Faculty of Medicine and professor of psychiatry at the University of Toronto, this career move amounted to his departure from the ranks of asylum psychiatry. He was now a powerful figure in Canadian medicine, respected by many physicians, but he left behind him ill will that further poisoned his already poor relations with provincial politicians and civil servants. As Clarke looked into the field of preventive mental health after 1911 he discovered that his outspokenness and ambition had made him many enemies. Rather than learning the lesson that diplomacy works best with bureaucrats and politicians, he continued to protest publicly whenever his views met resistance, whether or not the resistance was justifiable. This struggle between his steely stubbornness and the implacable inertia of government produced in him a bitterness that would both haunt his emotional life until the day he died and profoundly shape his interest in the medical inspection of immigrants.

II

As Clarke endured the frustrations of trying to reform asylum psychiatry in Ontario, Blumer was finding the politicization of mental health care in New York State equally demoralizing. Like Clarke he hoped to improve the circumstances of the practice of psychiatry in public hospitals. As a New York State psychiatrist he had even more reason to believe that the goal of genuinely curative psychiatry was realistic. A receptivity to change in the 1880s both in New York and elsewhere seemed propitious. When the antipsychiatric sentiments of the early 1880s abated, a broad medical and lay reform coalition took shape statewide, with Blumer in a pivotal role. He soon discovered however that the consequences of change were not all positive. The irony of so much reformism in turn-of-the-century psychiatry was that what started with such hope and optimism ended in such bitter discouragement. The resulting pessimism laid the ground for U.S. psychiatrists' support for "desperate remedies" as the century progressed.

When Blumer officially succeeded John Gray as medical superintendent at Utica in 1886 he had decided opinions about how to manage a mental hospital. As an assistant physician he had traveled to Edinburgh

G. Alder Blumer (center), with (from left to right) Edward N. Brush, Ogden Backus, Charles W. Pilgrim, and Theodore Deecke, on the steps of the Utica State Hospital, 1884. *American Journal of Psychiatry*, vol. 12, p. 379, 1932. Copyright 1932, The American Psychiatric Association. Reprinted by permission.

in the winter of 1883–84 to pursue further studies in psychiatry at the medical school he had briefly attended in 1877. There he had come into contact with Thomas Clouston (1840–1915), Edinburgh's reigning authority on psychiatry and a figure of growing prominence in psychiatry generally.[30] Clouston combined a lectureship at Edinburgh, awarded in 1879, with the post he had held since 1873 of medical superintendent of the Royal Edinburgh Asylum, the best-known mental hospital in Scotland. Blumer became a fervent admirer of the Scottish psychiatrist, and their cordial correspondence continued up to Clouston's death. It was no coincidence that Blumer and Clouston each combined asylum medicine, psychiatric teaching, and medical journalism in a single career.

The variety of clinical psychiatry Clouston was teaching when Blumer

30. Allan Beveridge, "Thomas Clouston and the Edinburgh School of Psychiatry," in *One Hundred and Fifty Years of British Psychiatry, 1841–1991*, ed. German E. Berrios and Hugh Freeman (London: Gaskell, 1991), pp. 359–88, 364. See also M. S. Thompson, "The Wages of Sin: The Problem of Alcoholism and General Paralysis in Nineteenth Century Edinburgh," in *The Anatomy of Madness: The Asylum and its Psychiatry*, ed. W. F. Bynum, Roy Porter, and M. Shepherd, 3 vols. (London: Routledge, 1988), 3:151–89.

arrived at Edinburgh stressed the theory that mental diseases were due to certifiably somatic conditions whose origins could be localized in specific regions of the brain. Clouston was heavily influenced by the ideas of Darwin, Lamarck, and Herbert Spencer and consequently rejected any metaphysical interpretations of the diseased mind. He also lectured tirelessly on the necessity of making the asylum into a hospital operated according to the most modern thinking in medicine. But along with most nineteenth-century psychiatrists he believed that asylum physicians should teach patients how to regain control of their emotions. If, as Clouston believed, insanity was essentially a breakdown in the physiological mechanism, then this kind of regimen was particularly suited to restoring nervous equilibrium.

Blumer's many notes written in his copies of Clouston's books show not only that he read the works of the Edinburgh psychiatrist closely but that Clouston's views shaped his approach to psychiatry as a medical superintendent. Where Clouston seems to have influenced Blumer most profoundly is in his interpretation of the asylum's corrective function. Like Clouston, Blumer was convinced that asylum life should teach patients how to control their behavior and obsessional thinking; accordingly, he introduced workshops, lectures, and formal schooling. He also relaxed institutional discipline by eliminating censorship of patients' letters, organizing outdoor games, and abolishing Gray's notorious Utica crib.[31]

In some ways Blumer was a throwback to the earlier generation of "alienists" who had emphasized the advantages of asylum-based moral treatment, the therapeutic approach that minimized the use of drugs and restraint and stressed the principle that psychological methods along with kindness, tact, and persuasion were the most effective techniques for treating insanity.[32] Thus though he favored new techniques of diagnosis and treatment he believed fervently in the theory that all these innovations were most effective in a medically supervised institution.

Besides succeeding Gray as head psychiatrist at Utica, Blumer also succeeded him as editor of the *AJI*.[33] Under Blumer the journal became more cosmopolitain and irenic. Published articles reflected an attempt to

31. For his memories of abolishing the Utica crib, see Blumer to George M. Kline, 18 July 1929, BP, box 35.
32. For Blumer's respect for the practices of mid-nineteenth-century psychiatrists such as Amariah Brigham, see Ellen Dwyer, *Homes for the Mad: Life inside Two Nineteenth-Century Asylums* (New Brunswick, N.J.: Rutgers University Press, 1987), p. 74. See also Blumer to Henry J. Coggeshall, 13 March 1889, BP, box 27.
33. In fact, Gray's poor health in the last years of his life meant that Blumer took over management of the *AJI* well before he was appointed medical superintendent. Edward Brush to C. B. Farrar, 18 June 1931, APA, RG (record group) Clarence B. Farrar, folder 43.

keep up with the scientific literature on the anatomy and physiology of the nervous system and the debates over psychiatric classification that were sweeping French, German, and Anglo-American medicine. The *AJI* also became a forum for theories about improving the quality of care of the insane.

Thus in a few years Blumer had established himself as a major figure in the nation's largest mental health care system. His reforms at Utica proved popular among his patients, and his wit and urbane manners also opened doors in local society. By the late 1880s his professional success seemed assured. But, like Clarke, he was soon to be reminded that employment as a public asylum psychiatrist had its difficulties.

In 1889 90 the New York State mental health care system underwent what Blumer and other psychiatrists saw as "revolutionary upheaval."[34] Legislation passed in Albany during these years produced sweeping changes in state care of the mentally ill. In keeping with other progressive reforms that were to transform the country between 1890 and the First World War, imposing centralized control over social services to the disadvantaged in the name of efficiency, New York State's progressive reforms set about making mental health care more accountable to government in Albany as a way of correcting alleged abuses and shortcomings.[35] Blumer and his colleagues tried to deal with these innovations as best they could, but in the end they found themselves caught up in a bureaucratic system that reduced their freedom to do what they thought best for their patients. Blumer finally escaped the predicaments of New York State asylum psychiatry in 1899, but psychiatrists across the country clearly faced a turning point in the practice of state hospital medicine. As one of them noted in 1899, "Many states look to New York for guidance in [lunacy] matters, and . . . 'As goes New York, so goes the Union,' is true in more than politics."[36] Psychiatrists could do little but regret the end of the relatively informal and localized management of the past.

Of course the care of the mentally ill in New York State had been

34. Blumer to P. M. Wise, 30 January 1891, BP, box 27.
35. For an overview of the debate over the U.S. progressive movement, see Arthur S. Link and Richard L. McCormick, *Progressivism* (Arlington Heights, Ill.: Davidson, 1983). The central works on the history of progressivism include Richard Hofstadter, *The Age of Reform: From Bryan to F.D.R.* (New York: Knopf, 1955); Samuel P. Hays, *The Response to Industrialism, 1885–1914* (Chicago: University of Chicago Press, 1957); Samuel Haber, *Efficiency and Uplift: Scientific Management in the Progressive Era, 1890–1920* (Chicago: University of Chicago Press, 1964); Robert H. Wiebe, *The Search for Order, 1877–1920* (New York: Hill and Wang, 1967); and Gabriel Kolko, *The Triumph of Conservatism: A Reinterpretation of American History, 1900–1916* (New York: Free Press, 1963).
36. William Russell to Blumer, 13 August 1899, BP, box 41.

evolving under pressure from reformers well before 1889–90. County authorities responsible for the local care and custody of the insane in almshouses and county asylums had conducted an ongoing debate with those who believed that this form of treatment was costly, inhumane, and medically ineffective. In a development matched by trends nationwide, the publicly supported almshouse (or poorhouse)—the main receptacle for the country's elderly persons with mental and physical infirmities—had come under increasing criticism. Reformers had claimed the typical almshouse was poorly constructed, ventilated, heated, and managed, indiscriminately mixing children, adults, lunatics, and the aged under one roof. In New York State, lunacy reformers had struggled to convince legislators to authorize the erection of asylums for the mentally ill so almshouse inmates could be placed in state-level facilities. Progress had been slow; as late as 1881 there were still 6,311 insane persons in county institutions but only 3,289 in the six state hospitals.[37] Nonetheless, as Gerald Grob demonstrates, "the conversion of the mental hospital into a surrogate home for elderly and other kinds of chronic cases" was well underway across the country.[38]

Although state asylum psychiatrists too disliked county care and agreed that transferring county patients to state asylums was in the best interests of these men and women, they departed from the reformers in believing that these patients should be hospitalized in institutions especially designed to accommodate the chronically ill. Their own asylums in the post–Civil War era were crowded with poor, violent, and long-term patients, so the last thing they wanted was the custodial responsibility for more of the same. Thus, by the late 1880s, psychiatrists and reformers in New York State had found themselves in an uneasy alliance. When, after the reform legislation of 1889–90, progressivism swept the state asylum system, psychiatrists found themselves caught in a difficult, middle position: sympathetic to the centralization of care but unwilling to accept the implication that this policy dictated close supervision of psychiatry by state officials. Much of their outrage over reforms to their asylums undoubtedly flowed from their realization that their own lobbying had helped to bring them about.

The first significant step in the reform of asylum psychiatry in New York State was the replacement in 1889 of the state commissioner in lunacy with a three-man commission authorized to set and impose stan-

37. David M. Schneider and Albert Deutsch, *The History of Public Welfare in New York State, 1867–1940* (Chicago: University of Chicago Press, 1941), p. 90.
38. Gerald N. Grob, *The Mad among Us: A History of the Care of America's Mentally Ill* (New York: Free Press, 1994), p. 120.

daids of patient care, financial accountability, and attendants' staffing and training on all state mental hospitals. The president of the new commission was a physician, Carlos MacDonald (1845–1923), soon to be Blumer's bitter enemy. Between 1873 and 1889, MacDonald had held the rank of medical superintendent at three different state asylums. He was more of a neurologist than a psychiatrist, which alone aroused suspicion in the eyes of the state's medical superintendents.[39] He was joined on the commission by two laymen, Henry Reeves and Goodwin Brown. In MacDonald's own words, the commission's powers were "practically unlimited, being probably greater than has heretofore been conferred by the legislature upon any similar body in any department of the State government."[40] Moreover, it quickly became clear that these broad powers would be exercised in ways that would arouse opposition not only from asylum psychiatrists jealous of their freedom to practice medicine but also from the unsalaried, public-spirited men and women who visited and inspected their local hospitals and oversaw the awarding of contracts for supplies and repairs. To psychiatrists and their managers the commission represented political centralization that would extinguish the spirit of charity in state hospitals. They agreed that all care of the dependent insane should be at the state level, but they could not endorse all the steps the commission imagined it had to take to reach that goal. For example, beyond its powers to visit, inspect, and recommend changes in the management of both private and public asylums, the commission lobbied the state legislature to break down the distinctions among the various state hospitals and establish uniform standards of record keeping, especially in financial matters. Perhaps most galling of all to state medical superintendents was the 1893 statute that reduced the per capita cost of maintenance for the six state hospitals from $208 to $184, a reduction that would inevitably be reflected in the quality of care.[41]

The creation of the Commission in Lunacy was followed by the State Care Act of 1890, legislation that ended county care for the insane in New York State (except for the counties of Kings, Monroe, and New York). By ordering the transfer of all the insane under county care to state asylums, the act also officially abolished the distinction between

39. "Dinner for Carlos F. MacDonald, M.D.," *New York State Hospitals Bulletin* 3 (1910–11): 165–70.
40. Carlos F. MacDonald, "Recent Legislation for the Insane in the State of New York," *AJI* 47 (1891): 354–83, 363.
41. Henry M. Hurd, ed., *The Institutional Care of the Insane in the United States and Canada*, 4 vols. (Baltimore: Johns Hopkins University Press, 1916–17), 3:121–27.

acute and chronic illness, thereby implying that seemingly incurable cases could be cured.[42] Unfortunately, most psychiatrists believed that nearly all the insane men and women from county institutions were well past the stage where recovery was possible. The presence of these patients in so-called therapeutic asylums such as Utica, psychiatrists argued, would depress the atmosphere and overcrowd the wards, making it even more difficult to cure patients who might recover. As one physician wrote Blumer in late 1890, "It is a pity that [the State Care Act] cannot distinguish more closely between the sheep and goats and leave a hospital where everything is so satisfactory as at Utica."[43] The act officially changed the name of all state lunatic institutions from "asylum" to "hospital," but ironically, just when psychiatrists had succeeded in improving the medical image of their institutions, their roles became more custodial than ever.[44]

One of the first practical consequences of the State Care Act was the transfer of some fifteen hundred mentally ill persons from county institutions to state hospitals. This influx had the predictable effect of swelling Utica's patient ranks with dependent syphilitic and senile persons, eroding the distinction between Utica—a supposedly acute-care facility—and the official State Asylum for Incurables at Willard. Between 1886 and 1899, Utica's patient population grew from 574 to 1,119. The percentage of announced recoveries among all patients fell from 20 percent in 1889 to between 7 and 9 percent throughout the 1890s.[45] Data at other New York State asylums confirm that the emptying of county institutions in the early 1890s translated into overcrowding and falling recovery rates.[46] The process was still going strong in 1900 when the head psychiatrist of the Binghamton State Hospital wrote:

42. Schneider and Deutsch, *Public Welfare in New York State*, pp. 94–97. For the public debate over the State Care Act and its emphasis on the curability of insanity, see *New York Daily Tribune*, 27 January 1891; *New York World*, 29 January 1891; *Binghamton Republican*, 15 February 1896; and *Newtown Register*, 3 September 1896.
43. Francis Metcalfe to Blumer, 27 November 1890, BP, box 27.
44. Dwyer, *Homes for the Mad*, pp. 208–12. See also Ian Dowbiggin, " 'Midnight Clerks and Daily Drudges': Hospital Psychiatry in New York State, 1890–1905," *Journal of the History of Medicine and Allied Sciences* 47 (1992): 130–52.
45. New York State Lunatic Asylum, *Fifty-Fifth Annual Report of the Managers of the State Lunatic Asylum at Utica* (Albany: James B. Lyon, State Printer, 1895), p. 52; 1896, p. 46; 1897, p. 64; 1898, pp. 41, 54–59; 1899, p. 50; 1900, p. 50. Hereafter cited as NYSLA.
46. See, e.g., the data for the St. Lawrence asylum, opened in 1891. St. Lawrence State Hospital for the Insane, *Tenth Annual Report of the Managers of the St. Lawrence State Hospital for the Year 1896* (Albany: Wynkopp Hallenbeck Crawford, 1897), pp. 47, 59; *Twelfth Annual Report, 1898*, p. 65; *Thirteenth Annual Report, 1899*, p. 65; *Fourteenth Annual Report, 1900*, p. 66.

We are receiving every year a large number of old people, some of them very old, who are simply suffering from the mental decay incident to extreme old age. A little mental confusion, forgetfulness and garrulity are sometimes the only symptoms exhibited, but the patient is duly certified to us as insane and has no one at home capable or possessed of means to care for him. We are unable to refuse these patients without creating ill-feeling in the community where they reside, nor are we able to assert that they are not insane within the meaning of the statute, for many of them, judged by the ordinary standards of sanity, cannot be regarded as entirely sane.[47]

This transfer of senile men and women from county to state facilities in New York reflected the growing use of the public mental hospital nationwide as the old-age home of choice for the mentally or physically impaired elderly.[48]

The socioeconomic status of Utica hospital patients also changed as county pauper cases were admitted. Some of these charity patients were of course respectable men and women whose families could not afford the costs of private care. Yet the testimony of New York State psychiatrists indicates that by the time most of them reached a public asylum they were in a disheveled, dirty, unruly and unhealthy state that evoked little sympathy from their future medical custodians.[49]

These changes were accelerated by a regulation of the State Commission in Lunacy that limited both the rate charged for private patients at state hospitals and the institutional space a medical superintendent could assign to privately paying persons. For most superintendents and managers of state hospitals, the admission of private patients was synonymous with the admission of curable, respectable, and socially agreeable persons.[50] Besides reducing the revenues of each hospital, cutting back on the number of paying patients, like absorbing the transfers from county facilities, threatened to upset the already delicate balance between poor and respectable inmates, lowering the status of the state institutions. Psychiatrists complained that the "pauperization" of their asylums was well underway.[51] The State Commission in Lunacy's position was that the regulation would make more room available for less fortunate and more

---

47. Charles G. Wagner, New York State Commission in Lunacy, *Annual Report*, vol. 12, 1900, pp. 22–36, cited in Grob, *Mental Illness and American Society*, pp. 186–87.
48. Grob, *Mental Illness and American Society*, pp. 179–87.
49. NYSLA, 1892, p. 7; 1894, p. 7. See also Wise to Blumer, 13 January 1894, BP, box 29, and 13 May 1892, BP, box 27. On the socioeconomic origins of Utica's patient population at the end of the nineteenth century, see Dwyer, *Homes for the Mad*, p. 105
50. NYSLA, 1891, pp. 15–16.
51. *New York Daily Tribune*, 27 January 1891.

seriously ill patients, implying that the resistance to this reform was due to class bias. That idea troubled some observers,[52] but others feared that if state hospitals admitted fewer and fewer paying patients, the gap between public and private hospitals would widen and, with it, the gap between rich and poor.[53]

Yet another contentious issue for the state's psychiatrists was the commission's 1890 order to each asylum to hire a female physician. In 1879, Pennsylvania had recommended that its state hospitals appoint women without making it mandatory. In the 1880s some states followed suit although they required women as assistant physicians, not as independent heads of women's wards.[54] A standard argument in favor of female psychiatrists, used by women's groups as well as some women physicians, was that female patients would prefer female doctors because physical lesions of the reproductive organs caused a large percentage of women's emotional disorders. Others rejected this theory, saying that "assuming this local trouble [of the reproductive organs] to exist, it is by no means clear that women are better qualified to treat it than men."[55] A further complication was that some women doctors began using this theory to justify ovariotomies just as enthusiasm for the procedure was in decline among male psychiatrists.[56] Psychiatrists' attacks on pelvic surgery thus became conflated with opposition to women psychiatrists, making it difficult now to distinguish plain misogyny from sincere resistance to a surgical procedure without proven therapeutic effectiveness. Certain male psychiatrists, trained in an era of therapeutic moderation, simply objected to invasive gynecologic surgery.[57] The issue was further clouded by the fact that some psychiatrists opposed women physicians because they disliked the notion of divided authority in state hospitals. They rejected out of hand sharing power with any other physician or layperson, much less a woman in charge of the female department and prepared to submit her patients to gynecologic operations. Above all, they disliked

52. *Albany Argus*, 30 December 1890, BP, Blumer Scrapbook.
53. *Middletown Daily Argus*, 17 July 1891.
54. See Constance McGovern, "Doctors or Ladies? Women Physicians in Psychiatric Institutions, 1872–1900," *Bulletin of the History of Medicine* 55 (1981): 88–107.
55. *Utica Daily Press*, 10 March 1890, BP, Blumer Scrapbook. See also Dwyer, *Homes for the Mad*, pp. 79–80, 241–42.
56. From his review of the literature on the history of ovariotomies, Edward Shorter has concluded that "women physicians often supported sexual surgery." Edward Shorter, *From Paralysis to Fatigue: A History of Psychosomatic Illness in the Modern Era* (New York: Free Press, 1992), pp. 348–49 n. 58.
57. Wendy Mitchinson, *The Nature of Their Bodies: Women and Their Doctors in Victorian Canada* (Toronto: University of Toronto Press, 1991), pp. 249–50.

taking orders in their own asylums from anyone but their own managers.[58]

Asylum physicians' opposition to the mandate to hire women physicians must therefore be seen in the broadest context, and in any case, medical resistance to the measure was far from doctrinaire. Although the state legislature in the end did not appropriate the necessary funds, most psychiatrists—including Blumer—went ahead and hired a woman physician anyway.[59] What mattered most to psychiatrists was their belief that their submission to the order to hire women physicians was another step in losing control over the management of their asylums to people whose good faith they deeply doubted.

New York State psychiatrists agreed on the need to take action to combat the perceived attempt to reduce them to the status of powerless bureaucrats. In this campaign Blumer played a leading role, and Peter Wise (1851–1907), the medical superintendent of the St. Lawrence Hospital in Ogdensburg, quickly became his chief ally and confidant. Early in 1891, in their second annual report, the commission recommended that each hospital's board of trustees be reduced from twelve to five members and that the commission take over from the State Board of Charities the duties of visiting and inspecting each hospital. To Wise this was a Machiavellian first step toward total abolition of asylum boards. Blumer also viewed the matter seriously; for on 30 January 1891 he wrote to Wise: "Your letter of the 28th inst. came as a balm to a sorely stricken soul. Thank heaven! there is at least one man in the State who seems to realize whither we are drifting. . . . We cannot afford to be passive in the presence of all this revolutionary upheaval. We cannot stand meekly by and see our system—the growth of years and the expression of the consecration of years of conscientious labor on the part of our brethren, living and dead—branded in lock, stock, and barrel with an iconoclastic N.G."[60]

In the midst of these problems Blumer received consolation and concrete assistance from at least one well-known source: he struck up a correspondence with Franklin B. Sanborn (1831–1917), a leading national authority on issues such as dependence, poverty, and penal reform.

58. At least one psychiatrist resisted the order to hire women physicians because he disliked appearing as if he were bowing to pressure from women's groups who supported the measure. See Judson Andrews to Blumer, 20 January and 7 February 1890, BP, box 27.
59. Edward N. Brush, "On the Employment of Women Physicians in Hospitals for the Insane," *AJI* 47 (1891): 323–30.
60. Blumer to Wise, 30 January 1891, BP, box 27.

Sanborn edited and wrote for the *Springfield Republican*, one of the country's finest newspapers, and had been instrumental in founding the American Social Science Association in 1865. He also was an original member of the Massachusetts Board of Charities, the first of its kind in the country, and had contributed in 1874 to the organization of the National Conference of Charities and Corrections, a national umbrella organization for state charity boards.[61]

Sanborn, like Blumer, saw value both in pre-Civil War individualism and in the more community-oriented postwar ethic that had resulted in institution building.[62] He agreed that trained experts were essential to improving the quality of life in the United States, but he had no illusions that they and their institutions were problem free, nor did he think that professionals alone knew everything about public charity. He was also skeptical about the progressivist urge to launch state-managed reform programs, which made him both Blumer's natural ally and a strident critic of the New York State Commission in Lunacy.

Sanborn thought, for example, that the mixing of curable and incurable cases in state hospitals was a disastrous policy:

From my point of view the so called improvements made by the Lunacy Commission in your State hospitals, are almost all retrograde steps, and the condition of insane care in New York is now decidedly worse than it was when I last visited the asylums in 1888. Perhaps as good an example of what I mean can be found in the fact stated by Dr. Wise, that the first patients at his new and costly hospital, in Ogdensburg, were old pauper cases from the county poor-houses, instead of acute cases susceptible of recovery, or particularly needing hospital care. The Lunacy Commissioners seem to imply that these old chronic cases are curable, and perhaps one in a hundred may be; but the duty of the State toward cases really curable, is so much more pressing than the duty of custodial care for these pauper dements, that I am grieved to see the chances of recovery, where recovery was possible, diminished by this forcing in of an incurable class, which will fill the St. Lawrence Hospital and overcrowd those at Buffalo, Utica, Poughkeepsie and Middletown. I can discover no compensation in the arbitrary projects

61. Thomas L. Haskell, *The Emergence of Professional Social Science: The American Social Science Association and the Nineteenth-Century Crisis of Authority* (Urbana: University of Illinois Press, 1977), pp. 51, 54, 55; for more on Sanborn, see chap. 3, "Frank Sanborn's Association," pp. 48–62. See also David J. Rothman, *The Discovery of the Asylum: Social Order and Disorder in the New Republic* (Boston: Little, Brown, 1971), pp. 251, 289.
62. Haskell, *Emergence of Professional Social Science*, p. 56.

and crude theories of the Lunacy Commission, for the excellent opportunities of recovery that existed in those hospitals when I last saw them . . . are now so seriously abridged and menaced.[63]

Naturally, Blumer was overjoyed to read this, and so began a long-running correspondence between the acerbic but clear-thinking reformer and the young and beleaguered asylum doctor.[64]

Blumer welcomed Sanborn's support; for he was in the process of mobilizing state psychiatrists against "the autocratic triumvirate at Albany."[65] Naturally his efforts earned them the enmity of the commission.[66] As one psychiatrist warned him in early 1894, "You are now the chief thorn in the side of the Commission and its pals. Don't leave any door unguarded."[67] Blumer hardly needed reminding; for 1893 the conflict had already turned nasty. The first solid indication that the commission's crusade to implement the letter and spirit of state care for the insane had grown personal had been the "Butterine" controversy. In February, Blumer had found himself the target of a public attack launched by no less than Roswell P. Flower, the governor of New York, who criticized him for purchasing for the Utica kitchen a butter substitute from a Chicago meat-packing firm rather than butter produced locally by Oneida County farmers.[68]

If there was any doubt as to what the Butterine controversy meant, there was none about the next series of events Blumer and his colleagues in psychiatry had to endure. In October, New York State began assuming full fiscal responsibility for the hospitalization of its dependent insane, provoking Carlos MacDonald to launch a public campaign to reduce what he deemed to be unnecessary expenditures. In November he charged that asylum spending abuses were rampant, citing as examples medical superintendents purchasing cigars, champagne, and sherry from their hospital budgets for personal use, and the four florists discovered at one unnamed New York State hospital. "That is as many as the late Jay Gould had," MacDonald, posing as a typically progressive enemy of

63. Franklin Sanborn to Blumer, 28 March 1891, BP, box 27.
64. Blumer to Sanborn, 30 March 1891, BP, box 27.
65. Blumer to Wise, 30 January 1891, BP, box 27; Blumer to Henry Hurd, 10 February 1891, BP, box 37.
66. Wise to Blumer, 17 December 1892, BP, box 27.
67. Edward Brush to Blumer, 8 January 1894, BP, box 28.
68. *Utica Daily Observer*, 2 February 1893, BP, Blumer Scrapbook. Blumer's explanation of his actions in the Butterine controversy are found in his letter to the commission, 3 March 1893, BP, box 27. See also Wise to Blumer, 13 January 1894, BP, box 28.

both big corporate trusts and civil service corruption, complained to the press.[69]

Matters came to a head in early 1894, with the culmination of a struggle going back to 1890. The commission had been campaigning to wrest control of the *AJI* from Blumer and the Utica Asylum. The effort seemed to be a personal affront to Blumer as well as a major threat to the autonomy of psychiatry itself. Presumably if the commission were successful in making the *AJI* the property of New York State, it could then exercise some sort of control over U.S. and Canadian psychiatrists. Blumer acted quickly, obtaining a ruling from the state attorney general that the *AJI* was in fact the property of the Utica hospital and its trustees. He then turned around and arranged for its sale in 1894 to the AMPA, thus narrowly keeping it out of the clutches of the commission.[70] Blumer's coup coincided with another attack by the commission. In a move widely acknowledged to be motivated by commission ill will, Blumer was forced on a technicality to undergo a civil service examination in order to keep his job at Utica. He passed the test, but no one was fooled about who was behind the incident.[71]

Blumer had the backing of most psychiatrists around the state, the country, and Canada; for all realized that what would happen in the Empire State would sooner or later affect them all. Many considered MacDonald to be little better than a traitor to psychiatry. "Some of you years ago were warned," one doctor wrote Blumer, "that your commissioner was a veritable Prince of Darkness." He "will stab any friend in the back to serve his own ends. He is a politician (in the worst sense of that word) to the backbone, and the knifing process comes perfectly natural to him."[72] Blumer wanted to have MacDonald expelled from the AMPA, but, as one colleague advised, "The moment we make MacDonald a martyr, that moment we strengthen his hands in certain localities and give opportunity to the enemy of repeating the old cry of tradesunionism and narrow-mindedness which they have hurled at the Association so often."[73] Psychiatrists in the 1890s had to be very careful about

69. *New York Daily Tribune*, 27 November, 4 and 6 December 1893; and *Buffalo Courier*, 27 November 1893; in Blumer Scrapbook, BP. For Blumer's complaints about the commission's estimates for the upcoming fiscal year, see Blumer to the State Commision in Lunacy, 25 November 1893, BP, box 27.
70. Blumer's account of this series of events is in his letter to A. R. Urquhart, 30 July 1894, BP, box 28. See also his letter to Farrar, 8 June 1934, APA, folder 24.
71. See *Albany Evening Journal*, 31 January 1894, BP, Blumer Scrapbook.
72. Walter Channing to Blumer, 5 December 1893, BP, box 27.
73. Brush to Blumer, 12 March 1894, BP, box 28. See also William Gorton to Blumer, 3 March 1894, ibid.

their public relations. As for Blumer, he fully supported a bill before the legislature which called for the abolition of the Commission in Lunacy and a return to the pre-1889 state of affairs.[74]

Much to Blumer's chagrin, however, Levi Morton, the new governor, reappointed MacDonald in early 1895 for another six-year term as commission president. Blumer and New York's medical superintendents thus had little to look forward to besides more battles with the commission. But there were surprises in store. On 30 September 1896, MacDonald resigned, stating his wish to enter private practice; but politics may also have been involved. The years 1893 to 1896 witnessed a shift in New York State political power from the Democrats to the Republicans, and MacDonald may have been so compromised by his years serving Democratic politicians that he was no longer trusted by his fellow Republicans.[75] MacDonald may also have decided that he could no longer tolerate the stress of serving on the commission. Although it is hard to know exactly what his motivations were during his battles with the state hospitals in the early 1890s, there is some evidence that he genuinely believed that the resistance he faced jeopardized the humanitarian principles of state care for the insane.[76]

An even greater surprise than MacDonald's departure was that he was replaced by Peter Wise. Blumer must have had an inkling of what would happen after Wise wrote him in September 1895 that the commission recently had behaved "in a manner not to call out any serious complaints. If they could expunge their past record and start anew, we might not have any great fault to find with them."[77] What Blumer thought about this is not recorded, but it hard to believe that he viewed Wise's elevation to the presidency of the commission as anything but a desertion to the enemy. In fact, after a temporary improvement, relations between state psychiatrists and the commission reverted to those of MacDonald's time. Relations between Blumer and Wise cooled. "I can assure you, dear Doctor," Wise wrote in 1898, "it makes a different impression whether you stand on the mountain top

74. D. R. Burrell to Blumer, 18 February 1894; and Blumer to John L. Wilkie, 9 February 1894, BP, box 28.
75. On New York's political history during these years, see Richard L. McCormick, *From Realignment to Reform: Political Change in New York State, 1893–1910* (Ithaca: Cornell University Press, 1979), esp. pp. 40–68.
76. For example, in 1891, MacDonald spoke to Henry Hurd of the Johns Hopkins Hospital about "the wearing character of his duties." As Hurd recounted, MacDonald blamed his unpopularity on "the necessity which seemed to exist for making the work of the Commission felt in behalf of State Care." See Henry Hurd to Blumer, 30 November 1891, BP, box 37.
77. Wise to Blumer, 24 September 1895, BP, box 28.

and see plainly in all directions, or whether you are merely on the mountain side and peek through a canon [sic]. Whatever I have done officially I have done conscientiously."[78]

Through the 1890s Blumer's optimism and enthusiasm for asylum medicine, like Clarke's, grew strained. As Utica's resident population reached a thousand he found himself increasingly unable to reconcile his commitment to maintaining an atmosphere conducive to moral treatment with the fact of his growing invalid and chronically ill patient class. The result in his eyes was nothing less than catastrophic: "Where the insane are massed together by the thousand," he wrote in 1893, "the danger is that routinism, the deadly foe of scientific medicine, may subjugate individualization, without which the highest aims of psychiatry cannot be realized."[79] Blumer's publications in the late 1890s reflected this state of affairs. Whereas earlier he had used occupational therapy to improve the chances of cure, he now saw it as valuable primarily because it made his many chronic patients "contented" and "peaceful."[80] The growing attention he paid to the virtues of work therapy stemmed from his discouragement with the difficulties of managing patients at a time when the standards of treatment, diagnosis, and scientific inquiry embraced by other U.S. physicians were getting higher and higher.

But Blumer was far from alone in his disillusionment. Even with the relatively favorable financial advantages of asylum psychiatry as late as 1900, young physicians choosing careers in medicine were not flocking to psychiatry.[81] Nor were state hospital physicians themselves cheerful about their specialty. As Wise lamented in 1894, "Oh! if I could only give up this unpleasant work, which has become so distasteful to me that I dread the day that dawns and retire with the feeling intensified. I am tired of everything and would rather live on a practice of a thousand a year than to continue it."[82] He daydreamed of running a private hospital that cared for only curable, "recent cases" of insanity. "The public ser-

78. Blumer to the State Commission in Lunacy, 28 May 1898; and Wise to Blumer, 18 September 1898, BP, box 29.
79. NYSLA, 1893, pp. 24–25; 1894, p. 23.
80. NYSLA, 1898, pp. 17–18. For Blumer's increasing preoccupation with work therapy in industrial shops or on farmland leased by state officials, see his "The Medical and Material Aspects of Industrial Employment for the Insane," *AJI* 54 (1897): 157–66, and "The Care of the Insane in Farm Dwellings," *AJI* 56 (1899): 31–40. For recognition that patients employed in the types of industrial and agricultural labor he recommended "are more easily handled," see George E. Dodge to Blumer, 11 January 1898, BP, box 29.
81. Grob, *Mental Illness and American Society*, p. 267.
82. Wise to Blumer, 13 January 1894, BP, box 28.

vice is becoming so distasteful to me," he added, "that . . . I think I would rather be a pauper."[83]

To Blumer, the spectacle of Wise, an erstwhile ally and friend, joining the very forces that had made life so difficult for them both, was disappointing and sobering. The fact that Wise's views had actually changed to suit his new office and responsibilities most likely confirmed for Blumer that, as he said later, the New York State system was no place for principled "gentlemen." The lesson was that if one were to survive professionally, then one had to come to terms with the powers that ran the state; if that meant following the official policy statements issued from Albany, then so be it. Like Clarke, Blumer was no longer young. Perhaps he concluded that the best way to practice public hospital psychiatry was to follow the path of least resistance and make peace with the state commission. One way to do this was to take a progovernment position on matters that affected state affairs. If nothing else, it would help defuse the tense conflict between psychiatrists and state officials, a struggle that asylum physicians knew in their most candid moments they could not win. This strategy would quickly become the keynote of state hospital psychiatry in the early decades of the twentieth century.

III

Convinced that there would be no respite in the struggles between Albany and the state hospitals, Blumer accepted the offer of the medical superintendent's post at the Butler Hospital for the Insane in Providence, Rhode Island. The years from 1899 to his retirement in 1921 saw him undergo a subtle and complex psychological and intellectual transformation with consequences for both the history of psychiatry and eugenics—consequences more manifest as the new century wore on. By following a career path different from that of so many other early twentieth-century U.S. and Canadian psychiatrists Blumer became the exception that proved the rule. While most psychiatrists found themselves unhappily mired in state and provincial hospitals, he was able to recover his enthusiasm and optimism about psychiatry, adumbrating attitudinal changes that would sweep the field only after the Second World War.

News of his acceptance of the Butler post spread rapidly through the community of U.S. and Canadian psychiatrists. As the congratulations

83. Wise to Blumer, n.d., probably 1899, BP, box 29. For a similar comment by a later commissioner in lunacy, see Albert Warren Ferris to Blumer, 24 August 1911, BP, box 31.

flooded in, it became obvious that most well-wishers agreed with Blumer that, as he himself said in his resignation speech, "the atmosphere of a well-endowed private hospital, with a self-perpetuating board of trust, offers, in its greater security, asylum to physician as well as to patient."[84] Or, in the words of another psychiatrist,

> I always thought that Providence would come your way after a while. In a short time you may be able to say farewell to printing-presses, and stocking machines, and brush and mat making toils, and glue factories, and coffee roasters, and other enterprises which perfume the air with odors that range from bouquet to borborygmal. In two more moons you may be able to say farewell to a system which has converted medical men into midnight clerks and daily drudges. Soon you will be able to rise from a system of compli-cated estimates to a higher estimation of yourself. In a few short weeks you will be able, I trust, to give up the manufacture of goods and figures, to doff the garb of a clerical and manufacturing expert, and to don the garb of a gentleman. Then you will be able to resume the practice of medicine! Then you will have an opportunity to study psychology, and to imitate, if not excel, the delightful and classical writings of Dr. [Isaac] Ray, one of your predecessors at Providence.[85]

These and other comments echoed the belief, widely held by psychia-trists at the turn of the century, that service in a state system of mental health care robbed doctors of their dignity and freedom to practice med-icine as they saw fit. They convey the strong impression that psychiatrists thought that the reforms of the 1890s had made them resemble prison wardens and "daily drudges" more than up-to-date physicians.[86] Their disappointment was tinged with ironic bitterness at having helped to create the reformist climate responsible for their plight.

Blumer's move to Providence did not, however, immediately end his emotional or active engagement in New York State mental health care politics. If anything he began speaking out more after his departure than

---

84. *Utica Daily Press*, 13 July 1899, BP, Blumer Scrapbook.
85. Selden Talcott to Blumer, 8 July 1899, BP, box 29. Henry Hurd agreed, saying that one advantage of the Butler job would be the "greater leisure for professional and literary work." Henry Hurd to Blumer, 12 June 1899, BP, box 37.
86. As one psychiatrist wrote Blumer, "How a number of Superintendents could attend those conferences as you did from month to month and have Com. Brown tell you about using potato peelers and gravely ask the question whether the farmers were to be compelled to wear their helmets and uniforms in the hay fields or might not occasionally put on a straw hat and suggest that the Utica Hospital photograph a genuine cod and distribute it so that the stewards might not be imposed upon in buying some other fish for cod etc., etc., *ad nauseum*, is beyond me." Brush to Blumer, 14 April 1900, BP, box 29.

he had at Utica. Having been ever mindful during the 1890s of the painful lesson that the more he said of a controversial nature, the easier it was for the commission to make life difficult for him, once he had left the state service he felt free to say what he had long held back. He also saw his chance to settle an old score with Carlos MacDonald.

Back in 1895, thanks largely to MacDonald's efforts, New York State had founded a research institution to study the pathology of insanity using the most modern laboratory techniques and equipment.[87] Named the Pathological Institute, it was placed under the guidance of Ira Van Gieson, considered an authority on histology and the pathology of the central nervous system. To many state psychiatrists it was bad enough that Van Gieson was an appointee; more galling was the fact that he seemed to share many of MacDonald's own, neurologically oriented views about the need to deploy advanced scientific methods to discover the causes and underlying biologic mechanisms of mental illness. Van Gieson stressed that psychiatry would be redeemed by what happened in his laboratories, not on state hospital wards. Being an extremely difficult person who closely resembled Sinclair Lewis's Martin Arrowsmith made him all the more unattractive to the state's psychiatrists. He had an undeniable streak of genius for laboratory research, but he could also be moody and prickly. He alternated bouts of laziness with spurts of intensely productive work. Unfortunately for Van Gieson, visitors sometimes observed the Pathological Institute during his inactive periods and came away with distinctly poor impressions.[88] Above all, he turned fiercely indignant when others tried to give him advice on how to run the institute. In other words, the situation surrounding Van Gieson and the institute was volatile.[89] Given Van Gieson's personality flaws, political connections, and theories about insanity, it was obvious after MacDonald's resignation in 1896 that an excuse would be found to fire him.

87. For the early history of the New York State Pathological Institute, see Grob, *Mental Illness and American Society*, pp. 127–31. See also Lawrence C. Kolb and Leon Roizin, *The First Psychiatric Institute: How Research and Education Changed Practice* (Washington: American Psychiatric Press, 1993); and David J. Rothman, *Conscience and Convenience: The Asylum and Its Alternatives in Progressive America* (Boston: Little, Brown, 1980), pp. 334–35. See also Theodore M. Brown, review of *The First Psychiatric Institute* by Kolb and Roizin, *Journal of the History of the Behavioral Sciences* 30 (1994): 439–40.
88. For example, one psychiatrist claimed to have visited the Pathological Institute without warning, at its headquarters in the Metropolitan Insurance Building in New York City in the fall of 1899. Not only was Van Gieson nowhere to be found, but there was little evidence that "anything was being done or had been done for some days [in the laboratories]. I judge entirely by the amount of dust on the majority of tables." Brush to Blumer, 1 February 1900, BP, box 29.
89. William A. White, "Obituary for Van Gieson," WAW, box 8.

The excuse presented itself in June 1899. Based on an interview with Van Gieson, a newspaper reporter alleged that, thanks to the work of the Pathological Institute, asylums themselves would be superfluous. Proclaiming the imminent discovery of "the germ of insanity," Van Gieson and his staff were widely believed to be saying that clinical psychiatry was useless. As one New York State psychiatrist put it, "No pains were taken [in the article] to avoid abuse of the Hospitals."[90]

Despite Van Gieson's official disclaimer in the *AJI*, the article provoked howls of protest from the *AJI* itself and many of New York State's psychiatrists.[91] Some complained that going to the press with such outlandish claims violated scientific responsibility and dignity. Others resented the way Van Gieson had intimated that the only scientific work being done on the question of insanity was that conducted at his institute, and not at state hospital laboratories.[92] But most found the notion of a "germ of insanity" plainly ridiculous; it called into question everything psychiatrists had been doing for almost a century to diagnose and cure mental illness. Extremely doubtful that the Pathological Institute would ever make good on its promise to reveal the microorganism, New York State psychiatrists believed that Van Gieson in the meantime was doing worse than nothing.[93]

No one wanted to oust Van Gieson more than Blumer, although his real objective most likely was less to hurt Van Gieson personally than to embarass MacDonald. In fact he was largely instrumental in mobilizing psychiatrists' discontent over Van Gieson and the Pathological Institute to the point where state officials could not ignore the issue.[94] In June, Butler began to strongarm Wise, who as president of the State Commission in Lunacy, initially wished to let the matter drop. "I should not want in trying to find an Esterhazy to create a Dreyfus," he told Blumer, obviously hesitant about making Van Gieson into a martyr whose complaints might bring down more opprobrium on the heads of psychiatrists.[95] But over the next few months Wise changed his mind. Rumors began to spread that New York State would not authorize a budget for the Pathological Institute beyond 1900. Faced with the possibility that

90. Arthur W. Hurd to Blumer, 29 January 1900, BP, box 29.
91. "A Deplorable Mistake," *AJI* 56 (1899): 177–79. For Van Gieson's disclaimer, see "Letter from Dr. Van Gieson," ibid., pp. 206–7.
92. See, e.g., Charles Wagner to Blumer, 29 January 1900, BP, box 29.
93. Arthur Hurd to Blumer, 29 January 1900; and Selden Talcott to Blumer, 2 February 1900, BP, box 29.
94. Blumer memorandum, 20 July 1899, BP, box 29.
95. Wise to Blumer, 14 June 1899, BP, box 29.

the state might lose the institute, Wise decided to make changes to make it appear more useful and accountable to Albany legislators. That meant getting rid of Van Gieson.

Early in 1900, Wise, making no effort to conceal his agenda, asked Blumer to serve on a committee that would ensure future funding for the Pathological Institute: "Personally and confidentially, I hope we may get a report from this committee which will disapprove the present line of inquiry now being conducted as a proper investigation by the Pathological department of the state hospitals, and also recommend that there will be a closer alliance with the state hospitals than now exists. I also hope the committee will fearlessly report that Dr. Van Gieson should be entirely relieved from administrative work." Wise added knowingly, "I think, undoubtedly, that we will, with you on the committee, get such a report as we want and as we need."[96]

Blumer was happy to oblige. As he and his committee hastened to complete their report they solicited the opinions of Adolf Meyer (1866–1950). At this date, Meyer was an outstanding young biologic researcher on the verge of becoming one of the leading U.S. psychiatrists of his generation. His main contribution to medicine was his theory of "psychobiology," an approach to psychiatry that took into consideration the life history of each patient as well as all germane physiological and biologic data. Unlike Van Gieson, he believed wholeheartedly that research into the anatomy and physiology of the brain should always be related to clinical practice. As he told Blumer in 1900, "My whole evolution has led me to the clinic as the source of all the laboratory needs." Meyer recommended that the institute's research be geared toward the clinical demands of the state hospitals as well as the teaching requirements of psychiatry.[97] These recommendations became part of the committee's report, which ultimately saved the Pathological Institute.[98]

For his labors, Meyer was rewarded with the offer of the directorship of the newly reorganized institute, renamed the New York Psychiatric Institute, an offer he accepted in 1901.[99] As for Van Gieson, his dismissal left him a broken man unable to perform any worthwhile research for

96. Wise to Blumer, 26 January 1900, BP, box 29.
97. Adolf Meyer to Blumer, 2 February 1900, BP, box 29.
98. Blumer to Meyer, 6 February 1900, AMCMA, series 1–355.
99. But first he hesitated, justifiably worried that he might someday share Van Gieson's fate. Blumer successfully allayed his fears; he had accurately appraised Meyer as a physician sensitive to the need to balance the clinical and scientific imperatives of psychiatry and capable of convincing state legislators of the need to continue funding the institute. Blumer to Meyer, 12 July and 21 July 1900, AMCMA, series 1–355.

the rest of his life. He felt betrayed and knew full well that Blumer had helped to engineer his removal.[100] Carlos MacDonald, for his part, never forgot nor forgave. In 1910 he told the *New York Times* that the institute had lost sight of its original aims, a tacit attack on Meyer's directorship from 1901 to 1908 and especially on the changes wrought in 1900–1901.[101]

Although vengeance was certainly one of Blumer's motives, the Pathological Institute incident was caused as well by the often acrimonious relations between clinical psychiatry and scientific medicine. Medical superintendents were always suspicious that the emphasis on "scientific" psychiatry might devalue their work of ministering to the mentally ill in state hospitals. They sincerely viewed clinical psychiatry as a humanitarian enterprise for the benefit of the less fortunate and worried that a dogmatic swing toward more scientific methods would have baneful results for their patients. They equated "scientific psychiatry" with the theories of the German psychiatrist Emil Kraepelin, who was then approaching the apex of his fame.[102] That Kraepelin's ideas seemed to countenance therapeutic pessimism was another reason for some U.S. and Canadian psychiatrists to distrust the most recent developments in German mental medicine. Van Gieson, in other words, was also a victim of this diffuse uneasiness about scientific psychiatry common to many physicians of Blumer's generation.

Blumer and Wise may have drawn satisfaction from the Pathological Institute incident, but Wise's smugness was cut short even before the incident had played out. In December 1900, Theodore Roosevelt, the progressive governor of New York, removed Wise from office, allegedly because Wise had solicited state hospital employees to purchase stock in a corporation in which he had a financial interest.[103] But his days were numbered anyhow because of his candid criticisms of Roosevelt's administration. "Embittered and broken," as one obituary was to call him, Wise spent the last seven years of his life trying to peddle patent medicines, a dose of which probably killed him at the age of fifty-six.[104]

Wise's fate was yet another sad reminder of the human casualties produced by the politicization of mental health care in the Empire State.

100. Ira Van Gieson to Blumer, 5 March 1900, BP, box 29.
101. *New York Times*, 4 September 1910, WAW, Box 4.
102. Brush to Blumer, 19 November 1902, BP, box 30; Blumer to Brush, 24 May 1919, BP, box 34.
103. On Wise's difficulties, see Henry Hurd to Blumer, 18 December 1900, BP, box 37.
104. "Obituary: Peter M. Wise, M.D.," *AJI* 64 (1907): 341–46. For expressions of pity and "disgust" at what had happened to Wise, see Henry Hurd to Blumer, 18 December 1900 and 12 July 1901, BP, box 37.

It proved that MacDonald's unhappiness serving on the commission was genuine. Wise's fate also confirmed that Blumer's departure from New York was no indicator of a normalization of relations between psychiatrists and state officials and politicians. In fact, relations worsened between 1899 and 1902, and New York State psychiatrists regretted Blumer's move to Providence all the more. One psychiatrist described them as "caught with our breeches down and our Bloomer gone."[105] Without their trusted leader to defend them, New York psychiatrists feared the worst, convinced that centralization, bureaucratization, and politicization would continue unremittingly.

The next chapter in the saga of New York State psychiatry was written in 1902 with the passage of what became known as the Brackett-Rogers Bill. That year Governor Benjamin Odell, committed to progressive reform in the name of economic efficiency, tried to have the New York State insanity laws amended to abolish asylum boards of managers and extend the central powers and duties of the Commission in Lunacy.[106] Odell's plans sparked protest. The State Charities Aid Association led the opposition and obtained a hearing in Albany before Odell himself on 17 February 1902.[107] State hospital medical superintendents were conspicuous by their absence from this meeting. In fact Odell admitted that "the medical gentlemen were requested not to come here and engage in log rolling." The SCAA asked Blumer himself to put in an appearance, which he declined to do. Without him, the hearings came to a rancorous conclusion.[108]

The Brackett-Rogers Bill did not end the battles over lunacy affairs in New York State. In 1905, in fact, asylum boards of managers were reinstated. But the other provisions of the bill augmenting the Commission in Lunacy's power were not repealed, strengthening the views of those who viewed the bill as the culmination of the events that had begun with the creation of the commission in 1889. Many agreed that the lesson of Wise's downfall and the commission was plain: power corrupts.[109]

105. E. H. Howard to Blumer, 26 January 1900, BP, box 29.
106. See McCormick, *From Realignment to Reform*, pp. 172–82; see also Schneider and Deutsch, *Public Welfare in New York State*, pp. 138–40; and Grob, *Mental Illness and American Society*, pp. 211–12.
107. SCAA, *Statement Adopted by the Board of the State Charities Aid Association, at a Meeting Held January 19, 1902, concerning the Recommendations relating to State Hospitals and State Charitable Institutions, Contained in the Annual Message of the Governor*, no. 81 (New York: SCAA, 1902).
108. For an extensive account of the meeting, see the *Utica Daily Press*, 18 February 1902, BP, Blumer Scrapbook. See also Herbert Brown to Blumer, 12 January 1902; and Charles Wagner to Blumer, 14 January 1902, BP, box 30.
109. Brush to Blumer, 14 January and 3 February 1902, BP, box 30.

Blumer himself was angry enough about Odell's policies to write a long letter to the *New York Evening Post* in early 1902 calling for "a halt ... to the policy of centralization that has demoralized" the state hospital service. According to Blumer, psychiatrists had been subjected to a regime of "monotonous and stunting *uniformity*, that accursed word that is writ so large in the bureaucrat's vocabulary."[110] For many New York State psychiatrists, then, the abolition of hospital boards of managers was the last step in a process that had turned asylums into warehouses of insanity.[111] "Ten years ago," wrote the superintendent of the Binghamton State Hospital in 1902, "there were 1140 patients in this institution, and 312 persons were employed to take care of them. Now we have 1375 patients and 265 persons to take care of them. Enough said."[112]

Blumer was not quite finished with his own attacks on the political management of New York State's mental health care system. In 1903 he became president of the AMPA and used his presidential address to publicize what he believed to be the calamitous course followed by Albany politicians and officials. The commission, he told his audience, had created a "system ... that checks ambition, subordinates the individual superintendent to the crippling spirit of bureaucracy and collectivism, and is in all respects inimical to the full and free growth not only of the medical officers themselves but of the hospitals over which they have been called to minister."[113] Blumer's address was the culmination of his thirteen years of confrontation with New York State officials. It is tempting to take his side and see the conflict as a Manichaean struggle between righteous psychiatrists and malevolent state politicians and administrators intent on creating a bureaucratic Leviathan, but probably some truth lay on each side. MacDonald's resignation and Wise's downfall proved that life on the commission could be as disheartening as life for medical superintendents.[114] Moreover, both sides in this civil war were guilty of using questionable tactics. Sometimes the press provoked conflict when it exaggerated the poor relations between psychiatrists and the commis-

110. *New York Evening Post*, 10 January 1902, BP, Blumer Scrapbook. His emphasis.
111. To Harry Palmer, Blumer's successor at Utica, the Brackett-Rogers Bill authorized "a most shameful centralization of power in the hands of the Commission," making each employee in the state system "a monkey on the string, to be made to dance by the Commission in Lunacy." Harry Palmer to Blumer, 11 January 1902, BP, box 30.
112. Wagner to Blumer, 14 January 1902, BP, box 30.
113. G. Alder Blumer, "Presidential Address," *AJI* 60 (1903): 1–18.
114. Nor did a commissioner's job necessarily get better with time; the president of the commission told Blumer in 1911 that he wanted to resign and obtain the post of "superintendent of a private institution for the insane." Albert Warren Ferris to Blumer, 24 August 1911, BP, box 31.

sion.[115] But ultimately it mattered little who was to blame. A formidable atmosphere of mistrust poisoned minds as well as relations.

Blumer's remarks before the AMPA indicated that psychiatrists imagined themselves to be living at the end of an age in the history of psychiatry, one marked by a subtle transformation in psychiatric self-perception. Nineteenth-century psychiatrists had defined themselves primarily in terms of what they could do *within* the asylum. Twentieth-century psychiatrists became increasingly receptive to new roles beyond the asylum's walls and new theories about the causes, diagnosis, and treatment of mental and nervous disorders.[116] Reform-minded physicians tried to integrate asylums into the community by linking mental hospitals to schools, juvenile courts, and outpatient and child guidance clinics. These were momentous changes for the country as well as psychiatrists, leading to "a new psychiatry, one that is the predecessor of psychiatry as we know it today," as Elizabeth Lunbeck has persuasively argued.[117]

Nonetheless, this orientation toward social psychiatry in the progressive era was symptomatic of a complex and uneasy psychological bifurcation between psychiatrists' public and private sentiments. Publicly psychiatrists extolled their own competence in preventive mental health; privately they felt a curiously involuntary resistance to cutting their ties to the asylum, their specialty's power base for almost a century. Despite bold talk, the "enduring asylum" continued to be the site of practice for the large majority of psychiatrists during this period.[118] The asylum's twentieth-century history overlapped with troubled economic times, especially the depression of the 1930s. Investment in state hospitals declined during the depression, leading to cutbacks in salaries, staff, treatment programs, and resources and a consequent decline in the quality of patient care. Meanwhile, state governments tended to expand their control over public mental hospitals, creating severe tensions between psychiatry's professional autonomy and public accountability.[119] If psychiatric demoralization was acute in a state system like New York's, it was even worse in states whose public welfare departments lumped the

115. This at least was the claim of the secretary of the Commission in Lunacy regarding its 4 December interview with a reporter from the *New York Daily Tribune*. See T. E. McGarr to Blumer, 7 December 1893, BP, box 27.
116. Grob, *Mental Illness and American Society*, p. 73.
117. Elizabeth Lunbeck, *The Psychiatric Persuasion: Knowledge, Gender, and Power in Modern America* (Princeton: Princeton University Press, 1994), p. 3.
118. For the history of the "enduring asylum" during the progressive era, see Rothman, *Conscience and Convenience*, esp. pp. 324–75.
119. Grob, *Mental Illness and American Society*, pp. 228–29.

mentally ill together with all other dependent groups. Thus Blumer's 1903 warnings were prescient, though they failed to reverse the course of events. Blumer was to live to see the passing of the "gentleman" medical superintendent, the "alienist" whose practice engendered the respect, deference, and trust in the hearts and minds of a grateful public. In the early twentieth century psychiatrists had laboriously to reconstruct this relationship with the public by affirming anew their accountability to the nation. The challenge laid the psychological and intellectual foundations for psychiatrists' dawning interest in the eugenics movement.

IV

Dispirited as he was over events in New York State between 1899 and 1902, Blumer's move to the Butler Hospital slowly weaned him emotionally from his obsession with the plight of psychiatry there. With a large and well-trained staff who cared for patients suffering from a wide range of mental and nervous disorders, he discovered that with some limitations he was able to practice psychiatry the way he wanted. Because Butler had been founded officially as a philanthropic enterprise by wealthy men with a desire to relieve the misery of insanity, Blumer was entitled to expect fewer financial pressures than he had experienced at publicly funded Utica.[120]

Butler's reputation as an attractive place to work was grounded in Rhode Island State policy toward the insane since the hospital's opening in 1847. Rhode Island had developed a "system of dual care" for the curably and incurably insane which was largely defined by wealth, national background, and social standing. Chiefly in response to rising admissions of poor Irish men and women in the 1850s, a plan to build a state-level public hospital to ease Butler's overcrowding had quickly arisen. The state would erect an asylum for incurable patients. But in planning, constructing, and managing this state asylum, Rhode Island politicians and patricians determined to make its provisions of care as inexpensive and stigmatizing as possible. State officials chose as their model the asylum on Blackwell's Island in New York City, one of the nation's worst institutional embarassments because of its frugal, unhealthy, and decrepit conditions. Rhode Island also decided to build the

120. "Dr. Blumer to Leave Utica," *Utica Daily Press*, 6 July 1899, BP, Blumer Scrapbook; P. W. A. Fitzsimmons to Blumer, 17 November 1899, BP, box 29; John Chapin to Blumer, 16 August, 19 August, and 7 September 1899, BP, box 29; Brush to Blumer, 22 July 1899, BP, box 29; Blumer to Brush, 24 February 1904, BP, box 30.

state asylum outside Providence on property to be shared by the state prison, almshouse, and workhouse in an institutional complex called the "State Farm." These and other features of the state asylum reinforced the impression that Rhode Island's mental health care system officially defined mental illness as little other than a form of combined dependence and deviance. In fact Rhode Island declared explicitly in 1870 that its state asylum had been erected "for the Insane Poor."[121]

From the few available accounts of the state asylum's early years, the atmosphere seems to have been depressing and treatment little better than perfunctory. Physical plant conditions were poor because construction costs had been held to a minimum. Over-crowding and patient abuse compounded the institution's problems. Asylum officials stressed discipline over remedial treatment. Thus, by the time Blumer arrived at nearby Butler, the state facility had a formidably negative reputation, as his correspondence with patients and their families amply proves. When, for example, the mother of a female patient learned in 1903 that Blumer wanted her daughter transferred to the state asylum, she wrote him, "I have some idea of how Eve must have felt when she was thrust out of Paradise."[122]

The policy that led to these conditions reflected the fact that by the time Rhode Island decided to build a public hospital for the insane, the optimism that had sustained the "cult" of asylum building across the continent in the 1840s and 1850s had evaporated. The very name "Asylum for the Incurable Insane" mirrored the widespread belief that state asylums would be custodial rather than curative. Attitudes toward the new asylum were also consistent with the state's traditional suspicion of governmental intervention in social matters and the frugality of its commercial and manufacturing elite, which assumed that poverty was largely a personal responsibility. Thus the obvious aim of the state's elite was to

121. See Fred Jacobs, "Private Care and Public Custody: Institutions for the Insane in Rhode Island, 1840–1900" (honors thesis, Brown University, 1978). See also Sarah M. Saklad, "Psychiatry in Rhode Island, 1725–1980," *Rhode Island Medical Journal* 68 (1980): 207–16; David A. Rochefort, "Three Centuries of Care of the Mentally Disabled in Rhode Island and the Nation, 1650–1950," *Rhode Island History* 40 (1981): 111–32; and Janet Golden and Eric C. Schneider, "Custody and Control: The Rhode Island State Hospital for Mental Diseases, 1870–1970," ibid. 41 (1982): 113–25. The similarities between what happened in Rhode Island and Massachusetts are striking; see, e.g., Gerald N. Grob, *The State and the Mentally Ill: A History of the Worcester State Hospital in Massachusetts, 1830–1920* (Chapel Hill: University of North Carolina Press, 1966), pp. 38–39, 91–92, 164–68, 246. Anti-immigrant sentiment in Rhode Island peaked in 1855 when the nativist Know-Nothing Party swept the state elections. By the end of the Civil War a full one-third of the state's population was foreign born. Fred Jacobs, "Isaac Ray and the Profession of Psychiatry," *Rhode Island History* 38 (1979): 99–111.
122. BPR, cases 4236, 4287, and 4312 (quoted).

build at public expense a facility that, by cutting every possible economic corner, would reinforce the fact that the fortunate and the unfortunate were to benefit from distinctly unequal treatment. They hoped the stigma surrounding state assistance would discourage families from availing themselves of state charity services and stand as a warning to paupers that the proper solution to personal problems was a combination of thrift, sobriety, hard work, and self-reliance. The implicit message was that Butler was not an option for them.

Rhode Island mental health care in the nineteenth century suggests, then, that as the century wore on, the Butler Hospital gradually abandoned its original obligations to all the state's mentally ill. Its wards, however, never were entirely cleared of the incurably ill; for when overcrowding quickly developed at the state asylum, Rhode Island decided to board some pauper lunatics at Butler. Nor did "disturbed" or violent patients ever disappear from the Butler Hospital.[123] Its evolution as a private, "corporate" hospital never totally blinded its managers to its origins and charitable mission. However much some of Butler's officials wanted to turn it into a rich persons' sanatorium for curable cases, they could never succeed entirely as long as the hospital presented itself to the community as a "charitable" institution. And this Butler's officials never stopped doing, if only because it was impossible; as a trustee admitted in 1920, "The community to which we appeal [for donations, subscriptions, and patients] and whom to serve is our first duty, would not sanction [emptying its wards of *all* these same] aged, imbecile, and incurable" patients. Or as Blumer himself put it in 1915,

> It is high time that the erroneous impression, still lingering in certain quarters, that this institution exists merely, or even mainly, for the wealthy and well-to-do were everywhere effaced. While there is always a demand for the high-grade accommodation which its well-appointed suites of rooms offer, and while we welcome the revenue arising in so far as it increases our ability to minister to a larger number of persons of moderate or meagre means, the claims of the proletariat are not, and never have been, sacrificed to those of the plutocracy.

If it was true, as a trustee wrote in 1911, that "many of the patients in [Butler] are well-to-do financially and pay large sums for board and treat-

---

123. As Blumer confessed in 1902, "We are at our wits end as regards the care of our more disturbed patients in Butler Hospital." Blumer to Walter Wightman, 13 March 1902, BPR, case 4416.

ment" while living in the comfort and luxury "to which they have been accustomed," then it was equally true that this "enables us to do better work for some poor man or woman who cannot pay us a cent but whom our physicians can cure."[124]

Butler's officials had therefore to perform a neat balancing act. They had to pay more than lip service to its charitable aims while at the same time competing successfully for affluent patients in the competitive marketplace for private, institutional mental health care. To ensure that Butler could operate year to year and admit state charity cases they had to publicize the advantages of the hospital to the wealthy so they could rely on a steady stream of paying patients. Potential clients had to be wooed by advertising Butler's luxury and class-segregated accommodations for prosperous patients and the high moral and behavioral quality of all patients.[125] Rich patients had to be convinced that there would be minimal contact between paying and nonpaying patients at Butler, and attempts were made to recruit patients whose manners, tastes, and social backgrounds matched its provisions for care. This policy risked depicting Butler as a haven for the wealthy, but there was no alternative for an institution that depended on philanthropic donations and bequests to survive. Neither could Butler's officials abjure its charitable commitment to the impecunious mentally ill without perhaps alienating the same public that made expensive building projects and charitable endowments possible at Butler. The history of Butler until at least the end of the Blumer era was a compromise between these two forces, one that, though it failed to satisfy everyone, satisfied enough people to ensure Butler's survival.[126]

124. Trustees and Superintendent of the Butler Hospital for the Insane, *Annual Report* (Providence: Snow and Farnham, 1920), p. 9; 1915, pp. 24–25; 1911, p. 13. Hereafter cited as B*AR*.
125. A good example of the way Butler's officials publicized the "luxury" and comfortable surroundings for "wealthy patients" can be found in B*AR*, 1911, pp. 12–13. For Blumer's own justification for admitting prosperous patients from out of state to help pay for the hospital's "charitable work," see Blumer to Brush, 11 February 1910, BP, box 41.
126. The views of Butler's medical superintendents reflected this ambivalence about its role. They wanted Butler to be a site for curative medicine and resisted anything that might lead to its becoming "a mere retreat for incurables." To entice the wealthy they had to firm up the distinctions between Butler and a state hospital for incurable paupers, but they also spoke out against the temptation to treat incurable paupers as second-class mental patients. One of Blumer's predecessors stands out in this respect. Isaac Ray (1807–81) was Butler's first medical superintendent and one of the "original thirteen" who founded the AMSAII. Ray was one of the most prolific and influential U.S. physicians of his generation, a pioneer in forensic psychiatry, asylum medicine, and the prevention of mental illness. Well before there was a mental hygiene movement he wrote a book on preventive psychiatry titled *Mental Hygiene* (Boston: Ticknor and Fields, 1863). See Jacques M. Quen, "Isaac Ray and Mental Hygiene in America," *Annals of the New York Academy of Sciences* 291 (1977): 83–93; "Isaac Ray on Drunkenness," *Bulletin of the History of Medicine* 41 (1967): 342–48; and "Isaac Ray and His Remarks on Pathological Anatomy," ibid. 38 (1964): 113–26. See also John Starrett Hughes, *In the Law's*

Blumer consequently viewed his practice at Butler as one that while serving the "plutocracy" also met some authentically charitable needs, and this appraisal was no mere rationalization that screened, ulterior motives. There were sound reasons for trying to exclude chronic, hopeless cases, poor or not, as well as disturbed and aggressive patients. As Blumer wrote in 1911, to make room for "acute cases of occurring insanity in urgent need of treatment," it was necessary to request families to make other provisions for chronically ill relatives, "even those who are well able to pay for all that their care costs." In other words, he wrote, "it is not a mere question of ability to pay, as so many people suppose."[127]

Blumer's inclination to stress curative hospital psychiatry at Butler was reinforced by the fact that the hospital was then in the middle of a fund-raising campaign to pay for a major rebuilding program. The success of the fund drive hinged on the hospital's ability to persuade the public, Rhode Island philanthropists, and wealthy patients and their families that Butler was now more devoted than ever to *curing* mental and nervous disorders. A symbolic step in this direction was taken in 1906 when "for the Insane" was dropped from the hospital's name, signifying that Butler was now "a hospital and not a place of confinement" and underscoring its commitment to the treatment of "patients suffering from neurasthenia and not technically insane." "Neurasthenia," a term coined in 1869 by the U.S. neurologist Charles Beard, was an ailment characterized by depression, fatigue, insomnia, dyspepsia, and other complaints that could be relieved through the rest, exercise, diet, and amusements available during an extended stay at a hospital like Butler. Neurasthenia was an "umbrella diagnosis" that psychiatrists and neurologists in late nineteenth-century North America used to cover a variety of nervous and emotional disorders. It was a far more flattering disease label for a paying patient than was insanity; for it defined nervous illness as the unintended yet correctable outcome of the struggle of respectable persons to excel in civilized society.[128] Naturally it was favored at places like Butler that

Darkness: Isaac Ray and the Medical Jurisprudence of Insanity in Nineteenth-Century America (Dobbs Ferry, N.Y.: Oceana, 1986); A. Warren Stearns, "Isaac Ray: Psychiatrist and Pioneer in Forensic Psychiatry," *AJP* 101 (1945): 573–85; and Jacobs, "Ray and the Profession of Psychiatry."

127. BPR, case 4447. Supporting evidence emerges in other correspondence in patient records, e.g., BPR, case 4241.

128. BAR, 1907, p. 21. F. G. Gosling, *Before Freud: Neurasthenia and the American Medical Community, 1870–1910* (Urbana: University of Illinois Press, 1987). See also F. G. Gosling and Joyce M. Ray, "The Right to Be Sick: American Physicians and Nervous Patients, 1885–1910," *Journal of Social History* 20 (1986): 251–67, esp. p. 252. For other thoughtful accounts of the diagnostic use of neurasthenia, see Charles E. Rosenberg, "The Place of George M.

tried to attract paying patients. The very name suggested an organic illness of the nervous system and thus sounded so much better than "depression," a psychiatric diagnosis that conjured up visions of asylums and the stigma of madness.[129] Blumer himself acknowledged this in 1907 when he wrote that neurasthenia was a term that was agreeable to "the patient and his friends [who] prefer that the mental defect [in insanity] shall be minimized while emphasis is given to the 'nerve' element in the case."[130]

As more and more men and women were realizing that one could be mentally sick without being a menace to oneself or the community, hospitals like Butler admitted increasing numbers of voluntary patients. In 1903, for example, 42 percent of Butler's admissions were voluntary, and by 1908 this figure had risen to 46 percent. Blumer believed that Butler's success in attracting voluntary patients was due in large measure to "the use of the term neurasthenia and its euphemistic variants" by hospital officials. To him, the positive feature of voluntary admissions was that these patients were usually of sound enough mind to admit themselves and hence stood a good chance of being cured. A substantial percentage of voluntary patients made Butler seem more like a rest home than a madhouse. He could promote it as a medical facility providing close, interpersonal treatment for "appreciative" patients who shared his manners and cultural tastes.[131]

The greater prospects for cure at Butler than at Utica subtly affected Blumer's views about the classification of mental diseases. The theories of Emil Kraepelin were making considerable inroads into U.S. and Canadian psychiatry, but to a Francophile like Blumer, German ideas were suspect—doubly so because of Kraepelin's stress on the incurability of most mental diseases. Underlying Kraepelin's patient and systematic clin-

Beard in Nineteenth-Century Psychiatry," *Bulletin of the History of Medicine* 36 (1962): 245–59; and Barbara Sicherman, "The Paradox of Prudence: Mental Health in the Gilded Age," *Journal of American History* 62 (1976): 890–912, and her "The Uses of a Diagnosis: Doctors, Patients, and Neurasthenia," *Journal of the History of Medicine and Allied Sciences* 32 (1977): 33–54. Gosling and Ray argue that, in contrast to disease categories such as degeneracy and hysteria, neurasthenia was a diagnosis that tended to exonerate patients from blame for their own illnesses. "Right to Be Sick," p. 258.

129. Edward Shorter, *From the Mind into the Body: The Cultural Origins of Psychosomatic Symptoms* (New York: Free Press, 1994), p. 132.

130. Blumer to C. Bertram Gay, 23 February 1907, BPR, case 4446. See also BAR, 1902, p. 17; and C. B. Burr to Blumer, 25 February 1902, BP, box 30.

131. BAR, 1904, pp. 21–22; 1907, p. 22. For similar developments at a Canadian private mental hospital, see Cheryl Krasnick Warsh, *Moments of Unreason: The Practice of Canadian Psychiatry and the Homewood Retreat, 1883–1923* (Montreal: McGill-Queen's University Press, 1989), p. 12.

ical method of study was his belief that there existed natural mental diseases, that is, psychological illnesses caused by physical lesions of the brain as authentic as the organic causes of diseases such as tuberculosis or general paresis. According to Kraepelin, that was where the similarity between mental diseases and the so-called organic ones ended, because though there was distinct hope for curing the latter, little obtained for the former.[132] Kraepelin's therapeutic pessimism dismayed the many psychiatrists critical of his terminology, especially his use of "dementia," usually to denote stupor and the deterioration of mental faculties. Blumer himself protested against what he called the "indiscriminate use" of "dementia" in early twentieth-century psychiatry. To him, misuse of the term led to confusion in matters of treatment.[133] Blumer preferred French theories of classification, notably those of Emmanuel Régis (1855–1918), professor of medicine at the University of Bordeaux, whose textbook on psychiatry Blumer had used when lecturing on mental diseases at Albany Medical College from 1893 to 1899. French psychiatry was then in transition from the popular theory of degeneracy, which emphasized the hereditary roots of insanity, to recognizably modern models of diagnosis, and Régis was a leader in these attempts to carve out a new classification system more therapeutically optimistic than Kraepelin's and less indebted to Kraepelin's notion of dementia praecox, or schizophrenia.[134]

Blumer also did his best in North America to popularize Pierre Janet's theory of "psychasthenia." Janet held that many of the psychological symptoms customarily ascribed to neurasthenia—such as anxiety, phobias, and lack of willpower—belonged more properly to a disease he

132. Gregory Zilboorg and George W. Henry, *A History of Medical Psychology* (New York: Norton, 1941), pp. 450–64. See also Eric J. Engstrom, "Emil Kraepelin: Psychiatry and Public Affairs in Wilhelmine Germany," *History of Psychiatry* 2 (1991): 111–32. On the impact of Kraepelin's views on the diagnosis of hysteria in the late nineteenth century, see Mark S. Micale, "On the 'Disappearance' of Hysteria: A Study in the Clinical Deconstruction of a Diagnosis," *Isis* 84 (1993): 496–526.

133. G. Alder Blumer, "The History and Use of the Term Dementia," *AJI* 63 (1907): 337–47.

134. For the theory of degeneracy and its place in the history of French psychiatry, see Robert A. Nye, *Crime, Madness, and Politics in Modern France: The Medical Concept of National Decline* (Princeton: Princeton University Press, 1984); Ian Dowbiggin, *Inheriting Madness: Professionalization and Psychiatric Knowledge in Nineteenth-Century France* (Berkeley: University of California Press, 1991); and Ruth Harris, *Murders and Madness: Medicine, Law, and Society in the Fin-de-siècle* (Oxford: Oxford University Press, 1989), esp. pp. 51–79. For the history of French theories of psychiatric classification, see P. J. Pichot, "The Diagnosis and Classification of Mental Disorders in French-Speaking Countries: Background, Current Views, and Comparison with Other Nomenclatures," *Psychological Medicine* 12 (1982): 475–92; and "The French Approach to Psychiatric Classification," *British Journal of Psychiatry* 144 (1984): 113–18.

called "psychasthenia." In Blumer's words, psychasthenia was "a lower order of mental activity, capable, it may be, of dealing with the past, future, the indefinite, the intangible, but woefully impotent to meet 'the various exigencies of times and occasions.' "[135] Janet's theory of psychasthenia was attractive to many American psychiatrists because it was in many respects a middle ground between the old somaticism of nineteenth-century psychological medicine and the new theories of Freud, Josef Breuer, and Carl Jung, which, while contending that emotional shocks or traumas were important causes of mental dissociation, also drew attention to distasteful sexual factors.[136] To Blumer the most impressive thing about psychasthenia was its "comparative curability, or at least improvability . . . as compared with the more hopeless diseases that are chronic and accumulate." Indeed he noted that a relatively high percentage of patients discharged from Butler Hospital between 1903 and 1905 could be diagnosed as psychasthenic.[137] His attraction to a concept like psychasthenia and his preference for French psychiatry reflected his growing therapeutic optimism the longer he practiced medicine at Butler.

But it was not only Butler's public commitment to curative psychiatry that appealed to Blumer. He also found Butler a good place to practice what he called "the newer psychiatry." Blumer kept abreast of current trends in North American psychiatry that stressed discovering the causes of psychological diseases through rigorous laboratory research and Adolf Meyer's method of observing all the social, biologic, and psychological influences on each mental patient. Meyer and other innovators had argued that nineteenth-century psychiatrists had been content to organize mental symptoms into neatly defined but static categories or prone to jump to unwarranted causal theories. This approach, most early twentieth-century psychiatrists agreed, ignored the fact that each patient's illness was the unique result of a failed attempt to adapt to specific environmental conditions, the systematic study of which enabled physicians to identify the lesions responsible and make an accurate prognosis. So every patient at Butler submitted to a thorough mental and physical examination upon admission, often including lumbar punctures and analysis of cerebrospinal fluid. Data were recorded scrupulously in order to make

135. G. Alder Blumer, "The Coming of Psychasthenia," *Journal of Nervous and Mental Disease* 33 (1906): 1–18, 6.
136. For Janet's impact on U.S. psychiatry, see Nathan G. Hale, Jr., *Freud and the Americans: The Beginnings of Psychoanalysis in the United States, 1876-1917* (Oxford: Oxford University Press, 1971), pp. 143–46.
137. Blumer, "Coming of Psychasthenia," p. 6.

differential diagnosis easier. "Where formerly observation was more or less passive," Blumer contended, "the watchword today is *investigate*. Search is made to discover the hidden symptoms. . . . With less care for the application of a name to the condition, the mere *nomen et flatus vocis*, we are now more eager to understand the patient himself."[138]

Blumer was also keen to introduce new treatment methods at Butler,[139] but actual treatment there represented a less abrupt departure from the past than did diagnosis. Treatment was still based mainly on the nine-teenth-century notion that early hospitalization and prolonged exposure to the hospital's "moral" environment improved the patient's chances for recovery. Like Clarke, Blumer thought dynamic psychology could contribute a great deal to the study of abnormal mental states, but he also thought that Freud and his followers were doing worse than nothing for their patients.[140] If Blumer and his assistants devoted time to some form of "talking cure," it was intended less as a way of exploring patients' innermost thoughts and emotions than as an attempt to enlist patients' cooperation in a morally rehabilitative process designed to restore ner-vous energy.[141] In 1911 he wrote that, although there was progress "along the lines of a closer relation between clinical and laboratory methods of examination" in diagnosis, "in the field of treatment there is little that is new which is good." Bathing and occupational therapy continued to be effective, he thought.[142] Blumer had always valued the latter and used it extensively at Butler, especially for female patients. Indeed Butler an-nual reports frequently included photographs of women patients doing needlework and making baskets. This form of occupational therapy was consistent not only with his traditional assumptions about women's work but also his fondness for genteel amusements and distractions as thera-peutic techniques. During his superintendency Butler offered picnics, dances, lectures, concerts, tennis and squash courts, a launch to take patients along the Seekonk River and out into Narragansett Bay, and teas at Blumer's own home on the hospital grounds for the better mannered patients. Thus, in spite of the many official tributes he paid to "the newer psychiatry," Butler's treatment program had not changed much since the mid-nineteenth century.

138. *BAR*, 1904, p. 18. His emphasis.
139. *BAR*, 1904, pp. 18–19.
140. See, e.g., Blumer to John Donley, 11 March 1911, BP, box 31.
141. On therapeutic techniques and styles in late nineteenth-century U.S. mental hospitals, see Constance M. McGovern, "The Myths of Social Control and Custodial Oppression: Pat-terns of Psychiatric Medicine in Late Nineteenth-Century Institutions," *Journal of Social His-tory* 20 (1986): 3–23.
142. Blumer to W. F. Drewry, 30 October 1911, BP, box 31.

There were other elements of psychiatry at Butler that proved congenial to Blumer's personal tastes, temperament, and ideas about what constituted enlightened mental medicine. As his correspondence with patients and their families and guardians shows, he performed his role as confidant, community leader, medical expert, and moral counselor with grace and tact. Once and awhile the nagging problem of reconciling charity with medical necessity threatened to upset the good relations with the community that Blumer so adamantly advocated, particularly when there arose the delicate subject of transferring a chronic patient from Butler to the state hospital or an out-of-state facility. Equally delicate were the times when it was necessary to write families and friends of patients to pay their bills, a task that often exasperated the normally polite and patient Blumer. But his diplomacy usually carried the day. It was the same in his capacity as moral adviser. Family members frequently wrote asking his advice about intimate domestic matters, such as how to deal with the myriad emotional problems associated with mentally ill relatives. At times his advice took on a didactic tone, especially when he preached the rehabilitative virtues of work therapy.[143] Whether the patient was male or female, Blumer believed there was something inherently uplifting about work, a moral quality that produced medically positive effects. In this respect he was merely repeating what had been standard advice for psychiatrists throughout the nineteenth century.

Perhaps the most important aspect of Blumer's performance as Butler's medical superintendent was his responsibility for sustaining the reputation of the hospital throughout Providence, the state, and the nation. In his own words, it was imperative for him to address "the attitude of the outside world to those things that concern the inside of Butler Hospital."[144] The best way to do this, he knew, was through his contributions to Butler's annual reports. Not only did ex-patients and the families and friends of patients read them carefully but the public that donated gifts and bequeathed endowments did so as well. By all appearances, the vast majority of Blumer's readers liked what they read, particularly Blumer's humorous asides, literary flourishes, and allusions to classical and biblical literature.[145] He genuinely seemed to enjoy this part of the job, welcoming the challenge of continually renewing the interest of patrons and benefactors, carefully detailing the improvements to the grounds and the buildings and the provisions for care and medical treatment. Practicing

143. See, e.g., BPR, cases 4148, 4314.
144. BAR, 1904, p. 15.
145. See, e.g., the comments of Sarah E. Doyle to Blumer, 21 February 1911, BP, box 31.

G. Alder Blumer, ca. 1930. *American Journal of Psychiatry*, vol. 12, p. 378, 1932. Copyright 1932, The American Psychiatric Association. Reprinted by permission.

medicine at Butler seemed to him to join the best of the old and the new in psychiatry. He enjoyed considerable local prestige and found that the doors of socially exclusive Providence clubs and institutions were soon open to him. He was on good terms with the city's mercantile, cultural, and social elite, as he had been in Utica. But the crucial difference was that in Providence he had to answer only to that same elite, not to state officials. The arrangement in Providence eminently suited his tastes, background, and character so much better than Utica had. If he encountered any disapproval, it was generally civil and often friendly, confirming for him that, no matter how much people might disagree with him on various matters, they nonetheless continued to admire him as a moral and intellectual pillar of the community.

Thus his life and career in Providence quietly yet inexorably shaped Blumer's disposition toward the practice of psychiatry. As early as 1903, four years after his move to Butler, it was obvious that his mood was changing. As Blumer himself admitted, "The longer I live in Providence and the more I see of the trend of things in New York, the more pleased I am to be in this particular field of labor."[146] One psychiatrist remarked in 1917 that when Blumer's troubles began to snowball at Utica in the late 1890s, "there was quite a change of attitude, for there seemed to be an exodus of enthusiasm." But he added that Blumer recovered his "pristine vigor" once he moved to Butler and its "more congenial surroundings."[147] Indeed in his two decades at Butler, Blumer's zest for work returned. Butler provided him with the opportunity "to study psychology," "don the garb of a gentleman," and "resume the practice" of curative psychiatry. In Providence he underwent a "process of identity-formation" or "self-fashioning" linked concretely to the politics of patronage.[148] There his professional identity depended more on his standing in the community and throughout the elite circles of New England than on his relations with state lunacy officials or public hospital psychiatrists. At Butler he learned that the success of psychiatry's endeavor to improve its low status as a medical specialty rested on far more than its ability to rationalize its therapeutic shortcomings. Blumer had to satisfy constituencies whose influence had been marginal at Utica: patients, their families and friends, and public-spirited men and women of the wealthy classes. His success in this project constituted an act of liberation, freeing him to practice psychiatry in ways more consistent with his own standards and expectations. This success testifies to his talent for recognizing the ties between patronage and professional image and his sensitivity to the differences between public and private hospital psychiatry.

146. Blumer to John Chapin, 18 February 1903; and Chapin to Blumer, 17 February 1903, APA, RG Clarence B. Farrar, folder 25.
147. J. Mosher to Blumer, 2 February 1917, BP, box 34.
148. On these factors in the history of early modern science, see Mario Biagioli, "Galileo's System of Patronage," *History of Science* 28 (1990): 1–62. See also Mario Biagioli, *Galileo, Courtier: The Practice of Science in the Culture of Absolutism* (Chicago: University of Chicago Press, 1993).

2

A CONFUSING WILDNESS OF
RECOMMENDATIONS: G. ALDER BLUMER,
EUGENICS, AND U.S. PSYCHIATRY, 1880–1940

The move to Providence not only brought back Blumer's "pristine vigor"; significantly it also engendered a subtle evolution in his views on the nature and prevention of mental illness. In his last years at Utica he had begun to be attracted to hereditarian models of insanity and eugenic approaches to the management of mental diseases. Like Francis Galton, Blumer had defined eugenics as the attempt to use the study of heredity and reproduction to improve the health and fitness of the human race.[1] Once in Butler's "more congenial surroundings," however, Blumer's attitude toward eugenics took another twist. As the years passed and he settled into psychiatric practice at a private mental hospital, he shed many of the eugenic opinions he had formed in the late 1890s. Thus, just when eugenics entered its "second stage" and enjoyed its greatest influence in the United States and Canada, Blumer became one of its loudest critics within psychiatry.[2] A close look at his evolving attitude toward eugenics and hereditarianism, then, helps explain why eugenics became popular in twentieth-century

---

1. For Galton's place in the history of eugenics, see Daniel J. Kevles, *In the Name of Eugenics: Genetics and the Uses of Human Heredity* (New York: Knopf, 1985), esp. pp. 3–19.
2. Mark H. Haller, *Eugenics: Hereditarian Attitudes in American Thought* (New Brunswick, N.J.: Rutgers University Press, 1963), p. 6.

North America in the first place and why certain occupational and social groups were attracted to the campaign to monitor reproductive behavior. In other words, the pattern and pace of Blumer's career offer clues to the complex integration of context and cognition within psychiatry in the early twentieth century, a time when eugenic concepts attracted the majority of U.S. institutional psychiatrists, some of whom actively lobbied to translate eugenic ideas into official practice.[3]

I

A decade of parsimonious funding, therapeutic frustration, and declining professional independence at Utica deeply affected Blumer's attitude toward mental illness and the mentally ill. As he faced mounting obstacles to the successful implementation of a moral treatment program, he became increasingly convinced that mental diseases were chronic ailments whose incidence could only be reduced through extreme preventive measures. In the late 1890s he began to voice his approval of eugenic policies designed to forestall the reproduction of nervous and mentally ill persons, policies such as sterilization, segregation, marriage laws, and immigration restriction. It was sterilization and marriage laws that most attracted him.

Blumer's interest in eugenics was far from exceptional. By the end of the nineteenth century many Anglo-American physicians, biologists, intellectuals, politicians, citizens' groups, and charity reformers were united in their conviction that one way to address the problems of poverty and dependence was to study the laws of inheritance to determine how to prevent the hereditary transmission of undesirable traits. The appeal of eugenics derived from two principal sources. The first was the German biologist August Weismann's theory of inheritance, which first became known in the English-speaking world in the early 1890s. Weismann argued that the information of heredity was found in human germ plasm, which was unaffected by environmental influences. His conclusion convinced some that, in the words of one U.S. reformer, "our only hope for the permanent improvement of the human stock would then seem to be through exercising an influence upon the selective process."[4]

3. Charles Rosenberg, "Woods or Trees? Ideas and Actors in the History of Science," *Isis* 79 (1988): 565–70. See also Gerald N. Grob, *Mental Illness and American Society, 1875–1940* (Princeton: Princeton University Press, 1983), p. 175.
4. Amos Warner, *American Charities* (New York: Thomas Y. Crowell, 1894), pp. 120–21. Cited in Haller, *Eugenics*, p. 60, and Robert C. Bannister, *Social Darwinism: Science and Myth*

The second source of the popularity of eugenics was the social Darwinist belief that charity institutions such as mental asylums worked against the laws of natural selection by making it easier for the poor and infirm to survive and thus outreproduce the "fitter" elite social classes. Under Galton's influence, Darwin himself complained in *The Descent of Man* (1871) that "civilized men" built "asylums for the imbecile, the maimed, and the sick" while "our medical men exert their utmost skill to save the life of every one to the last moment. . . . Thus the weak members of civilized societies propagate their kind." Darwin advised against curtailing this form of charitable activity, claiming it was "the noblest part of our nature" and the sacrifice human beings made for being civilized. By the end of his life, however, he grew so pessimistic about the effects of state charity on evolution and natural selection that he worried aloud about the danger to civilized progress posed by the fertile "scum" that made up Great Britain's lower classes.[5]

As an avid reader of British medical and scientific literature Blumer was well aware of the alarm in England over the sizable differential in fertility between the lower classes and the better-educated, economically successful middle and upper classes, and he knew it was part of a wider national anxiety about a declining national birthrate. These worries can be traced to the middle of the nineteenth century and the introduction of the theory of degeneration. Proponents, relying on the Lamarckian concept that pathological as well as healthy acquired characteristics could be inherited, prophesized the biologic decline of the human race unless significant reforms were made to the conditions surrounding the domestic and working lives of Europeans. The French psychiatrist Benedict-Augustin Morel, whose treatise on degeneration in 1857 did the most to popularize the term, contended that degenerate families died out by the fourth generation owing to a combination of hereditary and environmental factors.[6] Despite substantial public health improvements by

in *Anglo-American Social Thought* (Philadelphia: Temple University Press, 1979), p. 172. See also Frederick Churchill, "August Weismann and a Break from Tradition," *Journal of the History of Biology* 1 (1968): 91–112.

5. Charles Darwin, *The Descent of Man and Selection in Relation to Sex*, 2 vols. (London: Murray, 1871), 1:501–2. Cited in Richard A. Soloway, *Demography and Degeneration: Eugenics and the Declining Birthrate in Twentieth-Century Britain* (Chapel Hill: University of North Carolina Press, 1995), p. 53.

6. For the history of degeneration theory, see Robert A. Nye, *Crime, Madness, and Politics in Modern France: The Medical Concept of National Decline* (Princeton: Princeton University Press, 1984); Daniel Pick, *Faces of Degeneration: A European Disorder, c. 1848–c. 1918* (Cambridge: Cambridge University Press, 1989); and Ian Dowbiggin, *Inheriting Madness: Professionalization and Psychiatric Knowledge in Nineteenth-Century France* (Berkeley: University of California Press, 1991).

the end of century, many observers agreed that degeneration had set in and was evident especially in the mental and physical state of urban dwellers. The result was a tense debate over the future of the entire British Empire, a concern that seemed all the more urgent after the British army's unimpressive showing in the early campaigns of the Boer War.[7] Thus by the beginning of the twentieth century there was much talk in British educated and elite circles about race suicide and the need to take drastic steps to reverse what appeared to be the decline of Anglo-Saxon civilization.

When the Eugenics Education Society was formed in 1907, it became the first national organization in the United Kingdom dedicated to the task of race improvement. Always a small organization, with no more than two thousand members at any one time, it drew mostly from the educated, professional middle classes who exercised an influence over British public opinion. Within the society's ranks was a handful of psychiatrists, including the prominent doctor James Crichton-Browne (1840–1938). Psychiatrists, as specialists in chronic diseases customarily viewed as hereditary, were natural candidates for the label "eugenicist." Eugenics suggested preventive approaches to the eradication of mental illness and thus enabled psychiatrists to sidestep embarrassing questions about their persistent failure to cure their institutional patients.[8]

If the British debate over the future of the human race was refracted through an imperial and class-oriented prism, the growing U.S. interest in eugenics was based on deep-seated uncertainties about the ability of the country to both assimilate escalating numbers of newcomers and pay the skyrocketing costs of public charity as the nation's population rose dramatically around the turn of the century. With the organization and growth of state charity systems after the Civil War, many reformers and officials had argued that spending money on the institutional care of criminals, alcoholics, paupers, and the mentally handicapped was a wise investment because it enabled professionals to rehabilitate people who otherwise might stay in institutions and be a drain on the public purse for their entire lives. But it was not long before this optimism waned. By the final years of the nineteenth century, U.S. public opinion was very concerned about violent crime, increasing labor unrest, and the

7. Soloway, *Demography and Degeneration*, pp. 1–59, esp. p. 39.
8. For the history of the Eugenics Education Society, renamed the Eugenics Society in 1926, see Pauline M. H. Mazumdar, *Eugenics, Human Genetics, and Human Failings: The Eugenics Society, Its Sources, and Its Critics in Britain* (New York: Routledge, 1991). For Crichton-Browne and British eugenics, see Janet Oppenheim, *"Shattered Nerves": Doctors, Patients, and Depression in Victorian England* (New York: Oxford University Press, 1991), pp. 54–78, 278–83.

mounting toll of economic depression. Trends in ideas followed shifting social and economic conditions. The theory of degeneration, with its scenario of biologic descent, proved persuasive to many Americans. The Italian psychiatrist Cesare Lombroso's views on criminal anthropology, a variation on degeneration theory, were also highly influential among U.S. students of crime and mental illness. His assertion that murderers were atavistic relics whose behavioral patterns were no more reparable than their defective brains challenged many of the sanguine principles underlying the American tradition of reform and progress. The various strands of degeneration theory were woven together by Max Nordau in his immensely popular book *Degeneration*, translated into English in 1895; and the concepts of criminal anthropology surfaced in novels by Jack London and Frank Morris.[9]

Theories such as degeneration and criminal anthropology led public attention to focus on heredity and the allegedly high fertility of dependent men and women, especially the "feebleminded." Physicians who worked with the "feebleminded" used the term to describe the person who "differs from the insane in that he has neither delusions nor lucid intervals; an anti-social being, but of many grades of intelligence."[10] In fact custodians of institutions for the feebleminded played a pioneering role in the history of U.S. eugenics, so much so that by the 1890s the overwhelming consensus among physicians was that feeblemindedness was hereditary and constituted a distinct menace to society because, as superintendents and charity workers argued, the feebleminded were persons with "weak minds in strong and oversexed bodies."[11]

Perhaps nothing had helped to change U.S. opinions about the disadvantaged more than the publication of Richard Dugdale's *The Jukes* (1877). Dugdale, a merchant interested in social problems such as poverty and crime, examined the history of a particular family he called the Jukes, whose members included a surprisingly large number of derelicts, failures, criminals, and paupers. He concluded that the Jukes had cost taxpayers "over a million and a quarter dollars of loss in 75 years, caused by a single family 1,200 strong, without reckoning the cash paid for whiskey, or taking into account the entailment of pauperism and crime of the survivors in succeeding generations, and the incurable disease, idiocy, and insanity growing out of this debauchery, and reaching further

9. Haller, *Eugenics*, pp. 40–41.
10. Hubert Work, "The Sociologic Aspect of Insanity and Allied Defects," *AJI* 69 (1912): 1–15, 1.
11. Haller, *Eugenics*, p. 26.

than we can calculate."[12] Dugdale stressed that environment was as responsible as heredity in producing the Jukes family history, but hereditarians drew the conclusion that the Jukes case proved inheritance was far more potent than degraded surroundings. Dugdale's book quickly spawned similar family studies. Though often flawed, their message was clear: the unfit were particularly fecund; degenerate families often did not die out but continued to reproduce thanks in large part to charity and penal institutions; and the financial burden for supporting such degenerates was likely to get a lot worse in upcoming years unless states prevented them from reproducing.[13]

Thus by the 1890s there was a burgeoning literature in the United States and Great Britain on the threats degeneracy and the reproduction of society's dependents and deviants posed to civilization. As the debate widened, educated Americans sought means of limiting the fertility of those deemed most likely to produce unfit progeny. Although at least one extremist recommended "a gentle, painless death" as "the most humane means" of preventing the propagation of the unfit,[14] the solutions most eugenicists considered were segregation, marriage laws, and sterilization. Lifetime segregation enjoyed a wide appeal among officials. Such documents as the 1890 U.S. census, which indicated a large increase in the number of "idiots" and "imbeciles," shook the confidence of physicians who only fifteen years earlier had expressed the certitude that the feebleminded were corrigible. Medical superintendents began to insist on reducing the risk of pregnancy for feebleminded women by incarcerating them until they were past the reproducing stage.[15] The problem, according to expert opinion, was that the vast majority of feebleminded persons lived *outside* institutions, out of reach of segregation policies. The solution, then, had to be a policy that extended to defectives who were not institutionalized. The prohibition of marriage between defective persons quickly emerged as one of the most attractive remedies.

The first state to outlaw the marriage of defective persons was Con-

12. R. L. Dugdale, *The Jukes: A Study in Crime, Pauperism, and Heredity*, 4th ed. (New York: Putnam's, 1910), p. 167. Cited in Philip R. Reilly, *The Surgical Solution: A History of Involuntary Sterilization in the United States* (Baltimore: John Hopkins University Press, 1991), p. 15.
13. Reilly, *Surgical Solution*, pp. 12–18. See also Nicole Hahn Rafter, ed., *White Trash: The Eugenic Family Studies, 1877–1919* (Boston: Northeastern University Press, 1988), esp. her introduction, pp. 1–31.
14. W. Duncan McKim, *Heredity and Human Progress* (New York: Putnam's, 1900), p. 168. Cited in Haller, *Eugenics*, p. 42.
15. R. A. Mott, "Welcoming Remarks," in *The Proceedings of the Association of Medical Officers of American Institutions for Idiotic and Feebleminded Persons* (Philadelphia: Lippincott, 1890), p. 117. Cited in Reilly, *Surgical Solution*, p. 25.

necticut in 1895. Parties to a marriage in which at least one was feeble-minded, an epileptic, or an imbecile could be imprisoned for up to three years. So could unmarried persons. The only exception was for women forty-five years of age or older. Over the next twenty years, twenty-four states enacted similar laws. By the mid-1930s, forty-one states had laws prohibiting marriage of the mentally ill and feebleminded; seventeen, prohibiting marriage of epileptics; and four, prohibiting marriage of confirmed alcoholics. Eugenicists however were doubtful about the efficacy of such laws. Some claimed that marriage laws only discouraged the elite, fit classes from reproducing by making them think twice about wedlock, thus defeating a key objective of positive eugenics. One eugenicist criticized marriage laws for being unenforceable and inconsistent with what geneticists knew about inheritance. Marriage laws were in fact hard to enforce, and this realization soon undermined support for them among eugenicists, if not among legislators.[16]

If marriage laws did not effectively curtail the reproduction of the unfit, eugenicists reasoned, other solutions were necessary. Castration quickly emerged as an option. Arguments in favor of castration as a punitive or remedial measure were far from new. Advocates earlier in the nineteenth century had maintained that the threat of castration discouraged people from committing crimes, especially rape. Some also contended that castration actually transformed hardened criminals into law-abiding and caring citizens. But as eugenic ideas spread, the appeal of castration as a method of preventing the reproduction of undesirable persons extended to physicians and state officials. The first attempt to use castration systematically for eugenic purposes was at the Kansas State Home for the Feebleminded. Hoyt Pilcher, the superintendent, castrated forty-four boys and fourteen girls without legal warrant. When the news leaked out in 1894, the uproar cost Pilcher his job. Public opinion was not in favor of asexualization by castration. But some Kansas doctors supported Pilcher and hinted approvingly that surgeons at other institutions for the feebleminded had performed similar operations. Thus, while many recoiled at the idea of castration as a medical and eugenic procedure, a few physicians and charity officials were willing to try such a desperate remedy for what they perceived as a desperate situation, and a growing group of physicians could accept the idea of sterilization if a simple surgical technique could be discovered for rendering the patient sterile without affecting the internal hormones of the ovaries and testes.[17]

16. Reilly, *Surgical Solution*, pp. 26–27; Haller, *Eugenics*, p. 142.
17. Haller, *Eugenics*, pp. 48–49; Reilly, *Surgical Solution*, pp. 28–29.

The breakthrough came when the vasectomy and salpingectomy were introduced. Salpingectomy—the cutting and tying of the fallopian tubes—involved opening the abdomen and thus was often used in the late nineteenth century to sterilize women when they were forced to have children by Cesarean. A less dangerous operation was the vasectomy—the severing of the vas deferens through an incision in the scrotum. The first American case report of a vasectomy was in 1897 by A. J. Ochsner, a Chicago surgeon. Although he had performed the operation on two patients who complained of prostatitis, Ochsner argued that the procedure could also be used "to eliminate all habitual criminals from the possibility of having children." The same operation, he added, "could reasonably be suggested for chronic inebriates, imbeciles, perverts, and paupers."[18]

The next step came in 1902 when Harry C. Sharp, a surgeon at the Indiana Reformatory, announced his use of the vasectomy as a form of eugenic sterilization. In the words of one historian, Sharp's announcement "was virtually a manifesto for a sterilization movement."[19] Sharp reported that he had personally performed the vasectomy on forty-two prison inmates ranging in age from seventeen to twenty-five. Like Pilcher, he maintained that his patients actually felt better and were better behaved because of the alleged therapeutic effects of the operation, and this claim would become a prime justification for sterilization over the next forty years. Sharp also encouraged his colleagues in organized medicine to lobby their state legislatures in favor of sterilization laws. His advice was heeded; in fact enthusiasm for sterilization grew steadily in the pre–First World War period.[20] For example, in 1897 a Michigan bill calling for the sterilization of the feebleminded and some criminals was introduced but failed to pass. A similar bill did pass the Pennsylvania legislature in 1901 and 1905, only to be vetoed by the governor.

The first legislative victory for the eugenicists occurred in 1907 in Indiana, which passed the first sterilization law in the United States, thanks in no small way to Sharp, who fought energetically for it. This bill made mandatory the sterilization of confirmed criminals, idiots, imbeciles, and rapists upon recommendation by a board of experts. Over the next ten years, fifteen other states followed suit. In most of these

18. A. J. Ochsner, "Surgical Treatment of Habitual Criminals," *JAMA* 53 (1899): 867–68. Cited in Reilly, *Surgical Solution*, pp. 30–31.
19. Reilly, *Surgical Solution*, p. 31.
20. Reilly, *Surgical Solution*, pp. 38–39. See also James W. Trent, Jr., *Inventing the Feeble Mind: A History of Mental Retardation in the United States* (Berkeley: University of California Press, 1994), pp. 192–98.

laws the mentally ill were a specific target group. Then followed a series of constitutional challenges that resulted in seven of the first sixteen laws being struck down by federal or state courts. Consequently, between 1907 and 1927, only about eighty-five hundred patients were sterilized at state institutions.

But 1927 marked a turning point because that year the U.S. Supreme Court upheld the constitutionality of Virginia's sterilization law in the *Buck v. Bell* ruling. This judgment greatly accelerated the passing of other sterilization laws. Sixteen states in the late 1920s and early 1930s passed such measures. *Buck v. Bell* also emboldened state officials to put existing laws into practice, causing a tenfold jump in the average annual number of compulsory sterilizations. By 1940, thirty states had enacted statutes that permitted the sterilization of patients confined in state hospitals. The total number of legal sterilizations of mentally ill patients was 18,552, and more than half were performed in California alone. California's totals, when combined with those of Virginia and Kansas, accounted for approximately three-fourths of the nation's total. But it is clear that a good deal more were done than officially reported. According to Philip Reilly, "The actual number of eugenic sterilizations carried out in the United States *significantly exceeded* those allowed by state law."[21]

Spearheading the U.S. eugenic crusade were Charles Davenport (1866–1944) and Harry Hamilton Laughlin (1880–1943). Davenport, heavily influenced as a young man by the British eugenicists Galton and Karl Pearson, was able to convince the newly endowed Carnegie Institution of Washington to appoint him in 1904 as director of a biologic experiment station at Cold Spring Harbor on Long Island, where he soon decided to dedicate himself to a major study of human heredity. In 1910 he invited Laughlin, a high school biology teacher from Missouri, to become superintendent of his Eugenics Record Office (ERO) at Cold Spring Harbor. There Laughlin assumed responsibility for analyzing the massive collection of family data being compiled by the ERO's field workers. In 1912 he also assumed the post of secretary of the American Breeders' Association Committee to Study and to Report on the Best Practical Means of Cutting off the Defective Germ Plasm in the American Population. The association, begun in 1903 by W. M. Hays, a professor of plant breeding at the University of Minnesota, was renamed the American Genetics Association in 1913. It was the first national or-

21. Reilly, *Surgical Solution*, p. 90. My emphasis. See also ibid., pp. 88–110; and Grob, *Mental Illness and American Society*, p. 173.

ganization for promoting genetic and eugenic research in the United States.[22]

Laughlin soon became an outspoken and tireless campaigner for eugenics, including sterilization. But though he did a great deal to popularize eugenics, the clumsy and unsophisticated manner in which he mixed social Darwinism and outlandish policy proposals annoyed geneticists and other professionals who wanted to transform eugenics into a rigorous science. To Laughlin in 1914 it was "the bolstering up of the defective classes by a beneficent society that constitutes the real menace to our blood, because it lowers the basis of parenthood. . . . There must be selection not only for progress, but even for maintaining the present standard. To the degree we inhibit natural selection, we must substitute rational selection, else our blood will deteriorate." Given these kinds of ideas it was little wonder that in virtually the next breath Laughlin looked forward to "a future social status wherein selection for parenthood will not be held a natural right of every individual; but will be a prize highly sought by and allotted to only the best individuals of proven blood, and those individuals who are not deemed worthy and are by society denied the right to perpetuate their own traits in subsequent generations, will be held in pity by their fellows." Laughlin knew he was not alone in expressing these opinions. As Theodore Roosevelt said to him in 1913, "It is obvious that if in the future racial qualities are to be improved, the improving must be wrought mainly by favoring the fecundity of the worthy type and frowning on the fecundity of the unworthy types."[23] In 1936 the University of Heidelberg, with the encouragement of the Nazi state, awarded Laughlin an honorary degree for his contributions to eugenics.[24] By the Second World War, this and his other credentials had led many Americans to perceive Laughlin's brand of eugenics as unfashionable and unscientific, and his career as a eugenicist was virtually ended when the Carnegie foundation ceased funding the ERO in 1939.[25]

The momentum of the U.S. eugenics movement between the early

22. Barbara A. Kimmelman, "The American Breeders' Association: Genetics and Eugenics in an Agricultural Context, 1903–13," *Social Studies of Science* 13 (1983): 163–204, 163. On Davenport, see Kevles, *In the Name of Eugenics*, pp. 41–56; on Laughlin, see Reilly, *Surgical Solution*, pp. 56–70.
23. "Report of the Committee to Study and to Report on the Best Means of Cutting Off the Defective Germ-Plasm in the American Population," pt. 1, "The Scope of the Committee's Work by Harry H. Laughlin," ERO *Bulletin* no. 10A (February 1914), pp. 56–57.
24. Stefan Kühl, *The Nazi Connection: Eugenics, American Racism, and German National Socialism* (New York: Oxford University Press, 1994), pp. 86–87.
25. Garland Allen, "The Eugenics Record Office at Cold Spring Harbor, 1910–1940," *Osiris* 2 (1986): 225–64.

1890s and the First World War caught the attention of numerous psychiatrists including G. Alder Blumer. Though he became one of the earliest converts to eugenics in psychiatry, Blumer had held decidedly noneugenic views during his early years at Utica, which was hardly surprising, given his early devotion to the idea that asylums could be transformed into hospitals that cured mentally diseased patients. He emphatically believed then that under the firm yet benevolent guidance of a skilled psychiatrist, there were many potentially positive effects of hospital confinement on the depleted nervous systems of civilized men and women. Farthest from his thinking was that an asylum's main purpose should be to incarcerate congenitally defective people so they could not reproduce. Blumer's theories about insanity mirrored his youthful optimism. Rather than blame the statistical rise in cases of madness on marriages between people with family histories of insanity, as many physicians had done since the middle of the nineteenth century, he insisted that the hereditary effects of such marriages were little more than "a drop in the bucket." By emphasizing environmental factors—such as the demands made on physical and mental health by the feverish struggle for money and success—Blumer was proposing a theory of mental illness consistent with his faith in the power of institutional psychiatric treatment.[26]

As the 1890s wore on, however, Blumer's sanguine views began to change, as did those of other New York State psychiatrists. More and more physicians expressed alarm over what seemed to be the mounting numbers of incurable state hospital patients "suffering from constitutional degeneracies." This trend, physicians alleged, was fed by numerous "unphysiological" marriages. It seemed obvious that the most urgent challenge was to discover means to prevent mental illnesses before they had a chance to develop.[27] From this perspective eugenics made a great deal of sense. With the numbers of Utica's poor, aged, and chronically ill patients growing and with the beginnings of the asylum's transformation into an old-age home, Blumer gradually became receptive to

26. G. Alder Blumer, editorial on "The Increase of Insanity," *AJI* 50 (1893): 310–13. See also G. Alder Blumer and A. B. Richardson, eds., *Commitment, Detention, Care, and Treatment of the Insane: Being a Report of the Fourth Section of the International Congress of Charities, Correction, and Philanthropy, Chicago, June 1893* (Utica: Utica State Hospital Press, 1894), pp. 178–79; and G. Alder Blumer, "Progress in Mental Medicine" (paper read to the Oneida County Medical Society, 7 July 1891), BP, box 40. For criticism of Blumer's de-emphasis on heredity, see John M. Semple to Blumer, 18 November 1893, BP, box 27.
27. See, e.g., Smith Barker, "Causes and Prevention of Insanity," *Popular Science Monthly* 55 (1899): 102–13, 107–8.

these ideas; to late nineteenth-century social Darwinist literature, including the warnings of British physicians Thomas Clouston and Henry Maudsley; and to pro-eugenic articles appearing more and more frequently in English medical journals.

Blumer had kept in touch with Clouston since his postgraduate studies at Edinburgh. His library also contained several titles by the Scottish psychiatrist, notably Clouston's highly regarded *Clinical Lectures on Mental Diseases*, several editions of which Blumer read avidly. Like Blumer, Clouston emphasized that mental disease could be "counteracted by suitable environments" such as those found in a psychiatric asylum. Again like Blumer, he disliked intensely the growing pauperization and chronicity of his patient population at the Royal Edinburgh Asylum as the century came to a close. When exactly he began to entertain eugenic ideas is not clear. But in 1906 he advised Parliament to make "the breeding of a good race . . . an operative political motive" by encouraging residence in the countryside, where, he claimed, "the real breeding-places of the stable-minded, non-nervous element of our population" were to be found.[28] To Clouston it was not enough in the evolution of the human race "to trust entirely to 'favorable variations' and the gradual extinction of the unfit in mind, through their slowly dying out."[29] His *Before I Wed* appeared in 1915, a book of eugenic advice to young men stressing the importance of preventing mental and nervous illness by observing careful rules of healthy behavior. By then Clouston was showing the intellectual signs of treating the consequences of dissipation, alcoholism, syphilis, and general paralysis for thirty-five years, so much so that it is hard to imagine that his fondness for eugenics—like Blumer's—did not stem from this long and often futile struggle to conquer the ravages of madness.[30]

By contrast, Henry Maudsley (1835–1918) never seemed very hopeful about medicine's power to cure insanity. He was a visceral pessimist and convert to the theory of degeneration. Early in his career he served as an asylum medical officer, but he soon opened a private practice, taught medical jurisprudence at University College (London), and helped to edit the *Journal of Mental Science*. Thanks to his lucrative private practice,

28. Thomas Clouston, *The Hygiene of Mind* (London: Methuen, 1906), p. 264. Cited in Oppenheim, "*Shattered Nerves*," p. 296.
29. T. S. Clouston, *Unsoundness of Mind* (London: Methuen, 1911), p. 53. For other positive references to eugenics, see ibid., pp. 18, 29, 52–73, 299, 338, 345–46.
30. Margaret S. Thompson, "The Wages of Sin: The Problem of Alcoholism and General Paralysis in Nineteenth-Century Edinburgh," in *The Anatomy of Madness: Essays in the History of Psychiatry*, ed. W. F. Bynum, Roy Porter, and Michael Shepherd, vol. 3, *The Asylum and Its Psychiatry* (New York: Routledge, 1988), pp. 316–40.

Maudsley became quite wealthy and in 1907 offered the London County Council £30,000 to open a university psychiatric clinic.[31]

Maudsley was probably the best-known and most respected of all English psychiatrists in the second half of the nineteenth century. French, German, and Italian psychiatrists quoted him, as did Charles Darwin in *The Descent of Man*. Blumer's own copies of Maudsley's books, like his copies of Clouston's, were well thumbed. Maudsley proselytized on behalf of naturalist medical science and its capacity to discover the laws of society and politics. Like a growing number of educated late-Victorian professionals, he was a firm believer that anatomy, physiology, and pathology could ultimately unlock the secrets of the mind. He was also convinced that the effects of heredity on character, behavior, and health were far more powerful than was customarily thought.

Like many who subscribed to the theory of degeneration, Maudsley initially found solace in B. A. Morel's observation that degenerate families eventually died out and thus constituted no threat to evolutionary progress. But in 1883 he began to argue that degeneration was not a self-annihilating force but a regressive process that coincided with and rivaled evolution.[32] In the 1890s, still uneasy about the potential of degeneration to drag all of evolution down, he again and again cited heredity and its capacity to transmit unhealthy and antisocial traits from parent to offspring. The accumulation of all this bad heredity, he contended, left late nineteenth-century civilization in a precarious position. As he wrote in 1895, "The long, long time the world has lasted and the infinite travail of it to bring life on earth to its present development! The short time and the little change that will be necessary to bring it all to an end as a tale that is told!"[33] Elsewhere he asked, rhetorically, "Is it truly a well-based hope that the sum of morality on earth is growing steadily greater and the sum of immorality less?"[34]

31. Aubrey Lewis, "Henry Maudsley: His Work and Influence," *Journal of Mental Science* 97 (1951): 259–77; Trevor Turner, "Henry Maudsley: Psychiatrist, Philosopher, and Entrepreneur," *Psychological Medicine* 18 (1988): 551–74; reprinted in Bynum, Porter, and Shepherd, *Anatomy of Madness*, 3:151–89. See also Pick, *Faces of Degeneration*, pp. 203–16.
32. Maudsley believed that the human race was characterized by "a double flux of movement, as it were, ascendant and descendant, the ways or modes of degeneration in the descendant line being almost as many and divers [sic] as the varieties of evolution in the ascendant line. Some persons are high on the upward, others low on the downward path; many are just entering upon the one or the other; but there is no one who is not himself going in the one or the other direction and making the way which he takes easier for others to follow in." Henry Maudsley, *Body and Will* (London: Kegan Paul, Trench, 1883), p. 245. Cited in Pick, *Faces of Degeneration*, p. 209. See also Lewis, "Henry Maudsley," pp. 265–66.
33. Henry Maudsley, *Pathology of Mind* (New York: Macmillan, 1895), p. 92.
34. Maudsley, *Pathology of Mind*, p. 79.

Much of Maudsley's pessimism in 1895 was due to the fact that at age sixty he had begun to wonder if his life in psychiatry had been worth it. As a psychiatrist he had come to doubt the usefulness of a form of medicine that could never cure more than one-half of its patients and that "restor[ed] the other half to reproductive work." Although he did not proffer any concrete eugenic remedies, he did suggest that it was the responsibility of single men and women to follow elementary rules of mental and physical health; otherwise, a person's "sin will be avenged on him and on his children unto the third and fourth generation." Or, as he reminded his readers, in words that Blumer would later quote on more than one occasion, "The fathers had eaten sour grapes and the children's teeth were set on edge."[35]

This combination of professional disillusionment and therapeutic pessimism in Clouston's and Maudsley's writings deeply influenced Blumer in the late 1890s; for they seemingly made sense out of his own predicament as an asylum psychiatrist. Blumer was ready to applaud policies that might offer a way out of his impasse, but the move to the eugenicist camp did not come easily. He harbored a personal distaste for measures that infringed on fundamental liberties and prerogatives, such as the right to marry, and he had been decidedly ambivalent about Connecticut's eugenic marriage law.[36] But in 1897 he could argue that "our modern hospitals for the insane are in some measure responsible for the increase of insanity by promoting, not the survival of the fittest, but the survival of the unfit, as well as by permitting unstable persons to leave institutions and mate themselves with their kind, instead of allowing an affinity of contrast to prevail in selecting their wives."[37] Blumer's acceptance of this and other social Darwinist ideas confirms that he had read Maudsley carefully and had probably found numerous reasons for becoming a eugenicist.

By the turn of the century Blumer's ambivalence about heredity and eugenics had vanished. Quoting Maudsley, he argued in 1900 that "all diseases are hereditary." "The department of preventive medicine" most relevant to physicians was the eugenic prohibition of marriages between diseased persons. He hinted that his interest in eugenics stemmed from his work with the insane at Utica when he declared "that accident has forced it upon my consideration by reason of a special calling, and quite recent experiences have aroused an indignation

35. Maudsley, *Pathology of Mind*, pp. 563, 83, 79.
36. G. Alder Blumer, "Marriage of Epileptics," *AJI* 53 (1896): 163–64.
37. Blumer to Goodwin Brown, 19 November 1897, BP, box 29.

sufficiently righteous to give me at least temporary hardihood in attacking a giant evil." While applauding futuristic accounts of societies built on the principles of eugenics and euthanasia, he also cited similar practices among the ancient Scots, including the "rough and ready method" of burying alive babies and their epileptic or disturbed mothers. Blumer granted that the tactics of the ancient Scots were drastic, but he added that "from the point of view of science the cruel and remorseless Scot was more advanced than his descendants of our day." In reference to the 1897 Michigan asexualization bill, he noted that it was "a hopeful sign of the times." He went so far as to urge surgeons to aid "the survival of the fit" by removing both ovaries from women in whom only one was affected, thus "render[ing]" all their patients "as regards child-bearing, *hors concours*."[38]

Blumer's admonition to surgeons referred to a late nineteenth-century ovariotomy often called "Battey's operation." Named after its originator, Robert Battey, a surgeon from Georgia, it consisted of the removal of normal ovaries to induce premature menopause. Although ovariotomies were sometimes used to remove diseased ovaries, Battey's operation was also performed as a way of curing insanity, reducing sexual desire, preventing reproduction, or deterring antisocial behavior. Much of its popularity as a psychiatric therapy was based on the theory of reflex irritation, which stated that nervous connections running via the spine throughout the entire body regulated its organs, including the brain. It followed, then, that women's uteri might influence brain functioning, an assumption that, in the words of one historian, "provided the justification for massive medical intervention in the female organs of reproduction."[39] Mortality rates as high as 22 percent did not deter surgeons from performing Battey's operation repeatedly, with Battey himself operating on several hundred women between 1870 and 1890.

By the 1890s, however, more and more physicians were protesting that the operation was being abused, particularly for the relief of mental illness. In the words of one psychiatrist in 1893, asylums "might easily lose a portion of the slender hold they now have upon the public and friends

38. G. Alder Blumer, "Marriage in its Relation to Morbid Heredity" (lecture to the Providence Friday Night Club, 20 September 1900), BP, box 40. This lecture expressed the same ideas as those found in Blumer's "The Marriage of the Unfit," *AJI* 57 (1900): 375–77. The Friday Night Club was an association of Providence physicians who met at the prestigious Hope Club. On the importance of social clubs in turn-of-the-century Providence, see John S. Gilkeson, Jr., *Middle-Class Providence, 1820–1940* (Princeton: Princeton University Press, 1986), pp. 138–51.
39. Edward Shorter, *From Paralysis to Fatigue: A History of Psychosomatic Illness in the Modern Era* (New York: Free Press, 1992), pp. 40–94, 40.

of patients, if it were understood that the patients were subjected to experimental operations of a hazardous nature."[40] Despite this consideration, asylum gynecologic surgery did not immediately die out; indeed a surprisingly large number of female physicians both performed and approved of Battey's operation up to the end of the nineteenth century.[41] The Canadian psychiatrist Richard M. Bucke (1837–1902) authorized 226 such operations at the London provincial asylum between 1895 and 1900. One reason some physicians disliked giving up on Battey's operation despite its unfavorable reputation was its eugenic implications, and it was this eugenic dimension that particularly intrigued Blumer.[42]

In 1901 Blumer reaffirmed his support for eugenics. He praised the "recognition by physicians of the laws of heredity and an attempt on their part—for they have peculiar advantages as confidential advisors—to prevent the marriage of the unfit." He believed that the state was obliged to take legal action to monitor reproduction. It was also time, he declared, to convince everyone "of the solemn truth that the responsibility of making a human life is scarcely less serious than that of taking one."[43]

Blumer's strongest endorsement of eugenics was his 1903 presidential address to the AMPA in Washington, D.C. Speaking to a predominantly psychiatric audience, he conjured up a social Darwinist nightmare. He claimed the mentally ill and feebleminded were "notoriously addicted to matrimony and by no means satisfied with one brood of defectives." He then called for legislation outlawing the marriage of people with family histories of insanity and alcoholism, authorizing indefinite detention after a third admission to an asylum, and permitting divorce on the grounds of incurable insanity or chronic alcoholism. As long as the "myth that

40. John Chapin, "Removal of the Ovaries as a Cure for Insanity," *AJI* 49 (1893): 512–13.
41. Shorter, *From Paralysis to Fatigue*, p. 80.
42. See Haller, *Eugenics*, p. 30; Lawrence D. Longo, "The Rise and Fall of Battey's Operation: A Fashion in Surgery," *Bulletin of the History of Medicine* 53 (1979): 244–67; and Andrew Scull and Diane Favreau, " 'A Chance to Cut Is a Chance to Cure': Sexual Surgery for Psychosis in Three Nineteenth-Century Societies," *Research in Law, Deviance, and Social Control* 8 (1986): 3–39. For exceptions to the decline of ovary removal as a curative procedure, see Wendy Mitchinson, *The Nature of Their Bodies: Women and Their Doctors in Victorian Canada* (Toronto: University of Toronto Press, 1991), pp. 252–77; S. E. D. Shortt, *Victorian Lunacy: Richard M. Bucke and the Practice of Late Nineteenth-Century Psychiatry* (Cambridge: Cambridge University Press, 1986), pp. 143–59; and Cheryl Krasnick Warsh, *Moments of Unreason: The Practice of Canadian Psychiatry and the Homewood Retreat, 1883–1923* (Montreal: McGill-Queen's University Press, 1989), pp. 55–56. For the eugenic dimensions of Battey's operation, see William Goodell, "Clinical Notes on the Extirpation of the Ovaries for Insanity," *AJI* 38 (1882): 294–302.
43. G. Alder Blumer, "The Yesterday and To-Day of Mental Medicine," *Providence Medical Journal* 2 (1901): 101–11.

marriages are made in heaven" thrives, Blumer concluded, "infinite disaster" will follow. Quoting Maudsley, he warned that "the fathers have eaten sour grapes, and the children's teeth are set on edge."[44]

Thus Blumer's pro-eugenic attitudes and ideas, cultivated during his last years at Utica, persisted into his initial years at Butler. Yet, at almost the same time as he was uttering his remarks in Washington, his commitment to eugenics was faltering. As he became increasingly aware of the values and expectations of his clientele, he realized that it was a distinct liability for Butler's medical superintendent to hold eugenic beliefs, and his outward sympathy for eugenics faded away soon after the AMPA address. He never entirely rejected the eugenic paradigm, but he did grow more and more guarded about making pro-eugenic statements in public. His increasingly critical stance in the years after the Washington speech adumbrated the eventual views of most prominent psychiatrists on the eugenic enterprise in the twentieth century.

II

The first clear signs of Blumer's backing away from eugenics came in 1904 when he expressed his dissatisfaction with the hereditarian model of mental illness and its assumption that, beyond extreme prophylactic measures, institutional psychiatrists could do no more than provide patients with the basic necessities and segregate them from society. He had tolerated this model because it absolved psychiatrists—particularly public asylum physicians—of responsibility for curing patients. At Butler, though, his emphasis on hereditary weakness as the principal factor in mental and nervous illnesses proved incompatible with the expectations of patients, their relatives and friends, and the local community. Put simply, it would not do for Blumer to be constantly invoking the need for eugenic interference to erase the hereditary taint in the families of Butler's patients. Naturally the families of his patients would resent hearing that their maladies were due to the vices, delusions, and congenital inferiorities of their ancestors.[45] At a time when some New England patricians were campaigning for immigration restriction on the basis of their hereditary superiority over southern and eastern Europeans, they did not want to hear their own physicians casting aspersions on their

44. G. Alder Blumer, "Presidential Address," *AJI* 60 (1903): 1–18.
45. For the reluctance of Canadians to admit that their relatives had hereditary afflictions, see Mitchinson, *Nature of Their Bodies*, p. 292.

breeding and lineage.[46] Blumer was placed in the position of having to disavow publicly the eugenic views he had adopted since the late 1890s.

The result was a hasty retreat. As early as 1902, Blumer was aware of the touchiness of his new clientele and the need to destroy the popular prejudices against men and women suffering from emotional disorders. As he wrote that year, "People who are in a sanatorium for 'nerves' [like Butler], and whose friends flatter themselves that they are there for that purpose, do not like to intimate that their mental integrity is impaired."[47] In an attempt to erase the stigma of mental illness, he argued in 1904 that "in these New England communities of ours, where brains are more apt to be highly organized than in less favored parts of the country, it may even be a mark of distinction to possess a mind of sufficient delicacy to invite damage under the stresses of life."[48] If intermarriage among the prosperous families of the Northeast had produced sensitive nervous systems, Blumer seemed to be saying, it was less a cause for alarm than for congratulations. He implied that nervous illness was the price the social elite paid for being so civilized. Blumer was not alone among New England physicians in recognizing that the inhabitants of that region viewed their mental infirmities as a badge of honor, a symbol of their social and cultural success.[49] Indulging this bias, he was later to observe that some of the greatest minds of Western cultural history were also the most highly strung. "I am for prevention as earnestly as any man," he would then declare but go on to advise against the eugenic enterprise of "reduc[ing] mankind to the least common multiple in the effort to breed out the nervous temperament." "There cannot be complexity of the nervous system without what the world calls nervousness," in his view.[50] A neuropathic streak in a genteel family, then, was nothing to be embarrassed about. Quite the contrary, it was a sign of distinction.

More evidence of his shifting ideas appeared in 1906. Back in 1901, with memories of Utica fresh in his mind, he had barely been able to disguise his contempt for inebriate patients and his displeasure with the time he wasted trying to sober them up. His changed attitude by 1906 was, he admitted, due to his experience treating "men suffering from the liquor habit" and other addictions at Butler. Not surprisingly, Butler

46. Barbara M. Solomon, *Ancestors and Immigrants: A Changing New England Tradition* (Cambridge: Harvard University Press, 1956).
47. Blumer to Charles B. Rogers, 17 May 1902, BP, box 30.
48. BAR, 1904, pp. 15–16.
49. See, e.g., Robert T. Edes, "The New England Invalid," *Boston Medical and Surgical Journal* 133 (1895): 101–7, 101.
50. BAR, 1912, pp. 41–45.

"habit cases" tended to be wealthy persons who paid steep rates for their room and board during lengthy stays. They also tended to resist hospitalization more than less affluent patients, who often considered it an honor to be treated at a facility such as Butler with its provisions for private patients. "Habit cases," like other patients from prosperous backgrounds, disliked the idea of being treated in an asylum with all its associations with dependence and charity assistance. Faced with these patients for whom something remedial was expected, and to whom remarks about ancestral taint were bound to be offensive, Blumer refused publicly to condone their indefinite detention or rule out their marriage plans. Now attacking Maudsley's pessimism, he insisted: "I am not one of those who in the despair of fatalism, would excuse everything on the principle, so dear to many victims of habit, that it is impossible to escape the tyranny of a defective organization. We are all too ready to throw responsibility for our shortcomings upon preceding generations and complacently to reflect, in language that comes unctuously through the Bible, that the sins of the fathers having dieted on sour grapes, the children's teeth are set on edge, etc." Instead, he argued optimistically that "the constitution that, under injudicious training and environment, tends in the direction of inebriety or insanity, may be extraordinarily capable, under the rightful associations, of making a John Howard or a Martin Luther." The task of the physician, he concluded, was to exploit through hospitalization the positive tendencies in everyone's biologic inheritance. A hospital psychiatrist was not powerless when it came to treating a disorder such as alcoholism, which many thought to be hereditary. Alcoholics were not doomed by their family histories to chronic drunkenness or eventual madness.[51] All this optimism surely derived from the dawning realization that therapeutic pessimism did not suit the medical superintendent of a putatively curative mental hospital.

Were there still other experiences that taught Blumer to tread carefully on the sensitive topics of ancestry, marriage, and reproduction? An examination of his correspondence with patients, their families, and their friends discloses that during this period when his opinions about eugenics were changing he was encountering some difficulties in his relations with these interested parties. These difficulties had to do with Blumer's attempts to have pelvic operations performed for eugenic and therapeutic purposes. Shortly after his transfer to Butler in 1899 he began recom-

51. G. Alder Blumer, "Recent Experiences with Habit Cases," paper, 1906, BP, box 40. See also Edward M. Brown," 'What Shall We Do with the Inebriate?' Asylum Treatment and the Disease Concept of Alcoholism in the Late Nineteenth Century," *Journal of the History of the Behavioral Sciences* 21 (1985): 48–59.

mending gynecologic surgery for certain patients. Although it is impossible to determine the exact number of patients who submitted to these kinds of operations, it was probably not large.[52] In early 1903 he wrote to a patient's parent advising that the daughter undergo "the removal of the uterus, its appendages and the clitoris," adding, "Five such operations have been performed in this hospital during the past two years."[53] After 1904 there is no evidence that this operation was performed. The resistance Blumer faced in a handful of cases made it patent to him that by authorizing these operations he was jeopardizing his delicate relationship with "the outside world" whose "attitude . . . to those things that concern the inside of Butler Hospital" was of utmost importance to him.[54] That Blumer—ordinarily no admirer of surgical remedies for psychiatric cases—should have considered these operations in the first place attests to the strength of his conversion to eugenics around the turn of the century.

The women Blumer singled out for surgery of this nature tended to be paying patients and not state charity inmates. For the most part these women were noisy, destructive, violent, or obscene, making them a disruptive presence. For similar charity patients it was easy enough to make arrangements with state officials to have them transferred as incurables to the state hospital. But it was much harder to have paying patients in this category moved to another facility, partly because it was difficult to convince their parents or guardians that the move was warranted, and partly because Blumer did not like to discharge affluent patients who could pay for their treatment and stay at Butler. Therefore, one of the very few other options for this type of patient was surgery, and behind these operations lurked both medical desperation and economic motives.

According to Blumer, gynecological operations held out the hope of relieving patients' symptoms, if not curing the illness itself. He was relying on the theory that insanity was a genital reflex. This theory had led to a widespread insistence between 1850 and 1900 that removal of women's reproductive organs could clear up all or some morbid psychological and behavioral symptoms.[55] Blumer himself rarely cited the possibility of cure when broaching the topic of surgery, but sometimes he

52. The complete Butler clinical records for the Blumer years (1899–1921) are unaccountably lost. What is extant is Blumer's correspondence with Butler's patients and their guardians and parents.
53. Blumer to EFA, 28 February, 5 March 1903, BPR, case 3925. See also Blumer to SCH, 14 November 1902, BPR, case 4343.
54. RAR, 1904, p. 15.
55. Shorter, *From Paralysis to Fatigue*, p. 69.

held out the hope of improvement. For example, about one female patient who "made repeated assaults upon officers, nurses, and fellow patients," Blumer wrote that an operation would not lead to a "cure [of] the . . . morbid conditions of brain and nervous system." "We shall be satisfied," he added in his letter to the patient's concerned mother, "if we may render your daughter more comfortable and less prone to the distressing periods of excitement which have been a characteristic of the case for so long a time."[56] At least one raucous patient who submitted to the operation showed some progress. As Blumer had noted to the patient's mother in July 1902, "Having for over two weeks occupied myself the bedroom immediately under that in which your daughter sleeps, her deplorable condition has been painfully impressed upon me by her frenzied noisiness." In December, after "the artificial induction of the menopause," he was able to write: "I want you to rejoice with me that your daughter is in the sewing room, sitting quietly with other patients, hemming napkins. Before her operation, that would have been out of the question. She has also lent a hand in washing glass. The nurse told me that she wiped the tumblers carefully and held them up to the light knowingly to catch the sparkle that the experienced housewife likes to see after cleansing and friction."[57] Blumer's great relief over this relatively insignificant change indicates just how troublesome and disturbing he found "frenzied" patients like this one.

Few patients did improve after surgery, however, probably another reason why he stopped recommending it after 1904. After she had her ovaries and uterus removed in late 1902, one patient was described by Blumer in the next year as "dull, listless and controlled by fears of personal unworthiness." But because she was "not especially difficult of management," he considered the operation "a decided success." Nonetheless, by May 1904 that patient was "quite depressed" and had suffered "a mental deterioration." In 1907 she was transferred to the state hospital. If the operation had improved her condition, it was only temporarily.[58]

The responsibility for these operations did not rest entirely on Blumer. Among the few cases when the topic of an operation surfaced in his relations with the public, at least twice the possibility of surgery was raised by the patients' families or friends. As one distressed parent of an agitated thirty-six-year-old asked Blumer in 1903, "Could there be any

---

56. Blumer to SCH, 24 November 1902, BPR, case 4343.
57. Blumer to TLS, 18 July, 10 December 1902, BPR, case 3852.
58. Blumer to SCH, 27 November 1903, 9 May 1904, BPR, case 4343.

trouble with her ovaries? I know of two patients, after the organs was [sic] removed, they recovered their health." Blumer replied that there was no reason to think that her ovaries were diseased or that an operation would succeed. He gave roughly the same answer in March 1904 when the father-in-law of a patient asked his opinion about an ovariotomy. The patient apparently had acted in an overtly erotic manner toward her female nurse and used "grossly vulgar" language with other patients. "Considering the erotic manifestations, would there be a faint hope— we expect nothing more—of restoring her by an operation?" asked the father-in-law. Again Blumer advised against an operation, citing the possibility that the patient's condition would worsen if surgery were performed.[59] These overtures from patients' families are evidence of what Edward Shorter has called "a characteristic American phenomenon: addiction to surgery as a sequel of . . . medically suggesting the population into the belief that vague, nonspecific" conditions like insanity were linked to the reproductive organs.[60]

Blumer's willingness to have surgery performed on reproductive organs was not confined to his female patients; he authorized vasectomies as well. They too were not numerous and were limited to the pre-1904 period, but it is clear from his own records that Blumer imagined eugenic purposes could be served by this form of surgery. As with ovariotomies, he also believed that vasectomies might have a beneficial effect on patients' unruly behavior. He recommended vasectomies, for example, for a few male patients who were destructive or inclined to masturbation.[61] But underlying his enthusiasm for surgery as a curative measure was a deep conviction that in these instances he was dealing with families with bad heredity. As he wrote to a fellow physician in 1902 regarding one patient and his wife: "Was there ever a more striking illustration of the marriage of the unfit?"[62] But when he broached the topic of a eugenically oriented vasectomy with the families of patients, he sometimes received emphatically negative answers. To the family of a particularly aggressive and noisy patient, Blumer wrote that though an operation would likely have "immediate results" for the patient's mental condition, it was also "surely wise to place such men *hors de combat* by getting rid of their reproductive potency." This patently did not sit well with the patient's brother, who replied to Blumer that he did not enjoy hearing that his

59. S. B. to Blumer, 23 March, and Blumer to S. B., 28 March 1904, BPR, case 4597.
60. Shorter, *From Paralysis to Fatigue*, p. 91.
61. BPR, cases 4442 and 4498.
62. Blumer to Henry R. Stedman, 13 January 1902, BPR, case 4463. See also Blumer to E. H. Pomeroy, 4 February 1902, ibid.

brother was "being threatened by the doctors of Butler Hospital of having an operation performed on him." The brother's opinion was unequivocal: "It is fully understood after careful consultation [among the family] that *no operation* is to be made."[63]

That these operations carried a strong hint of reproach about a family's ancestry was also evident in the reaction of another patient's relative. Blumer had remarked that the patient's family showed "a neurasthenic background" and a "predisposition" to mental illness. A sister indignantly wrote back: "The records of the family for two hundred years show not a single [one] of our ancestors either nervously or mentally afflicted. In fact any member of this generation [of the family] having a chronic disease cannot blame the past, for our ancestors died at good ages of acute troubles or old age."[64] Blumer certainly realized that he ran the risk of offending relatives if he persisted in advising operations with eugenic overtones, and he discovered that these operations were controversial for another reason: as at least one case indicates, carelessness about obtaining the proper consent for pelvic operations could lead to embarrassing legal problems that jeopardized a hospital's public relations.[65] Publicity surrounding questionable practices such as reproductive surgery at mental hospitals threatened to destroy the "slender hold" those institutions had on the public and patients' families.

Yet Blumer's abandonment of eugenics was not total. In 1907 he testified at a Providence hearing into the need for a school for the feebleminded, urging that the school be erected to provide custodial control for this class of the mentally handicapped. "Feebleminded women who are loose in the community are often notoriously loose in another sense," he warned, and every step should be taken to keep them from roaming the streets freely and reproducing their own kind. By recommending the eugenic segregation of the feebleminded he was giving his assent to a eugenics-based policy that enjoyed wide popularity in the pre-war years.[66]

63. Blumer to CGW, 27 May, and Blumer to HW, 26 May 1903; MWW to Blumer, 3 October 1903 (his emphasis), BPR, case 4498.
64. HHC to Blumer, 6 June 1905, BPR, case 4533.
65. See BPR, case 4256, for an example of this dilemma.
66. *Providence Journal*, 22 February 1907; cited in David A. Rochefort, "Three Centuries of Care of the Mentally Disabled in Rhode Island and the Nation," *Rhode Island History* 40 (1981): 111–32, 124. Some eugenicists backed the opening of sexually segregated training colonies for the feebleminded because they thought that the public was not ready for sterilization laws. Once the feebleminded were confined in these facilities, prosterilization lobbyists hoped to use the sterilization argument to justify discharging inmates into the community. Other people committed to new colonies for the feebleminded for humanitarian and corrective reasons may have used eugenic reasons to "cinch . . . the argument" in favor of such establishments, as Edward Larson suggests. Blumer was probably closer to the latter position. On the debate

Indeed, at almost the same time that he was flattering the delicate nervous systems of his New England patients and patrons, Blumer was saying very different things to his psychiatric confreres. At the annual meeting of the AMPA in 1908 he stated: "I happen to come from a State in New England which was settled by a crank, Roger Williams, who brought with him to Rhode Island a great many men of his type. Those old families have been breeding and interbreeding ever since, insomuch that there are few of the old families in Rhode Island to-day which do not reveal the unhappy consequence in neuroses of some sort, and the evil work is still going on." Although he hesitated to endorse coercive legal steps to prevent the reproduction of these Rhode Islanders, he did express his opinion that psychiatrists "ought not to weary in well-doing, or tire from preaching from the housetops the dangers that follow in the wake of the marriage of the unfit."[67] Evidently Blumer still took a dim view of the unwise marriages his patients continued to contract in defiance of his advice, though he was careful to conceal his real thoughts from the lay public.[68] The dangers of pathological heredity among his patients were as daunting to him as ever, only he was much more reluctant to openly express his misgivings about the reproductive practices of his clientele.

The dissimilarities between Blumer's official and informal attitudes surfaced sporadically throughout the balance of his career at Butler. In 1916 he wrote a friend that "insanity is to a large extent a degeneracy" and added that mental illnesses were not nearly as curable as some people thought.[69] Four years later he told another psychiatrist that there was little truth to the "comforting view that there is less in heredity than most of us believe. The awkward facts cannot be blinked and the 'damned spot' will not out. There is no getting away from the simple scriptural doctrine that 'the fathers have eaten sour grapes and the children's teeth are set on edge.' The tyranny of inherited organization is something that neither you nor I can escape."[70] Was he aware that earlier he had denied the scientific validity of precisely the same biblical passage? It is hard to believe that he was not, which means that he must have known that he

---

over sterilization versus segregation in the Deep South, see Edward Larson, *Sex, Race, and Science: Eugenics in the Deep South* (Baltimore: Johns Hopkins University Press, 1995), pp. 64–65.

67. "Discussion," *AJI* 65 (1908): 35.

68. For another physician's similar sentiments, see Henry R. Stedman, "On Medical Advice regarding the Marriage of Subjects with a Personal or Family History of Insanity," *Journal of Nervous and Mental Disease* 14 (1889): 1–11. Stedman complained that physicians' "counsel" on the question of marriage "is seldom asked, and when accepted rarely followed" (p. 2).

69. Blumer to William Foster, 8 August 1916, BP, box 34.

70. Blumer to L. Vernon Briggs, 4 March 1920, BP, box 34.

was tailoring his words on eugenics and heredity to fit his audiences. His approving use of this Maudsley quotation also shows that as late as 1920 he had not shaken off that Victorian doctor's influence. When confiding in other physicians who knew all too well what it was like to cater to the psychological health care needs of North America's mentally ill, he revealed his distinct respect for the power of inheritance; but when addressing the regional public on which he depended, he muted the significance of heredity and eugenics.

Blumer's most emphatic and candid criticism of eugenics was a lecture delivered in Providence in 1914. It illustrates how he could reject extreme eugenic measures such as sterilization while simultaneously retaining an interest in eugenics as a springboard to the study of the effects of heredity on mental and physical health. Drawing attention to his eugenics-slanted presidential address to the AMPA in 1903, he distributed a cartoon (see illustration) and told his audience: "It is a comforting saying that a wise man changes his mind, a fool never." Indeed what he had to say constituted a significant departure from the 1903 speech. Blumer confessed to having undergone "a certain process of deSumnerization as the years have rolled by and experience has given pause and poise."[71] This was a reference to the Reverend Walter T. Sumner, the dean of the Cathedral of St. Peter and St. Paul in Chicago. In a 1913 pro-eugenic sermon Sumner had announced that no men and women would be married at his cathedral without "a certificate of health from a reputable physician." Sumner declared that he was no longer willing to be a "party to the marriage of persons who, because of their physical condition, should never be allowed to enter into the marriage state and propagate their species."[72]

By now Blumer was not only growing skeptical about this type of eugenic sentiment but was also becoming impatient with social Darwinists who warned—as Blumer had in the late 1890s—that eugenic measures would be necessary if society were to continue interfering with the laws of natural selection by building charitable institutions for the "unfit" classes. Instead, Blumer argued that adverse publicity about the financial costs of public charity would be sufficient to develop in men and women "a consequent repugnance for socially and economically improper unions" and thus that involuntary sterilization programs like Wisconsin's

71. G. Alder Blumer, untitled paper, 1914, BP, box 40.
72. Quoted by Martin W. Barr, "The Imperative Demand for Legislation to Arrest the Rapid Increase of Degeneracy," *Alienist and Neurologist* 34 (1913): 400–408, 401–2.

When the Eugenic Marriage Supplants the Old Fashioned Love Marriage

By John T. McCutcheon

Scene—A Drawing Room. Time—The Loveless Age of the Future.
Characters—Gentleman, with Matrimonial Intent and Lady.

THE WOOING.

He—"This is a very pleasant evening."
She—"It is indeed."
He—"Will you be my wife?"
She—"Is your temperature normal?"

He—"Always the same—winter and summer."
She—"And your pulse?"
He—"Absolutely normal."
She—"Blood pressure?"
He—"Approved by the best physicians."
She—"Have you ever been sick?"
He—"Never in my life."
She—"Have your ancestors ever been sick?"
He—"Never to the best of my knowledge."
She—"Are they still living?"
He—"Yes; all living and in excellent health."

She—"Very well. If you will please go before a notary and make an affidavit to the truth of your statements, I will marry you."

THE NEW CUPID

"I'll have my best man attend to it this afternoon."
She—"By the way, I didn't catch your name."
He—"My name is Eugene—Gene for short And yours?"
She—"Eugenia."
He—"A very pretty name."
She—"Here! Cut out that sentimental stuff. Have you ever been married before?"
He—"Yes; five times, but have secured divorces."
She—"Upon what grounds?"
He—"Ill health. My doctor signed the decrees."
She—"Very well. If you wish to study my health certificate, which hangs on the wall over there, you may do so, and if you find it satisfactory, we will call in a notary and sign the marriage contract."
He (rising)—"Thank you very much. I will do as you say. Have you any preference as to where we shall spend our honeymoon?"
She—"Venice, I think, will do."

IN THE DISCARD

THE HONEYMOON.

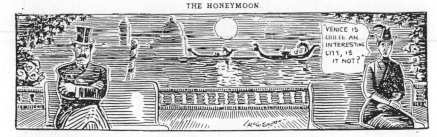

"VENICE IS QUITE AN INTERESTING CITY, IS IT NOT?"

Cartoon distributed by G. Alder Blumer at his 1914 Providence lecture, taken from Blumer's personal papers (BP, box 40). There is no indication where it was published.

of 1913 were unwise.[73] Thanks to public education, he maintained, people would voluntarily put eugenic principles into practice.

Moreover, Blumer told his Providence lecture audience, sterilization was "unscientific" because it did not square with what geneticists knew about heredity. Here he relied on the arguments of a growing number of scientists, such as the Princeton zoologist Edwin Grant Conklin (1863–1952), who were beginning to have reservations about negative eugenic measures.[74] Blumer declared that Mendelian genetics showed that neither a defective person nor the offspring of one defective and one healthy parent were fated to have defective progeny. Similarly, as the example of hemophilia illustrated, "two normal individuals may have dormant within one of them at least an ancestral 'recessive' characteristic which their union may transmit to one of their offspring in a patent form."[75] To Blumer's mind, sterilization was liable to do as much harm as good. In the case of certifiably hereditary diseases like hemophilia it was useless.

Blumer then cited three more reasons why he opposed much of negative eugenics, such as laws requiring a clean bill of health from a physician before marriage. First, he was alarmed about the potential for professional embarrassment to doctors from any failure to detect a predisposition to disease while examining men and women engaged to be married. Second, involuntary eugenic reforms ran counter to his libertarian sentiments. As he had written in 1904, "No one knows better than I that the government that governs best is usually that which governs least."[76]

The third reason was also one that reflected changes in medical and scientific thinking. In his own words, "To eugenics, properly defined as by Galton, for instance, opposition is practically unthinkable but the pretensions and doings of many who profess to be exponents of eugenics

73. In his annual report for 1914, Blumer drew distinctions between "the concomitant advantage of unhampered mating" throughout Rhode Island's history and "ill-digested, haphazard prohibitions affecting the freedom of the subject," such as Wisconsin's 1913 eugenic law. As Blumer wrote, "Wisconsin, a weanling in wisdom and rather new on the map, may perhaps learn something of Nature's law of compensation from the study of the commonwealth which Roger Williams founded nearly three hundred years ago." BAR, 1914, pp. 29–30.
74. See Kenneth M. Ludmerer, *Genetics and American Society: A Historical Appraisal* (Baltimore: Johns Hopkins University Press, 1972), pp. 35, 36–37, 38, 42, 121–22, 159. "Negative" eugenics entailed the use of measures—often involuntary—to prevent the "unfit" from reproducing, whereas "positive" eugenics entailed campaigning to encourage the biologically "fit" to reproduce, and the distinction was reflected in two camps of eugenicists.
75. Blumer, unititled paper, 1914, BP, box 40.
76. Blumer to CFT, 22 October 1904, BPR, case 4627.

are a wholly different matter." Like others, Blumer worried that genetics would become dominated by popularizers, zealots, and amateurs whose efforts would make the scientific study of inheritance a target of satirists. He had come to believe that the typical eugenicist was nothing more than a meddlesome "crank" or "fanatic with an imagined single remedy for all human ills [who] clamors for the instant application by law of his panacea."[77] Even some eugenicists were unhappy with the direction in which the movement seemed to be heading,[78] and this opinion was still being expressed by psychiatrists more than twenty years later. As one wrote in 1935, "Overenthusiastic proponents [of eugenics] . . . hurt it more than do its enemies. . . . Eugenics is . . . being made ridiculous."[79]

Blumer ended his lecture with a stirring defense of "the love marriage," the notion that marriage should be a "love match" rather than a contract drawn up according to imagined medical considerations. It was better to leave men and women free to decide whom they wished to marry. Citing the British psychiatrist Crichton-Browne and quoting Alfred Wallace, the cofounder of the theory of evolution according to natural selection, Blumer argued that any "direct interference with the freedom of marriage" was "not only totally unnecessary but would be a much greater source of danger to morals and to the well-being of humanity than the mere temporary evils it seeks to cure."[80] To him, the issue at stake was not that there was no hereditary component to mental illness but that eugenic measures constituted undue interference in the lives of people whose mental troubles might simply be the neurasthenic consequence of the stress of civilized existence. Rather than "risk the displeasure of lovers who seldom brook interference where the affections are engaged" (as he had put it years before), he muted the pathological significance of heredity and challenged the wisdom of eugenics as it pertained to the reproductive practices of his southern New England audience.[81]

At the same time it was clear that Blumer had not given up hope that some day eugenics would become a genuine science whose study might yield feasible measures governing heredity and reproduction. He was too

---

77. Blumer, untitled paper, 1914, BP, box 40.
78. See, e.g., the Illinois State Charities Commission, *Annual Report* 4 (1913): 9–10.
79. Abraham Myerson, "A Critique of Proposed 'Ideal' Sterilization Legislation," *Archives of Neurology and Psychiatry* 33 (1935): 453–66, 454.
80. Blumer, untitled paper, 1914, BP, box 40. For Wallace's opinions of Galton's *Hereditary Genius* (1869) and his disagreement with Galton over the issue of marriage laws, see Emel Aileen Gokyigit, "The Reception of Francis Galton's *Hereditary Genius* in the Victorian Periodical Press," *Journal of the History of Biology* 27 (1994): 215–40, 220–21.
81. BAR, 1901, p. 23. See also Stedman, "On Medical Advice."

much of a Darwinist to categorically reject the implications of natural selection for mental health care social policy. His references to Crichton-Browne and Conklin show that his attitude had modified but not changed radically. The example of Crichton-Browne is instructive. He was a believer in Lamarckian theories that held that improvements in people's physical and moral environment could positively affect what they passed on to their offspring through heredity. As president of the Sanitary Inspectors' Association, Crichton-Browne loudly criticized slum dwellings in 1905 for their adverse effects on the health of England's poor. He also worried that the popularization of eugenics would ultimately discourage precisely those who could afford to have children from marrying. He was less than enthusiastic about "preaching [eugenics] from the housetops" because he feared that "at that rate we should very soon have no marriages at all." At the same time, he was a long-standing member of the British Eugenics Education Society and freely expressed his anxieties about the socially unbalanced state of the British birthrate. Thus Crichton-Browne remained a eugenicist while simultaneously resisting the indiscriminate policy recommendations of other eugenicists.[82] Blumer was less worried than Crichton-Browne and other British eugenicists that eugenic "preaching" would reduce the fertility of the "fit" classes; his clinical experience at Butler had destroyed any illusions he might have had about the hereditary fitness of the privileged classes. Still, he shared the general uneasiness of many Britons about compulsory negative eugenic policies.

Blumer's refusal to give up on eugenics entirely as an approach to the study of genetics was also similar to Edward Conklin's position. Conklin was what Daniel Kevles has called a "reform eugenicist." He believed heredity was a powerful force—as a geneticist it is hard to imagine he would think otherwise—and he worried about the allegedly dysgenic effects of "the differential birth rate in favor of the poorer elements." But he emphasized the importance of the environment on human development, discounted the dangers of miscegenation, and denied that segregation or the sterilization of large numbers of "undesirables" would do any good. It would, he said, "be like burning down a house to get rid of the rats." Like other reform eugenicists, Conklin tried to separate eugenics from the political, social, and racial biases that characterized much of the prewar movement. Reform eugenicists stressed instead the biologic qualities of *individuals*. What compelled eugenicists such as Conklin to

82. James Crichton-Browne to Francis Galton, 5 March 1905, Galton Papers, University College, London. Cited in Oppenheim, *"Shattered Nerves,"* pp. 280–81.

spread the "reform" eugenic message may have been tactical considerations as much as dislike of prejudice. Reform eugenicists were intent on placing eugenics on a neutral and less controversial footing. They hoped to disarm critics who accused eugenicists of serving vested interests. As one stated, eugenics had to reject "the idea of encouraging or discouraging either Park Avenue or Hester Street."[83] Conklin wrote bluntly, "We should avoid indiscriminate condemnation of whole races or classes."[84] Blumer's and Conklin's views were in fact so similar by 1914 that Butler's medical superintendent might be described as a reform eugenicist. But tactical considerations alone cannot explain the actions and words of reform eugenicists. Many were sincerely uneasy about the prejudices of others who claimed to endorse eugenics.

Thus, by 1914, Blumer had moved a long way from his early 1900s eugenicism. Essentially he had changed from a "mainline" to a "reform" eugenicist, at roughly the time when many other psychiatrists were beginning to gravitate toward the movement. That his overall fervor cooled just as eugenics theory began to attract converts in significant numbers testifies to the impact his occupational switch had on him. Like many psychiatrists and geneticists, he eventually concluded that mainstream eugenics was increasingly falling under the sway of fanatics such as Harry Laughlin, and he began to rethink his commitment to the cause.

III

As Blumer began growing skeptical about eugenics, his colleagues at the American Medico-Psychological Association were just beginning to take it seriously. Interest in involuntary eugenic policies was scattered throughout the membership, and a handful of psychiatrists were strong supporters. Never, however, did the AMPA officially approve sterilization or marriage laws. The mixed membership, consisting, as it did, of not only state hospital physicians but also neurologists, private hospital

83. Frederick Osborn, "Significance of Differential Reproduction for American Educational Policy," *Social Forces* 14 (1935): 23–24. Cited in Kevles, *In the Name of Eugenics*, p. 174. For Kevles on "reform eugenics," see ibid., pp. 164–75; on "mainline eugenics," see ibid., p. 88. See also Matthew Thomson, "Sterilization, Segregation, and Community Care: Ideology and Solutions to the Problem of Mental Deficiency in Inter-War Britain," *History of Psychiatry* 3 (1992): 473–98, 494.
84. E. G. Conklin, *Heredity and Environment in the Development of Man*, 6th ed. (Princeton: Princeton University Press, 1930), pp. 307–8, 310, and his "Some Recent Criticisms of Eugenics," *Eugenical News* 13 (1928): 61–65. Cited in Bentley Glass, "Geneticists Embattled: Their Stand against Rampant Eugenics and Racism in America during the 1920s and 1930s," *Proceedings of the American Philosophical Society* 130 (1986): 130–54, 136–37.

doctors, public health officials, medical scientists, and devotees of new dynamic theories of psychopathology, militated against any broad consensus in favor of negative eugenics. This situation conflicted sharply with conditions at the local state level where state hospital psychiatrists often endorsed involuntary eugenic laws. Such a contrast illustrates how psychiatrists' opinions about eugenics, like Blumer's, frequently shifted according to occupational circumstances.

U.S. psychiatrists' interest in sterilization and marriage restriction largely coincided with the first flurry of laws governing these practices. After Connecticut passed its 1896 law regulating marriage, Kansas (1903), New Jersey and Ohio (1904), and Michigan and Indiana (1905) followed suit. Then came Indiana's sterilization law of 1907, followed by California (1909), Washington (1909), and Connecticut (1909). Between 1911 and 1915, nine states passed sterilization laws without gubernatorial veto, making this period the high-water mark in the history of sterilization. At roughly the same time, opposition to these statutes started to mobilize. Between 1912 and 1921, constitutional challenges were mounted against eight eugenic laws, and seven were overturned.[85] It is hardly surprising, then, that AMPA psychiatrists should also been debating the virtues of sterilization and marriage restriction.

Against this background, some psychiatrists cautioned that segregation was preferable to sterilization or marriage laws. Many argued that, though the hereditary sources of insanity were undeniable, eugenic practices were ineffective or downright counterproductive. Some maintained the popularization of eugenics simply discouraged healthy people from having children without having any impact on the target classes.[86] Others pointed to the lack of convincing evidence that sterilization reduced the rate of insanity.[87] Some objected that sterilization was primarily used to punish. Others joined Blumer in decrying the therapeutic pessimism implied by eugenics; psychiatrists could pose all they wanted as experts on marriage and reproduction, but the public still wanted them to cure patients.[88] These considerations, combined with the fact that there was no sure way of predicting whether offspring would inherit their parents' traits, led one New York State psychiatrist to write in 1912, just as a

85. Reilly, *Surgical Solution*, pp. 50–55.
86. "Report of the Inter-Hospital Conference of Physicians Held at the Middletown State Homeopathic Hospital, Middletown, New York, April 25–26, 1912," *New York State Hospitals Bulletin* 6 (1913): 250.
87. Henry R. Stedman, "Sterilization from the Eugenic Standpoint," *Boston Medical and Surgical Journal* 168 (1913): 311–13.
88. Henry Hurd, "Psychiatry as a Part of Preventive Medicine," *AJI* 65 (1908): 17–24, 20.

sterilization bill was being debated in the New York State legislature: "What is now required is not so much the precipitate enactment of laws, which may subsequently be repealed, found inadequate or allowed to fall into disrepute, but rather State appropriation for the investigation of the still nebulous problems of heredity, and a more exact determination of the type of individual in whom the more strenuous methods for the prevention of reproduction will represent a eugenic advance."[89] Thus, just as Blumer refused to give up on eugenics as a legitimate subject of scientific inquiry while withholding his support for some of its policy consequences, so other psychiatrists remained eugenicists while severely criticizing measures such as sterilization.

Yet some psychiatrists believed differently, often advocating sterilization of the feebleminded as a more effective preventive measure than simple segregation in an institution. In fact their advocacy was so forceful that it made the issue of feeblemindedness the most prominent eugenics issue at the time.[90] The tone of the debate was set by two physicians in particular, Walter Fernald (1859–1924) and Henry H. Goddard (1866–1957). Goddard, who coined the term *moron* and worked at the Vineland Training School, a private institution for the mentally retarded in New Jersey, urged intelligence testing using the methods of Theodore Simon and Alfred Binet. He also published a highly influential book titled *The Kallikak Family* in 1912. This study of a family descended from a Revolutionary War soldier offered two chief conclusions. The first was that feeblemindedness was most likely a dominant hereditary trait; the second, that the feebleminded were highly fertile. Despite the lack of proof for either hypothesis, Goddard's book went through several editions, suggesting a significant effect on educated opinion.[91]

Fernald too was nationally recognized as an authority on feeblemindedness. The superintendent of the Massachusetts School for the Feebleminded from 1889 to his death in 1924, he was a firm believer in the accuracy of intelligence tests and the notion that the feebleminded were, in Blumer's words of 1907, "notoriously loose" in the reproductive sense. By the 1920s both men would retract most of their claims, Fernald concluding that, contrary to professional opinion, the feebleminded actually had a low marriage rate and a very low birthrate.[92] In the prewar period,

89. Clarence P. Oberndorf, "The Sterilization of Defectives," *New York State Hospitals Bulletin* 5 (1912): 106–12, 112.
90. Haller, *Eugenics*, p. 96.
91. H. H. Goddard, *The Kallikak Family* (New York: Macmillan, 1912). See also Reilly, *Surgical Solution*, pp. 20–22; and Kevles, *In the Name of Eugenics*, pp. 77–79.
92. Reilly, *Surgical Solution*, p. 122. Even before his defection from the eugenics movement

however, his and Goddard's views found a receptive audience among other physicians working with the mentally handicapped. Citing Fernald's publications, the president of the AMPA declared in 1908 that although "society may not be able to prevent the marriages of the unfit, it can and should prevent the marriages of the feebleminded." Four years later the chief physician of the Pennsylvania Training School for Feebleminded Children attacked the opponents of sterilization laws and their insistence on individual rights. "How in the light of all the teaching that nature, history and experience supplies," he exclaimed, "anyone can object to the unsexing of the unfit as the only assurance for the survival of the fittest, on the grounds of interference with individual rights, is inconceivable." He urged "the affirmative action" of asexualization, including removal of testicles and ovaries, not only for eugenic reasons but also for the way these operations supposedly made patients "more tractable" and less sexually promiscuous.[93]

Naturally, these views were aired at the AMPA annual meetings. At the 1908 meeting, Blumer's complaints about "those old families" of Rhode Island echoed the general sentiments of the members. As one psychiatrist declared, "I do not believe in legislation. Some States, as you know, have passed stringent laws in matters of heredity, but unless they have behind them an educated public opinion, they do not amount to much, except as they themselves may be educational." Other psychiatrists contended that the best way to begin educating the public about eugenics was to start with the common schools. One member recommended introducing Clouston's *Hygiene of Mind* into secondary school curricula. The prevailing view was that though "stringent" eugenic laws were ineffective and impractical, medical advice on reproductive and marital matters was urgently needed.[94]

By 1912 eugenic opinions within the AMPA had become more extreme. At the annual meeting, Hubert Work, the president, warned,

---

Fernald along with other institutional superintendents had been trying to limit the influence of Davenport's ERO. See Trent, *Inventing the Feeble Mind*, pp. 205–6. Goddard's change of heart was evident by 1917. See the minutes of the 7 February 1917 meeting of the National Committee for Mental Hygiene, AMFH, Thomas Salmon Papers, box 1, folder 3, where Fernald said the feebleminded have been "slandered as a class," that feeblemindedness was not increasing, that the feebleminded were not necessarily prone to criminal nor promiscuous behavior, and that there were "dangers" in popularizing psychological testing. By the end of the First World War he admitted that he was "as guilty as anybody in my small way in the past in emphasizing the menace of the feebleminded." See "Discussion," *Journal of Psycho-Asthenics* 23 (September 1918–June 1919): 130. Cited in Haller, *Eugenics*, pp. 119, 122.

93. Martin W. Barr, "The Asexualization of the Unfit," *Alienist and Neurologist* 33 (1912): 1–9, 4, 7, 8.
94. "Discussion," *AJI* 65 (1908): 30–37.

"The unlicensed transmission to offspring of incurable mental and physical defects will in time encompass our decadence." Citing the threat of "race suicide" and the staggering costs to states like New York of caring for their insane, he gave a ringing endorsement of sterilization. For too long, he argued, states had relied on the method of segregating the mentally ill, an approach that had proven inadequate. He even chided Blumer for the latter's criticisms of eugenics in his 1912 annual report. Blumer's temperate views clearly were not shared by all.[95]

Reaction to Work's address is hard to gauge precisely. No one criticized it, but that was hardly surprising because AMPA presidential addresses were at worst politely received. The comments of some psychiatrists, however, signify that a handful did approve of sterilization. One said that Work had "sounded the war-cry and it behooves us to enlist in the battle which he proposes to lead us in." The Canadian psychiatrist Thomas Burgess added indignantly that he knew "of a certain Journal that went so far as to refuse to publish an article on 'Sterilization,' " "a disgrace," in his eyes. "It is for us to start the ball rolling and make the rest of the men 'toe the mark,' " he announced, presumably calling for the AMPA to assume the psychiatric leadership in the struggle to enact sterilization laws. To another member, Work had addressed "a matter of vital importance at the present time, one which is very much discussed, and one which will probably be brought before the Association for future discussion."[96]

Indeed the AMPA did strike a committee of three members, named the "Committee on Applied Eugenics," with Work as chairman. The next year Work presented the committee's report at the AMPA meeting in Niagara Falls. Containing little that most psychiatrists had not already heard, the report warmly endorsed sterilization. It did not, however, advocate *involuntary* sterilization, which it simply recommended as a last resort for overcrowded institutions that sought to discharge inmates. The report sparked at least one critical comment: a psychiatrist correctly objected that the committee's assertion that acquired mental retardation could be transmitted through heredity was unproven. But there were indications that opinions were sharply divided. Conceding that the report

<hr>

95. Hubert Work, "Sociologic Aspect of Insanity." In what was probably a typical view among hard-line eugenicists, Work considered any opposition to sterilization to be evidence of psychiatric disorder itself. He described the courts that struck down sterilization laws as unconstitutional as "fruitful fields for studies in abnormal psychology." Similarly, he accused state governors who vetoed sterilization laws of "appeal[ing] to the emotions of the hysterical." Hubert Work, "Legislation in Reference to Sterilization," *PAMPA* 21 (1914): 501–3.
96. "Discussion," *AJI* 69 (1912): 216–17.

was "carefully prepared" and provided "much ground for thought," Blumer's good friend Edward Brush (1852–1933) hastily moved that it be "received, but not adopted."[97] When Blumer called for the question, defenders of the report scrambled to amend Brush's motion so that it provided for the report's publication as well as a discussion of "applied" eugenics at the 1914 annual meeting. This amended motion was seconded and carried. But the proceedings of the 1913 meeting confirm that reaction to the report was mixed.[98]

Differences came to a head at the 1914 meeting, thanks largely to AMPA president Carlos MacDonald, Blumer's former nemesis from New York State. MacDonald thought that much good would be done "if every feebleminded person, every incurably insane or epileptic person, every imbecile, every habitual criminal, every manifestly weak-minded person, and every confirmed inebriate were sterilized." He offered several resolutions for consideration, but unaccountably, none referred to sterilization. His principal resolution—one that could hardly have generated any dissent—was that special charitable institutions be provided

97. Born in Glenwood, New York, Brush was chief editor of the *AJI* and *AJP* from 1905 to 1930. After graduation from the University of Buffalo Medical School, he accepted an invitation in 1877 from John Gray to pursue pathological studies at the Utica Asylum. Brush's stay at Utica, where he cemented his friendship with Blumer, lasted until 1884. In 1891 he became the first medical superintendent of the Sheppard and Enoch Pratt Hospital in Towson, Maryland, where he stayed until 1920. As editor of the *AJI* he relied heavily on the advice of Blumer and such others as Clarke, demonstrating what a later editor of the *AJI* would call an "always conservative but catholic and tolerant" attitude toward psychiatric matters. Brush agreed wholeheartedly with Blumer that the centralized reorganization of New York State psychiatry around the turn of the century was anathema because it undermined the ability of psychiatrists to meet these obligations. Like Blumer he maintained a keen interest in New York State mental health care politics long after he left the state. For biographical information, see "Correspondence," *AJP* 88 (1932): 1190–97. See also C. B. Farrar, "Edward Nathaniel Brush," APA, RG Clarence B. Farrar, folder 43. As Brush himself admitted, "My relations with Blumer for the past half century have been most cordial and intimate[,] indeed affectionate. We have never had a difference and we have freely come or gone to each other with our worries and perplexities as well as our successes. More like brothers than professional associates and friends." Edward Brush to C. B. Farrar, 9 December 1931, ibid. See also Edward Brush to Blumer, 2 July 1899, BP, box 29.

98. "Report of Committee on Applied Eugenics," *AJI* 70 (1913): 232–40. The 1913 presidential address was James T. Searcy's "Have We a Specialty?" (ibid., pp. 263–72). Searcy was superintendent of the Alabama Insane Hospitals, a past president of the Medical Association of the state of Alabama, and "the dean of southern mental health officials." His top assistant and successor was William D. Partlow, a leading advocate of eugenic sterilization in the Deep South. Searcy had adopted eugenics late in his career after favoring neo-Lamarckian theories of inheritance which emphasized the effects of habit and environment on heredity. Convinced like so many eugenicists that civilization was actually dysgenic, he admonished the AMPA to think deeply about ways of "discouraging the increase of the less capable, as well as encouraging the multiplication of the more capable." But Searcy was representative of Deep South psychiatrists before the 1920s in that he preferred eugenic segregation to sterilization and recognized the formidable difficulties facing those who sought the "practical application of eugenics." Larson, *Sex, Race, and Science*, pp. 43–44, 47, 55, 60.

for the feebleminded rather than housing them in "jails, almshouses or other institutions" that neither catered to their educational needs nor offered facilities for care. His most controversial resolution called for AMPA approval of "a marriage law which will require a clean bill of health and evidence of normal mind before a marriage license is issued."[99]

If MacDonald hoped that this proposal was moderate enough to achieve consensus, he was sadly mistaken. When it was moved and seconded that MacDonald's resolutions be accepted and adopted, the motion was voted down by fifty-two to twenty. In an effort to salvage something of the original motion, Brush moved that the resolutions be amended with the "objectionable clause" regarding the marriage law deleted. The now-toothless motion was carried. Officially the AMPA was not ready to recommend sterilization and marriage laws for eugenic reasons without further study.[100]

The pro-eugenics bloc received another setback at the same meeting. In accordance with the motion from the 1913 meeting, a symposium on "applied eugenics" was held, featuring four papers on a variety of eugenics-related topics. The original purpose of the symposium was to provide an opportunity for further debate on what certain members plainly believed was a crucial topic. At the symposium it was decided that the discussion would be canceled owing to "to the lateness of the hour" and the fact that the crowded schedule of papers the next morning left no time for debate. It is hard to believe that time could not have been found had members been as vitally supportive of eugenics as some claimed to be.

Part of the opposition to MacDonald's resolutions may have been due to memories of his days as an unpopular New York State Commissioner in Lunacy in the early 1890s. Opponents included William A. White (1870–1937), who with the possible exception of Adolf Meyer was the most authoritative voice in North American psychiatry by 1914. From 1903 until his death in 1937, White was the medical superintendent of St. Elizabeths, the huge federal mental hospital in Washington. With Smith Ely Jelliffe (1866–1945) he was among the first physicians to embrace psychoanalysis and prepare the way for the subsequent penetration of psychiatry and neurology by dynamic models of the mind.[101] At the Long Island College Medical School and during brief stints as a hospital

99. Carlos F. MacDonald, "President's Address," *AJI* 71 (1914): 1–12.
100. "Discussion," *AJI* 71 (1914): 196–98.
101. John C. Burnham, *Jelliffe, American Psychoanalyst and Physician: His Correspondence with Sigmund Freud and C. G. Jung*, ed. William McGuire (Chicago: University of Chicago Press, 1983).

William A. White. Courtesy of the American Psychiatric Association.

physician, White developed an interest in psychiatry. In 1892 he had decided to take the civil service examination to qualify for an assistant physician post at Blumer's Utica Asylum. He had ended up finishing fourth, but thanks to Blumer's help, he had secured an equivalent position at the Binghamton Asylum.[102] At Binghamton, White had met Jelliffe and Boris Sidis, a former student of William James at Harvard and another pioneer in dynamic psychiatry. Sidis was then performing research at Ira Van Gieson's Pathological Institute. Later White had collaborated with Sidis on numerous experimental projects in psychology using techniques such as hypnotism. By his own admission, White had learned during these experiments how to trace mental symptoms to their roots in life experiences. It was this lesson that paved the way for his later interest in psychoanalysis.[103] Nonetheless, like Blumer, White had

102. "In a sense I have always thought of you as being responsible for my entering the State service." W. A. White to Blumer, 13 November 1928, BP, box 35.
103. Arthur P. Noyes, "Lecture 23: William Alanson White," in *History of Psychiatry*, APA, Unpublished MSS, pp. 278–88. See also William A. White, *William A. White: Autobiography of a Purpose, 1906–1936* (New York: Doubleday, Doran, 1938); and Arcangelo R. T. D'Amore,

taken a deep interest in hereditarian theories while employed in the New York State service. As late as the 1908 AMPA meeting, and five years after he had taken the St. Elizabeths job, he had declared "that the time is ripe when this association ought to take some stand" regarding "the subject of eugenics—the welfare of the race."[104]

By 1908 there were also signs, however, that White was heading off in directions that would take him far from the hothouse world of eugenics. In 1907 he and Jelliffe had founded the Nervous and Mental Disease Monograph Series designed to publish in English translation some of the most recent European books on psychiatry—a clear sign that both were open to innovative and eclectic theories of pathology, diagnosis, and treatment. Then in 1913 the two men began the *Psychoanalytic Review*. Dissociating themselves from any one of the emerging factions in the troubled psychoanalytic movement, they committed themselves firmly to publishing articles that drew on the insights of Freudian psychology. White expressed his own attitude toward Freud in 1917: "None of us feel that we should be slavish followers of any theory or any school. We do, however, believe that Prof. Freud has pointed the way which is leading to an absolute remodelling of our understanding of mental disease."[105] Of course there was no absolute incompatibility between psychoanalysis and an interest in heredity or eugenics.[106] But just as psychotherapy in general taught that the influence of heredity was secondary to the impact of education and environment, so there was a distinct inconsistency between psychoanalysis and the hereditarianism of degeneracy theory which both White and Jelliffe had accepted early in their careers.[107] When White and Jelliffe turned their backs on degen-

ed., *William Alanson White: The Washington Years, 1903–1937* (Washington: St. Elizabeths Hospital, 1976).
104. W. A. White, "The Physical Basis of Insanity and the Insane Diathesis," *AJI* 50 (1894): 530–37; "Discussion," *AJI* 65 (1908): 36.
105. White to Mrs. Winnifred Springer, 2 March 1917, WAW, box 16.
106. In fact Jelliffe invited the eugenicist C. B. Davenport to submit an article on heredity to his *Psychoanalytic Review*. S. E. Jelliffe to C. B. Davenport, 17 November 1914, Davenport Papers, American Philosophical Society, Philadelphia. Cited in Burnham, *Jelliffe*, p. 62.
107. For Jelliffe's flirtation with degeneracy theory, see Burnham, *Jelliffe*, pp. 33, 38. As one New York psychiatrist optimistically observed in 1911, "If the mental habits and surroundings of an individual are largely responsible for the onset of a psychosis, we can look forward to accomplishments which may rival the success achieved in the crusade against tuberculosis." James V. May, "The Modern Trend of Psychiatry," *Interstate Medical Journal* 18 (1911): 1098. Cited in John C. Burnham, *Paths into American Culture: Psychology, Medicine, and Morals* (Philadelphia: Temple University Press, 1988), p. 203. Freud's creation of psychoanalysis—particularly his theory of infantile sexuality—as an alternative to degeneracy theory is described in Frank J. Sulloway, *Freud, Biologist of the Mind: Beyond the Psychoanalytic Legend* (New York: Basic Books, 1979), pp. 289–97. The anti-Semitic implications of degeneracy theory perhaps provoked Freud into devising a new theory to account for neuropathic symptoms. See Larry

eracy theory they demonstrated a readiness to question the hereditarian and somatic models of disease at the root of eugenics and to champion the therapeutic optimism many like-minded psychiatrists simultaneously favored. Somatic models stressed hereditary neurological defect as a cause of mental illness and—drawing on the example of general paralysis—the localization of insanity in various parts of the brain.[108] White believed that Freudian methods could even be applied to the treatment of patients suffering from dementia praecox, or schizophrenia.[109] This approach to therapy naturally undermined the therapeutic pessimism that sustained the taste for eugenics.

By 1913, White's condemnation of negative eugenics was a matter of public record. He wrote that "eugenics bids fair to increase its field of operations as time goes on and to become progressively a more and more valuable asset to preventive medicine." But he insisted that the state of positive knowledge about heredity did not warrant the practice of sterilization.[110] In 1914 he expressed similar thoughts on eugenic marriage laws:

> I think it is very ill-advised for this Association to go on record as recommending the enactment of marriage laws in this blanket sort of way. These things have been tried elsewhere and have been shown to be hopeless failures, in many instances at least, and where there is effort made to restrict marriage under certain laws it has led to discouragement of marriage to a certain extent, and also naturally toward illegitimate sexual relations. Whereas, in an abstract way the thing is all right, I believe it would be unwise to recommend its adoption and by so doing tend to cause legislators to rush into ill-advised legislation.[111]

Stewart, "Freud before Oedipus: Race and Heredity in the Origins of Psychoanalysis," *Journal of the History of Biology* 9 (1977): 215–28. Freud's relationship with the Parisian neurologist Jean-Martin Charcot, a major adherent of the theory of degeneracy, was also crucial in the origins of psychoanalysis. See Toby Gelfand, " 'Mon Cher Docteur Freud': Charcot's Unpublished Correspondence to Freud, 1888–1893," *Bulletin of the History of Medicine* 62 (1988): 563–88, and "Charcot's Response to Freud's Rebellion," *Journal of the History of Ideas* 50 (1989): 293–307.

108. For a history of this trend in U.S. psychiatry and neurology during the progressive era, see Nathan G. Hale, Jr., *Freud and the Americans: The Beginnings of Psychoanalysis in the United States, 1876–1917* (Oxford: Oxford University Press, 1971).

109. White to W. A. Robinson, 6 March 1917; and White to E. Stanley Abbot, 4 November 1920; reproduced in Gerald N. Grob, ed., *The Inner World of American Psychiatry, 1890–1940: Selected Correspondence* (New Brunswick, N.J.: Rutgers University Press, 1985), pp. 107–8. See also White to T. W. Galloway, 9 March 1919, WAW, box 20.

110. William A. White, "Eugenics and Heredity in Nervous and Mental Diseases," in *The Modern Treatment of Nervous and Mental Diseases*, ed. William A. White and Smith Ely Jelliffe (Philadelphia: Lea and Febiger, 1913), pp. 17–55, esp. pp. 51–54.

111. "Discussion," *AJI* 71 (1914): 196–97.

In his private correspondence he was even less charitable. In 1908, he had admitted his deep interest in the subject of eugenics but added that "prohibitory laws" were "usually worse than useless."[112] Or as he had written in 1912 to a California physician, "To enact into law a scheme for the sterilization of so-called defectives . . . is inviting disaster." His main complaint about sterilization was that it was impossible to predict in even the most degenerate families what a single member's heredity would be. "Now if we cannot predict we have no right to interfere," he asserted.[113]

Nor was White alone when he also admitted to a visceral antipathy to fanatics who when campaigning for causes such as temperance and eugenics were "forever overstating their case."[114] Underlying psychiatric skepticism about eugenics was an unwillingness to appear like "fools rushing in where angels fear to tread," as White put it.[115] Psychiatrists may have been anxious to discover remedies for insanity to relieve grave overcrowding problems, but many could sense the potential for professional embarrassment should eugenic practices prove bogus. Psychiatry was, after all, anxious to look as scientifically and clinically respectable as possible.

We must not, though, overestimate the misgivings about eugenics. The psychiatric fold continued to include eugenic zealots willing both to propagandize and to lobby legislators. Those opposed to eugenic laws nonetheless tended to consider eugenic study of heredity a valuable component of the science of genetics. White, even after he had come to the conclusion that sterilization and marriage laws were unwise, continued to employ a fieldworker supplied by Harry Laughlin's and Charles Davenport's ERO.[116] By the 1920s it was public knowledge that he did not share the eugenicists' belief in sterilization and marriage laws, but his relations with eugenicists such as Laughlin and Davenport remained cordial throughout his career. White's behavior in this regard was probably due to his resilient expectation that some valuable information could still be extracted from the efforts of the eugenicists.

112. White to Heber Butts, 21 May 1908, WAW, box 2.
113. White to J. T. Fisher, 15 November 1912, WAW, box 7. This letter is reproduced in Grob, Inner World of American Psychiatry, pp. 172–74; see also White to Arthur P. Herring, 4 November 1916, ibid., pp. 171–72.
114. White to Irving Fisher, 11 January 1916, WAW, box 13.
115. White to J. T. Fisher, 15 November 1912.
116. White to H. H. Laughlin, 22 January 1912, WAW, box 8.

IV

Yet no matter how interested in eugenics psychiatrists continued to be during the interwar period, the years just before the First World War witnessed the zenith of eugenic enthusiasm in mental medicine at the national level. After 1914 uneasiness about involuntary measures escalated, especially as evidence mounted that negative eugenic policies did little to eliminate mental defects or improve mental and physical health.[117] Skepticism was evident at the 1917 AMPA meeting when Charles W. Burr, professor of mental diseases at the University of Pennsylvania, asked, "what can be done to lessen the number of marriages" between defective persons? Burr then answered his question: "Confinement for life of the imbecile, the habitual criminal and certain of the insane, with asexualization of a certain group of the insane." He conceded that he had "painted a sad, hopeless, pessimistic picture" of the effectiveness of existing charitable and penal institutions and policies, but only because he, like other militant eugenicists, truly believed that the United States was at a biologic crossroads.[118]

The reaction showed that alarmist eugenic and social Darwinist rhetoric was going out of fashion in the AMPA. All four psychiatrists who responded to Burr's comments rejected them in no uncertain terms. Adolf Meyer, in his typically tortuous prose, described Burr's views as "an example of confusing wildness of recommendations." E. E. Southard (1876–1920), head psychiatrist at the Boston Psychopathic Hospital, called Burr's statements "alarmist" and agreed with White's remark that "we make a great mistake when we lay at the door of heredity so many things."[119] Southard was unexceptional among early twentieth-century psychiatrists in believing that the presence of the feebleminded proved heredity was a powerful component of certain mental states.[120] Yet, like Clarke and others, he believed that when asylums incorporated "the hospital ideal" they would become places where recovery was a distinct possibility for many patients. Like Southard, White thought that blaming

117. See A. J. Rosanoff, "A Study of Eugenic Forces: Particularly of Social Conditions Which Bring About the Segregation of Neuropathic Persons in Special Institutions," *AJI* 72 (1915): 223–49; and "Intellectual Efficiency in Relation to Insanity," ibid. 73 (1916): 77.
118. Charles W. Burr, "The Prevention of Insanity and Degeneracy," *AJI* 74 (1918): 409–22.
119. "Discussion," *AJI* 74 (1918): 422–24.
120. For evidence of Southard's interest in heredity and eugenics, see Harvard Medical School, Countway Library of Medicine, Elmer E. Southard Papers, contents of box 7, esp. "Appendix to Memorandum Presented at Meeting of Board of Scientific Directors of the Eugenics Records Office: Concerning the Study of Eugenics in Massachusetts."

"the germ plasm" for all mental abnormalities was simply "building up a program of doing-nothingness" for institutional psychiatrists. As physicians committed to exploring new methods of diagnosis and treatment, all three men stood for innovative intellectual trends and growing impatience with eugenic pessimism. And this triumvirate of luminaries only became more uncomfortable with eugenics as time went on.[121]

The war itself changed the thinking of many psychiatrists. Some returned from their medical service overseas armed with new theories about the diagnosis and treatment of mental diseases. After observing soldiers who succumbed to the shock and strain of combat, they concluded that mental conditions thought to be degenerative and incurable were in fact highly treatable and could be redefined as "personality disorders." Army psychiatrists not already converted to Freudian concepts were quickly convinced of the effects of trauma and environmental stress on the incidence of mental and nervous diseases. They also became persuaded of the existence of psychological mechanisms that translated unconscious, instinctual conflicts into physical and emotional symptoms.[122] Consequently, psychodynamic models of the mind grew increasingly popular in the 1920s and 1930s. This change of thinking coincided with an interest in more benign forms of preventive psychiatry such as child guidance clinics, psychiatric social work, and hospital outpatient wards for patients with relatively mild symptoms. Psychiatrists in general felt more and more optimistic. As early as 1917 the AMPA president captured the mood of many North American psychiatrists when he said to his audience, "Serious, thoughtful students of psychiatry are busily at work on problems of vital importance, and I venture to predict that within the period of a decade or two their labors will result in a much better understanding of the etiology, pathology, diagnosis and treatment of mental diseases than we now possess."[123] Nonpsychiatrists, for example the neurologist Charles L. Dana, also noticed that the world war was ushering in a new era of psychiatry.[124] Psychiatrists' rising hopes that

121. "Discussion, " *AJI* (1918). On Southard and his Boston Psychopathic Hospital, see Elizabeth Lunbeck, *The Psychiatric Persuasion: Knowledge, Gender, and Power in Modern America* (Princeton: Princeton University Press, 1994).

122. Nathan G. Hale, Jr., *The Rise and Crisis of Psychoanalysis in the United States: Freud and the Americans, 1917–1985* (New York: Oxford University Press, 1995), esp. chap. 1, "The Great War: The Human Laboratory," pp. 13–24.

123. Charles G. Wagner, "Recent Trends in Psychiatry," *AJI* 74 (1917): 1–14, 14.

124. Charles L. Dana, "Discussion," *AJI* 74 (1917): 224–25. According to Pearce Bailey, another prominent U.S. neurologist, the war taught the American public to think more highly of psychiatry than could any peacetime events. Earl D. Bond, *Thomas W. Salmon: Psychiatrist* (New York: Norton, 1950), pp. 99, 104. Cited in Hale, *Rise and Crisis of Psychoanalysis*, p. 20. For other testimonials to the significance of the war for psychiatry, see Thomas Salmon to

their specialty might at last become a science, an efficacious branch of medicine, dampened—if they did not extinguish—eugenic ardor.

A good example of brightening attitudes and prospects was Arthur Hiller Ruggles (1881–1961), Blumer's successor at the Butler Hospital from 1921 to 1948. Born in Hanover, New Hampshire, he received his medical degree from Harvard in 1906. In 1909 he joined the staff of the Butler Hospital, where except for brief periods he practiced psychiatry for the rest of his career. Ruggles had a vital interest in changing psychiatry in ways that would ultimately make it unrecognizable to those who, like Blumer, remembered what asylum medicine looked like in the late nineteenth century. Eventually he served as president of the National Committee for Mental Hygiene (NCMH) and in 1946 helped to found the Group for the Advancement of Psychiatry, which sought to reform psychiatry by promoting psychiatric social activism and dynamic theories of mental illness.[125]

Ruggles's years in psychiatry illustrated how much the profession had changed since the turn of the century, the heyday of Blumer's career. The 1920s found countless psychiatrists still wrestling with what seemed to be timelessly tiresome conditions in state hospitals, but Ruggles and others looked confidently beyond the walls of the mental hospital for opportunities to put their expertise into practice. Thirsting for new approaches, Ruggles had served as psychiatrist to the U.S. Expeditionary Force's Second Division in 1917–18. Although he would later concede that "the psychiatric lessons learned in World War One" were not really applied until the Second World War, he was emphatic about their value.[126] The war confirmed for him that many more people were psychologically impaired than anyone had previously realized; it also proved to his satisfaction that even a psychiatric patient who presented the classic symptoms of severe psychosis could recover if "immediately removed from the intolerable situation in which he had found himself." The experience of treating soldiers suffering from "shell shock" in 1917–18 convinced him that mental distress is due more to "emotional stresses

Walter B. James, 9 April, and Frederick Tilney to Salmon, 5 April 1919, AFMH, Thomas Salmon Papers, box 2, folder 5.

125. For the history of the GAP, see Gerald N. Grob, *The Mad among Us: A History of the Care of America's Mentally Ill* (New York: Free Press, 1994), pp. 198–202. At Butler Hospital from 1939 to 1943, Ruggles treated Clifford Beers, author of *The Mind That Found Itself* and the founder of the North American mental hygiene movement, during his final illness.

126. Arthur H. Ruggles, "Psychiatry's Part in Preventive Medicine," *Bulletin of the New York Academy of Medicine*, 2d ser., 6 (1930): 453–60, 453–54. See also Arthur H. Ruggles, *The Place and Scope of Psychotherapy: Viewing Fifty Years in Psychiatry* (New York: Salmon Committee on Psychiatry and Mental Hygiene, 1952), pp. 9–14, 12–13.

and strains" than to irreversible and degenerative physiological or anatomic conditions. This insight, Ruggles and many other physicians believed, entitled psychiatrists to exercise social leadership by employing psychotherapy and other treatments to create "a mentally healthier community."[127]

After the war these matters tended increasingly to engage the minds of leading U.S. psychiatrists, as sympathy for eugenics grew thinner and thinner, particularly among the psychiatrists considered to be the intellectual pacesetters. White's psychoanalytic collaborator Jelliffe confessed in 1935: "I am not very strong on 'eugenics,' and am far from clear in my own mind just what is really sound about the general eugenic situation."[128] Another esteemed U.S. psychiatrist, James K. Hall (1875–1948), the most prominent southern psychiatrist of the interwar period, wrote, facetiously, "Sterilization represents the only absolutely perfect method of prevention. The unconceived human being cannot possibly be feebleminded or insane . . . Sterilization with equal certainty will prevent poverty, plutocracy, atheism, communism, selfishness and prodigality. The unconceived mortal can assuredly obtain a bill of perfect health, if he can lay his handless hands upon it."[129]

Adolf Meyer, for his part, was a member of the Committee on Eugenics of the American Breeders' Association. He also belonged to the American Eugenics Society (AES) and even served on its advisory council from 1923 to 1935. Yet Meyer's AES affiliation was due more to his eclectic interests than to any deep commitment to the cause. He abjured dogma and denounced "systematizers" in psychiatry. He preferred instead to "swear allegiance to the rich harvest of fact." Meyer often behaved as if he believed assembling all the facts about a patient's life history was sufficient.[130] Thus, his affiliation with the AES reflected his conviction that it was unwise to rule out any potential source of empirical knowledge. In fact he was highly skeptical about much that tried to pass

127. Ruggles, *Place and Scope of Psychotherapy*, p. 71. For the history of shell-shock theory in Great Britain and Canada, see Martin Stone, "Shellshock and the Psychologists," in *The Anatomy of Madness: Essays in the History of Psychiatry*, ed. W. F. Bynum, Roy Porter, and Michael Shepherd, vol. 2, *Institutions and Society* (New York: Tavistock, 1985), pp. 242–71; and Thomas E. Brown, "Shell Shock in the Canadian Expeditionary Force, 1914–1918: Canadian Psychiatry in the Great War," in *Health, Disease, and Medicine: Essays in Canadian History*, ed. Charles G. Roland (Toronto: Hannah Institute, 1984), pp. 308–32.
128. S. E. Jelliffe to Victor Robinson, 3 October 1935, Library of Congress, Jelliffe Papers. Reproduced in Grob, *Mental Illness and American Society*, p. 176.
129. James K. Hall, "Sterilization?" *Southern Medicine and Surgery* 99 (1937): 514.
130. Adolf Meyer to William Healy, 29 October 1917, AMCMA, ser. I; Grob, *Mad among Us*, pp. 143–44; C. P. Oberndorf, *A History of Psychoanalysis in America* (New York: Grune and Stratton, 1953), p. 84. Cited in Grob, *Mad among Us*, p. 146.

for eugenics. Not only was he dubious about segregating the "defective and dangerous because they are apt to reproduce their kind;" but he also admitted he was willing to allow people with hereditary defects to marry as long as they provided healthy environments for their children.[131] As he revealed in 1935, many AES documents were "extremely embarrassing" to a scientist's eyes, and he vehemently opposed eugenicists' legislative solutions. "I hate the word compulsory in a democracy," he wrote an AES member in 1927. By the end of his life he had concluded that most of eugenics was little more than an ill-disguised attempt by one group to subordinate another.[132]

Perhaps the most potent attack on sterilization by a psychiatrist was the broadsides fired by Abraham Myerson (1881–1948). Born in Lithuania, he came to the United States in 1886. As a young man he caught the eye of Southard, who selected him as a staff psychiatrist for the Boston Psychopathic Hospital. Irreverent and iconoclastic, Myerson fit in well at Boston Psychopathic, with its orientation toward dynamic and innovative approaches to the study of mental disease. Although he conceded as late as 1935 that he was "in sympathy with limited sterilization laws," for most of his career he took pleasure in mocking the claims of eugenicists.[133] Like Blumer he believed that many privileged New England families had more than their share of genetic mental and nervous illnesses. He liked to point out that if sterilization were applied to these families "the 'Who's Who' of American development" would read quite differently.[134]

Myerson's chief attack on sterilization came in 1934. That year he chaired a committee of the American Neurological Association investigating conditions of commitment and sterilization in mental institutions. The committee's report epitomized the complexities surrounding eugenics by the 1930s. The study was supported by a grant from the Carnegie Institute, which at the same time was funding Harry Laughlin's pro-eugenic campaign. Nonetheless, the study's conclusions were extremely critical of eugenics, rejecting compulsory sterilization and emphasizing the role of environment as opposed to heredity. The ANA report stated

131. Adolf Meyer, "The Right to Marry: What Can a Democratic Civilization Do about Heredity and Child Welfare?" *CJMH* 1 (1919): 145–54.
132. Adolf Meyer, "Discussion," *Archives of Neurology and Psychiatry* 33 (1935): 463–66, 465; Adolf Meyer to Leon Whitney, 24 September 1927, AMCMA, ser. II; "Sterilization," ser. II.
133. Abraham Myerson, "A Critique of Proposed 'Ideal' Sterilization Legislation," *Archives of Neurology and Psychiatry* 33 (1935): 453–66, 453.
134. Lunbeck, *Psychiatric Persuasion*, pp. 33, 339 n. 29. See Abraham Myerson and Rosalie D. Boyle, "The Incidence of Manic-Depressive Psychosis in Certain Socially Important Families," *AJP* 98 (1941–42): 11–21.

that "so far as mental disease is concerned, the race is not rapidly going to the dogs, as has been the favorite assertion for some time." It also found "no sound scientific basis for sterilization on account of immorality or character defect." Yet the committee did say that a patient, guardian, or family member could consent to surgery, and it approved voluntary sterilization for diseases such as Huntington's chorea, schizophrenia, epilepsy, and feeblemindedness. Myerson believed in any case that most of eugenics was "a mess of incomprehensible bias."[135] His report was negative enough to kill a sterilization bill in New York in 1936.[136]

The plummeting status of eugenics was evident as well in the pages of North American psychiatry's main journal. In 1921 the AMPA changed its name to the American Psychiatric Association (APA) and the name of its journal from the *AJI* to the *American Journal of Psychiatry* (*AJP*). Under Blumer's friend Edward Brush's editorship, papers on eugenics and heredity were a rarity for the next two decades; a survey of the interwar period shows only a handful on either subject. Ordinarily when heredity was discussed it was in the context of genetic research, not eugenics.[137] Psychiatrists had other matters to pursue. They recognized that the reorganization of general medicine and medical education had threatened to leave psychiatry behind. Mainstream medicine appeared more innovative and exciting than state hospital psychiatry, not least to young physicians, and by the depression, psychiatrists were among the lowest paid of all medical specialists. How was the field to attract promising students to a profession perceived as synonymous with asylum medicine? The remedy seemed obvious to some: psychiatry must broaden its scope. In this regard, the change of names in 1921 was highly symbolic. The APA would in future pay increasing attention to clinical, scientific, and educational psychiatry rather than the practical challenges of asylum management which had absorbed its attention since its founding in 1844.[138]

Two issues had acquired considerable importance by the depression: credentialing and medical school education for psychiatrists. More and more psychiatrists saw these issues as linked to their specialty's status. The transformation of medical education since 1870 had for the most

135. Abraham Myerson et al., *Eugenical Sterilization: A Reorientation of the Problem* (New York: Macmillan, 1936), p. 4; Myerson, " 'Ideal' Sterilization Legislation," p. 454. For a positive review of the ANA's report in a psychiatric journal, see "The Sterilization Question: Abstract," *Psychiatric Quarterly* 10 (1936): 158–64.
136. Reilly, *Surgical Solution*, pp. 123–24.
137. Trent, *Inventing the Feeble Mind*, p. 205.
138. Grob, *Mental Illness and American Society*, pp. 266–69. See William L. Russell, "Presidential Address: The Place of the American Psychiatric Association in Modern Psychiatric Organization and Progress," *AJP* 89 (1932): 1–18.

part left psychiatry out,[139] so as the APA sought in the 1930s to meet the challenges of integrating psychiatry into the medical school curriculum and founding psychiatry departments in medical schools, it also struggled to secure board certification for psychiatrists. Psychiatry would have to wait until after the Second World War to achieve significant participation in medical schooling, but it would become one of the first medical specialties to have board-certified practitioners. The founding of the American Board of Psychiatry and Neurology in 1934 was not an entirely happy event; for it grew out of a compromise between psychiatry and neurology which led to squabbles. Still, the APA's Committee on Psychiatric Standards and Policies was hopeful about the new board and looked forward to the day when hospital psychiatrists would be board certified.

The APA also expressed the hope that psychiatry would soon enjoy a clientele in no way limited to the patient population of state hospitals. Although the majority of psychiatrists continued to be employed in those institutions, the commitment to the traditional mental hospital along with its patients and its forms of treatment was steadily weakening. Growing numbers sought to strengthen psychiatry's ties to general medicine and began stressing its curative potential over its caring functions.[140] Perhaps the outstanding feature of this evolution was the effect psychoanalysis had on the popularity of psychiatry. By the late 1940s psychiatry was almost synonymous with the image of the analyst, who in the words of John Burnham "embodied . . . knowledge and power."[141] In short, psychiatrists increasingly wanted to be known for what they could do for their emotionally disabled patients as well as for public mental health. Psychiatric support for sterilization and marriage laws seemed like an admission of failure.

V

Nonetheless, the many psychiatrists unable to extricate themselves from state hospital psychiatry assured continued, if uneven, regional psychiatric support for sterilization well into the 1930s. With state and local eugenic organizations preaching the eugenic gospel and pressuring legislators to pass eugenic legislation, state hospital psychiatrists undoubt-

139. See Kenneth M. Ludmerer, *Learning to Heal: The Development of American Medical Education* (New York: Basic Books, 1985).
140. Grob, *Mental Illness and American Society*, pp. 269–87.
141. Burnham, *Paths into American Culture*, p. 100.

edly found it difficult to resist the demands of these constituencies, even if they wanted to. Just as Blumer discovered in the 1890s that employment in a state mental health care system predisposed him to accept eugenic measures, so twenty and thirty years later, psychiatrists in certain states had the same experience. They too discovered quickly that appeals to a putatively humane and cost-cutting policy like sterilization found receptive listeners among state officials and politicians. Thus, in their annual reports to state charity and welfare organizations, countless medical superintendents either urged the introduction of sterilization laws or praised their operation. Rarely were there words of dissent from the theory behind eugenics or of caution about the potential abuse of sterilization. Indeed many medical superintendents spent a great deal of time reassuring the public about the actual sterilization operations and their impact on the physical and mental health of patients. Some self-serving psychiatrists, sniffing which way the political winds were blowing in cash-starved states, supported sterilization programs as adjunct policies to custodial segregation. Others did so simply because sterilization looked to be the only option—albeit a desperate one—in the face of overcrowded, deteriorating, and underfunded institutions.

Among state psychiatrists, Robert P. C. Wilson, a Missouri physician, and L. Potter Harshman from Indiana stood out in the campaign to publicize the virtues of sterilization in the interwar period. In 1936 Wilson conducted what one historian has described as an unsuccessful "one-man statewide campaign for a sterilization bill." The aptly named Harshman studied the attitudes of Indiana judges toward sterilization between 1931 and 1934 and concluded that physicians ought to pressure county bar associations and law schools to convince half-hearted judges to approve sterilizations.[142] As these examples indicate, state hospital psychiatrists of the period were far from lukewarm on the issue.[143]

But few North American psychiatrists promoted sterilization more vigorously and consistently than William Partlow. By the mid-1930s he was not only his region's leading eugenicist but one of the few southern eugenicists with a national audience for his views.[144] Superintendent of the Alabama State School (or Home) for Mental Deficients (renamed after him in 1927), he had also been appointed superintendent of the

142. Reilly, *Surgical Solution*, pp. 91–93.
143. For another example of state hospital medical superintendents and their State Board of Charities and Corrections lobbying for sterilization laws, see Kentucky State Board of Control for Charitable Institutions, *Biennial Report* 5, 1911–13, pp. 15 16; 6, 1913–15, pp. 17–18; 13, 1927–29, pp. 80–82, 95–96; and 16, 1933–35, pp. 72–73.
144. Larson, *Sex, Race, and Science*, pp. 139–40.

Alabama Insane Hospitals in 1923 and continued to hold the two posts for three decades. Partlow had leaned initially toward the neo-Lamarckian theory of degeneracy that stressed environmental causes of mental illness as well as heredity.[145] Over time, though, he had joined the hereditarian and negative eugenicist camp. Heavily influenced by James T. Searcy, then the superintendent of Alabama Insane Hospitals, Partlow had asked in 1916: "Then how shall we avoid the increasing numbers of cases of feeblemindedness?" His answer: "By segregation and possibly by sterilization during the productive period."[146]

In 1919, Partlow had had his opportunity to put his eugenic theories into practice. That year Alabama legislation had created the State Home for the mentally retarded. Probably by Partlow's own initiative, a clause had been inserted in the law empowering Partlow as superintendent to sterilize any inmate as long as he obtained the approval of the superintendent of the state mental hospitals.[147] Once Partlow occupied both posts, he alone determined who would and would not be sterilized, and took maximum advantage of this provision. He carefully segregated both sexes at the home and sterilized all inmates upon discharge. By 1932 he had sterilized 129 persons, the slight majority being male. In 1934 he wrote that "up to the present time" he had been responsible for 184 sterilizations of inmates discharged from his school for the feebleminded, though none for patients at mental institutions. As he admitted, "For many years I have advocated the sterilization of certain types of constitutional hereditary deficients, including feebleminded, insane, repeating criminals, chronic drug and alcoholic addicts, epileptics, etc."[148] Partlow was thus poised to lead the campaign for a sterilization law in Alabama that would cover operations performed on additional categories besides the mentally retarded; his draft bill called for the sterilization of "any sexual pervert, Sadist, homosexualist, Masochist, Sodomist, or any other grave form of sexual perversion, or any prisoner who has twice been convicted of rape." Moreover, his proposal provided fewer procedural protections than any other U.S. sterilization law. Decisions were to be strictly the province of mental health experts without provision for ju-

145. William Dempsey Partlow, "Degeneracy," *Transactions of the Medical Association of the State of Alabama* (1907), p. 224. Cited in Larson, *Sex, Race, and Science*, p. 43; according to Larson, Partlow still believed in the same theory of heredity as late as 1910 (p. 187 n. 23).
146. W. D. Partlow, "Proceedings," ibid. (1916), pp. 33–34. Cited in Larson, *Sex, Race, and Science*, p. 44.
147. Larson, *Sex, Race, and Science*, pp. 105–6.
148. William D. Partlow to E. S. Gosney, 26 March 1934, Association for Voluntary Sterilization Records, Social Welfare History Archives, University of Minnesota, Minneapolis. Reproduced in Grob, *Inner World of American Psychiatry*, pp. 174–75.

dicial review. One of Partlow's political allies even praised Hitler's "bold experiment in mass sterilization" and urged Alabama to follow Nazi Germany's example. After vigorous debate in both houses of the state legislature the bill passed, only to be unexpectedly vetoed by the governor. The governor's firm stand and a subsequent Alabama Supreme Court ruling also had the effect of stifling Partlow's own program at the home.[149]

By the end of the 1930s, Partlow's cause looked doomed. More and more Alabamans were troubled about the extent of the Nazi eugenics programs. In addition, the national eugenics movement suffered a substantial setback in 1939 when the Carnegie Institute removed Laughlin from his post as the head of the ERO and closed down the ERO entirely the next year. But Partlow was indomitable. Undaunted even by the news leaking out from the Allied liberation of German concentration camps, or by the signs of the emphysema that would kill him a decade later, he managed in the 1940s to put together another coalition of prosterilization forces. As before, he enjoyed the support of the state's medical society and a host of women's groups. His principal ally was Birthright, a New Jersey-based, nonprofit organization that had assumed the leadership of the national eugenics movement. Birthright was committed to propaganda in favor of selective sterilization for parents who violated the Child's Bill of Rights (drafted by the White House Conference on Child Health and Protection in 1930). It enjoyed the patronage of Clarence Gamble, a militantly eugenic physician and heir to the Gamble soap fortune.[150] With this assistance Partlow helped to draft a new sterilization bill that was introduced in the state legislature on the day Germany surrendered. Despite passing the state senate by a two-to-one margin, the bill died in the house health committee a week later. Still, Partlow struggled resourcefully but futilely until his death in 1954, by which time the opportunity for sterilization legislation countrywide had long passed.[151]

The activism and influence of psychiatrists was also evident in California and Wisconsin. California was one of the first states to pass a sterilization law (1909) and followed up with expanded laws in 1913 and 1917. By 1921 California surgeons had performed 2,558 of the nation's 3,233 official sterilizations. Between 1923 and 1926 the annual number

149. 1935 Alabama House Bill 87, secs. 1–6, in Alabama State archives; J. N. Baker, "Sterilization in Alabama," *Montgomery Advertiser*, 6 February 1935, p. 4, col. 3. See also Larson, *Sex, Race, and Science*, pp. 139–46.
150. Reilly, *Surgical Solution*, pp. 131–35.
151. Larson, *Sex, Race, and Science*, pp. 146–52.

Relying on the theory that there was a neurophysiological link between the brain and reproductive organs, Hatch maintained that sterilization often reduced the severity of mental symptoms in addition to curtailing reproduction.[156] Given his official power over appointments and policies, it is not surprising that most of California's state hospital superintendents agreed. As one California psychiatrist stated in 1926,

> In talking to male patients who have been benefited by the operation, many claim that in about two weeks after the operation they begin to feel better, that is, their mentality improves and they feel stronger both mentally and physically. I have had a number of men at the hospital ask me to sterilize them after they have seen the beneficial effects of the operation on other patients. In cases of the women we have no direct beneficial effects excepting the fact that their minds are relieved from the fear of further pregnancy. Many of our patients who have had a psychosis following childbirth, refuse to leave until they have been sterilized, feeling that another pregnancy would mean a recurrence of the psychosis.

F. O. Butler of the Sonoma State Home for the Feeble-Minded added that in about 37 percent of the young women sterilized at his institution the operation weakened their sexual instincts. Thus he thought sterilization could be justified for four reasons: it prevented the reproduction of the unfit, curbed sexual desire, prevented women from becoming psychotic owing to gestation and parturition, and improved the mental and physical health of male patients.[157] Faced with such arguments, it is easy to understand how eugenicists may have swayed public as well as official opinion.

Indeed, if the testimony of psychiatrists is to be believed, public opinion was highly educable when it came to sterilization. As Blumer had discovered, some families opposed it because they resented the implication that they were tainted with a hereditary defect, but as one psychiatrist contended, others withheld consent only because they were afraid that sterilization brought inconvenient relatives one step closer to discharge.[158] According to more than a few state psychiatrists and charity officials, some families and patients themselves actually requested the

156. Laughlin, *Eugenical Sterilization*, p. 53.
157. F. O. Butler, "Sterilization Procedure and Its Success in California Institutions," California Department of Institutions, *Biennial Report* 3 (1924–26), pp. 92–97, 96.
158. R. J. Hathaway, "Report on Eugenics Law and Sterilization of Patients," Montana State Hospital, *Biennial Report* 24 (1923–24), p. 24.

operation (something that Blumer too had encountered), simply because it was a means of birth control or because it was a condition for discharge into the community. Others, like the patients cited by Butler, believed that sterilizations genuinely improved their mental conditions.[159]

Private citizens also made the case for eugenic sterilization. One was a mother from Helena, Montana, calling herself "a tax payer" and defender of "helpless children." She cited ghoulish reports of children murdered allegedly by "beastly morons, the treacherous insane, the silly imbecile and the dangerous criminal." To her mind, the prospect of sterilization—which she mistakenly equated with castration—was not only a deterrent to potential criminals but a way to curb the fecundity of these classes of society, saving taxpayers money and preventing innocent children from being fathered by irresponsible men. "In God's name haven't little helpless children any rights?" she asked in 1924. "Haven't heart broken mothers any rights? Hasn't a constantly menaced society any rights? Hasn't a tax burdened people any rights?"[160] Eugenicists could capitalize on such alarm over child welfare to promote sterilization programs.

Thus state campaigns for sterilization were mainly but not exclusively driven by elite and professional opinion. A quantitative study of commitment proceedings in California from 1870 to 1930 shows that citizens and local authorities exploited the mental health care system of state hospitals in order to remove troublesome persons whose mental and behavioral traits jeopardized neighborhood peace and the tranquility and financial survival of their families. Psychiatrists' interests were of course served by encouraging the idea that many people could be sane individuals yet still in need of psychiatric treatment, and some psychiatrists did indeed recognize that their influence over public opinion could be used to artificially stimulate demand for their services. But psychiatry was undeniably also responding to public pressure.[161] The same was true for sterilization. It is impossible to quantify public sentiment, but there is no reason to dismiss out of hand the testimony of state psychiatrists who claimed that patients and their families were growing increasingly receptive to sterilization as a form of medical intervention by the 1930s. As a Kansas psychiatrist reported in 1924, "Our experience along this line has led to the belief that there is a widespread and growing indorsement of

159. See the testimony of one sterilized ex-patient in North Dakota Board of Control of State Institutions, *Biennial Report* 2 (1912–14), p. 126.
160. Hathaway, "Eugenics Law and Sterilization of Patients," pp. 27–28.
161. Fox, *So Far Disordered in Mind*, pp. 10–11, 163, 168–69.

the principle of sterilization, for eugenic purposes, by society in general, and an approval of our work in this field by the more intelligent and serious-minded of the public."[162]

Public acceptance of sterilization programs was furthered by the fact that the depression made asexualization seem justifiable for a host of noneugenic reasons, including birth control for indigent single mothers. Depression-era eugenics proved that hereditarianism need not be central to eugenic policy.[163] Eugenicists in the interwar period often emphasized environment as much as heredity. Officials argued that preventing parenthood in persons thought to be unable to raise children was eminently advisable. Sterilization, they averred, would save countless innocent children from the pathogenic parenting of irresponsible men and women. Among patients' families and the public, many thought like the Montana mother: sterilizing improper parents meant defending the rights of helpless children. The steady increase in the sterilizations of young women in the United States after 1930 attests to the mounting public willingness to treat sterilization as a catch-all solution to a host of social problems linked to reproduction.[164]

There is another reason why psychiatrists do not deserve all the blame for the enactment of state sterilization laws. The eugenics movement in the United States drew much of its energy and leadership from Progressivism, which was an unprecedented attempt on the part of Americans—usually affluent, well educated, and professionally trained—to solve the country's social, political, and economic problems in the early decades of the twentieth century. Progressives tended to argue that these problems were due to the failure to apply scientific expertise and techniques to the management of society. Significantly they also contended that as voluntary, informal approaches to charity had proved inadequate, it was necessary for the state to assume the responsibility for administering reform policies.[165] Eugenics closely conformed to this conception of Progressivism. It appealed to physicians, scientists, engineers, academics, policy makers, and social workers who believed that the reproductive

162. M. L. Perry, "Sterilization," Topeka State Hospital, *Biennial Report* 24 (1922–24), p. 4.
163. Matthew Thomson, "Sterilization, Segregation, and Community Care: Ideology and Solutions to the Problem of Mental Deficiency in Inter-War Britain," *History of Psychiatry* 3 (1992): 473–98, 496.
164. Reilly, *Surgical Solution*, pp. 94–95.
165. Arthur Link and Richard L. McCormick, *Progressivism* (Arlington Heights, Ill.: Harlan Davidson, 1983). See also Richard Hofstadter, *The Age of Reform: From Bryan to FDR* (New York: Knopf, 1955); Samuel P. Hays, *The Response to Industrialism, 1885–1914* (Chicago: University of Chicago Press, 1957); Robert H. Wiebe, *The Search for Order, 1877–1920* (New York: Hill and Wang, 1967); and Samuel Haber, *Efficiency and Uplift: Scientific Management in the Progressive Era, 1890–1920* (Chicago: University of Chicago Press, 1964).

practices of dependent men and women were responsible for the apparent increase in the rates of poverty, criminality, immorality, and mental illness. Progressive eugenicists looked to the growth of scientific knowledge for ways to reduce these rates.[166] It was no accident that Blumer's flirtation with eugenics coincided with the New York State governorship of the Progressive Theodore Roosevelt, a staunch supporter of eugenics.[167] The influence of Progressivism was felt even more demonstrably in California. It was in Wisconsin and the Deep South, however, that the close connections among Progressivism, psychiatrists, and eugenics were particularly evident.

The eugenics movement in Wisconsin had begun in the 1890s for many of the reasons it had started in other states; the economic crisis of that decade had prompted educators and charity and correction officials to consider drastic policies. Believing custodialism would prevent the reproduction of the "defective classes," state reformers had applauded the opening of a home for the feebleminded at Chippewa Falls in 1895. Yet confinement as a eugenic measure had seemed insufficient, and the home's first superintendent, Albert W. Wilmarth, had quickly proved to be a leading advocate of eugenic marriage and sterilization laws.[168] Richard Dewey, medical superintendent of the Milwaukee Sanitarium from 1895 to 1920 and Blumer's successor as editor of the *AJI* from 1894 to 1897, had felt strongly as well that preventive measures were overdue but had thought legislation providing for "the permanent imprisonment, electrocution, or castration of insane, imbecile, epileptic, inebriate, or degenerate beings" would "at present fail of enactment, or if enacted, fail of enforcement."[169]

Dewey's doubts did not discourage Wisconsin eugenicists, however; for they knew their recommendations would receive a sympathetic hearing from state politicians. The state was, after all, already famous for the "Wisconsin Idea," favored by the Progressive governor Robert La Fol-

166. Haller, *Eugenics*, pp. 5, 76, 86, 110, 124, 178; Donald K. Pickens, *Eugenics and the Progressives* (Nashville, Tenn.: Vanderbilt University Press, 1968); Ludmerer, *Genetics and American Society*, pp. 15–18; Kevles, *In the Name of Eugenics*, p. 101. For the links among eugenics, psychiatry, and Progressivism, see Burnham, *Paths into American Culture*, pp. 189, 223.

167. Pickens, *Eugenics and the Progressives*, pp. 119–29; Kevles, *In the Name of Eugenics*, pp. 74, 85, 88, 94.

168. See A. W. Wilmarth, "Report of Committee on Feebleminded and Epileptic," National Conference of Charities and Correction, *Proceedings* (1902), pp. 152–61. Blumer cited this paper in his 1903 AMPA presidential address. See also Trent, *Inventing the Feeble Mind*, pp. 195–98.

169. Richard Dewey, "Remarks on Mental Contagion and Infection," *Transactions of the State Medical Society of Wisconsin* 33 (1899): 502–6. Cited in Rudolph J. Vecoli, "Sterilization: A Progressive Measure?" *Wisconsin Magazine of History* 43 (1960): 190–202, 194.

lette. It authorized public policy making based on the advice of experts in the biologic, psychological, medical, and social sciences.[170] Once Indiana had introduced the nation's first sterilization law in 1907, Wisconsin eugenicists had quickly swung into action. One sterilization bill was introduced and failed. Another was introduced in 1909, and its failure had only intensified the fervor of state eugenicists, including the state Medical Society and psychiatrists such as Charles Gorst. Superintendent of the Wisconsin State Hospital for the Insane, Gorst stressed the link between eugenics and Progressivism, urging the state legislature in 1910 to pass a sterilization bill as soon as possible. In his superintendent's report he wrote that it was "wicked that the persons suffering from periodical insanity should be allowed to return to their homes to propagate and scatter their children about the state as dependents. Several states have passed the sterilization law and Wisconsin should wake up and be equally as *progressive*. . . . It is the duty of the State to regulate this condition of affairs."[171]

Gorst's call to action simply echoed other state progressives such as the officials of the Wisconsin Board of Charities and Corrections. Wisconsin academics also joined the campaign to convince legislators that opposition to sterilization was unscientific and fiscally irresponsible. Finally, Governor Francis E. McGovern signed a sterilization bill into law on 30 July 1913.[172] The message that sterilization was the experts' method of choice for solving the problem of rising rates of mental illness intrigued Wisconsin Progressives, who often mistakenly equated humanitarian reform with ideas that looked modern and scientific. Progressivism provided a nurturing intellectual climate that helped to translate psychiatrists' eugenic views into reality.

The connection between Progressivism and sterilization was equally strong in the Deep South, though to the vast majority of southerners eugenics had an imported, alien image.[173] As a result, eugenic statutes arrived there late, coinciding with the emergence of New Deal Progressive politics in the interwar period. But the ground had been laid during the first two decades of the twentieth century by psychiatrists, physicians, and mental health officials in every state in the region. These constituencies made up one of the most dedicated activist groups in favor of

170. Kevles, *In the Name of Eugenics*, p. 101.
171. Charles Gorst, "Superintendent's Report," Wisconsin State Board of Control, *Biennial Report* 10 (1908–10), pp. 75–76. My emphasis.
172. Vecoli, "Sterilization," p. 201.
173. Larson, *Sex, Race, and Science*, p. 17.

compulsory sterilization.[174] Drowning out the voices of the few medical dissenters, such as C. F. Williams of the South Carolina State Hospital for the Insane, southern psychiatrists produced a steady stream of provocative pro-eugenic rhetoric. Some private physicians readily and publicly supported eugenics, but the bulk of the southern medical community joined the eugenic crusade only at the prompting of state mental health officials.[175] As elsewhere, southern psychiatrists introduced the topic to the people of the region because patient populations were growing disproportionately fast, a seemingly sure sign that these groups reproduced faster than so-called normal persons. Psychiatrists advocated segregation, which meant building more custodial facilities. This would be expensive, they conceded, but would in the long run translate into savings for state budgets and lower taxes for responsible citizens.[176]

During the second decade of the twentieth century the eugenic gospel in the Deep South was also preached by NCMH officials. Thanks chiefly to the efforts of Clifford Beers, an ex-state hospital patient and author of *The Mind That Found Itself* (1908), the NCMH had been founded in 1909. Beers's original hope was that the organization would work primarily to improve conditions in mental hospitals, in one of which he claimed to have been abused as an inmate. But the NCMH quickly shifted its orientation. It sought to publicize the need for more research into mental disease and funding for policies addressed to preserving public mental health as an alternative to the custodial treatment of the severely and chronically mentally ill. A major NCMH tactic was the use of surveys to study the extent of mental defectiveness not just in mental hospitals but also in prisons, schools, reformatories, and homes for the feebleminded. This use of surveys run by trained professionals and designed to compile abundant statistical data was characteristic of the Progressive era. NCMH officials believed the information gathered would help legislators and administrators make policy decisions. Thus the organization stressed the prevention of mental illness and the public reliance on experienced professionals such as psychiatrists.[177]

Some of the first NCMH surveys were conducted in the Deep South and helped to generate a consensus in the region in favor of the eugenic segregation of the mentally retarded. The NCMH's influence on south-

174. Larson, *Sex, Race, and Science*, p. 106.
175. Larson, *Sex, Race, and Science*, pp. 46, 49.
176. Larson, *Sex, Race, and Science*, pp. 42–49.
177. Grob, *Mental Illness and American Society*, pp. 144–66. See also Norman Dain, *Clifford W. Beers: Advocate for the Insane* (Pittsburgh: University of Pittsburgh Press, 1980).

ern policy makers can be measured by the fact that by 1920 every state had begun building special facilities for the feebleminded. In achieving this result the NCMH had worked hand in hand with eugenically inclined physicians and psychiatrists. A critical figure in the campaign was Thomas Haines, NCMH field representative in the Deep South. Haines visited Alabama and Mississippi, praising the work of Partlow and others. His message was eugenic, fiscal, and humanitarian. He urged the transfer of the mentally disabled from the prisons, orphanages, and poor farms, where they were often found living in deplorable conditions, to new, clean, medically supervised institutions where they might receive some training and their quality of life would presumably be much better. But at the same time, Haines justified institutionalization on the grounds that it also prevented inmates from propagating, thereby preventing crime and immorality and lowering the costs of future treatment. Haines, like other mental health officials across the country, did not reject the sterilization option out of hand, but in the period between the outbreak of the First World War and the landmark 1927 Supreme Court ruling of *Buck v. Bell* he and like-minded mental hygiene figures were reluctant to recommend sterilization until popular opinion should become more receptive and the constitutionality of the measure be assured.

The NCMH itself never took an official stand on sterilization, as the anti-eugenicist C. F. Williams learned in 1926.[178] A handful of members including the internist Lewellys Barker and psychiatrist Stewart Paton were ardent eugenicists. Over time, though, the organization grew skeptical about sterilization's virtues. One reason may have been the uneasiness of its principal financial backer, the Rockefeller Foundation, without whose grants the NCMH could not survive. The foundation preferred to fund projects dealing with medical research, medical education, and the collection and dissemination of public health information; like other foundations it tried to steer clear of politics and social activism. It was willing to support surveys of feeblemindedness that could be construed as eugenic, but it drew back from what one Rockefeller official called "propaganda favoring sterilization legislation."[179] Sterilization was simply too controversial for Rockefeller representatives. This position

178. Edith M. Furbush to C. F. Williams, 5 January 1926, South Carolina State Hospital (Columbia), Department of Education and Training, Sterilization File. Cited in Larson, *Sex, Race, and Science*, p. 194 n. 117.
179. Katherine B. Davis to Raymond Fosdick, 2 February 1921, Rockefeller Archive Center, Bureau of Social Hygiene Papers, ser. 3, box 8. Cited in Barry Alan Mehler, "Sources in the Study of Eugenics," pt. 2, "The Bureau of Social Hygiene Papers," *Mendel Newsletter* 16 (1978): 6–15.

became even more firmly established in 1931 with the appointment of Alan Gregg, who had little sympathy for psychiatry in the first place and emphasized disinterested laboratory medical research, as director of the Rockefeller Foundation's Division of Medical Sciences. Over the next eight years he proceeded to reduce the foundation's contributions to the NCMH until Rockefeller support for its general activities ceased in 1939. The NCMH, increasingly anxious about declining revenues during the depression, endeavored to please Gregg and the foundation all the more as grants dwindled, which further discouraged any NCMH impulse to approve of sterilization. Indeed by the 1930s some NCMH officials were quite hostile toward it.[180] In other words, in its applications for funding to the large foundations "conservative in their outlook," the NCMH had to practice "circumspection."[181] The NCMH, then, seems to have been a good barometer of respected opinion in psychiatry: initially supportive of segregation for eugenic reasons, when state hospital psychiatrists were a strong constituency in its membership, and dubious about eugenics in general and sterilization in particular in the interwar period as those members retired and were replaced by psychiatrists more interested in such topics as child guidance.[182]

Nonetheless, the NCMH surveys did bolster the sterilization cause in the Deep South, though only Mississippi passed a sterilization statute (1928) before the depression. Far more sterilizations took place at the state's two psychiatric hospitals than at the Mississippi School and Colony for the Feebleminded. C.D. Mitchell, medical superintendent of the huge Mississippi State Hospital, produced a good example of how sterilization and the "scientific" therapy of patients could be combined as

180. For NCMH criticism of sterilization as a public health measure, see AFMH, Frankwood Williams Papers, box 5, ser. III.A, folder 9; box 7, ser. III.C, folder 10; and box 7, ser. III.D, folder 13. As one physician wrote to Frankwood Williams, medical director of the NCMH in the 1920s, "Among existing State laws now on the statute books there are probably none that would find endorsement by most of the modern psychiatric groups." George Pratt to F. Williams, 3 March 1931, box 7, ser. III.C, folder 10. Thomas Salmon, an important psychiatric figure in the early history of the NCMH, was similarly opposed to sterilization. See Salmon to Charles Davenport, 20 June 1922, AFMH, Salmon Papers, box 3, folder 5. See also Grob, *Mental Illness and American Society*, p. 173. According to Barbara Sicherman, NCMH officials only approved of segregation for the feebleminded, not for people with other mental defects. Barbara Sicherman, "The Quest for Mental Health in America, 1880–1917" (Ph.D. diss., Columbia University, 1967), p. 350. I thank Hans Pols for sharing with me his conclusions based on his work on the history of the NCMH. On Gregg's career with the Rockefeller Foundation, see Theodore M. Brown, "Alan Gregg and the Rockefeller Foundation's Support of Franz Alexander's Psychosomatic Research," *Bulletin of the History of Medicine* 61 (1987): 155–82.
181. Dain, *Clifford W. Beers*, p. 290; Grob, *Mental Illness and American Society*, pp. 162–64, 266–67, 308.
182. Grob, *Mental Illness and American Society*, p. 166.

part of an allegedly progressive and humane treatment program. Like his peers in the 1930s, Mitchell believed that sterilization not only guaranteed "the survival of the fittest by abrogating defectives of power to procreate" but relieved discharged patients of "the burden of child bearing and rearing," which, he was certain, would reduce readmissions. So convinced was he of the efficacy and humaneness of sterilization that he hoped to perform the operation on *all* patients.[183]

In South Carolina, the next-to-last American state to enact a sterilization law, eugenicists had to contend with C. F. Williams. Until his retirement in 1945 he opposed eugenic theories because they lacked scientific proof and conflicted with his professional optimism. But he faced a formidable foe in B. O. Whitten, superintendent of the State Training School for the Feebleminded. Heartened by the Supreme Court ruling of 1927, Whitten in the 1930s launched a major drive in the state senate and house of representatives for a sterilization bill. After some setbacks, the bill became law in 1935. The next year Whitten was elected president of the American Association on Mental Deficiency. But Williams resisted the opportunities provided by the new law, permitting only one sterilization to be performed at the state hospital until his retirement. Whitten himself set a moderate pace at his institution in contrast to what was being done at other institutions. In the first ten years after the law was passed, his facility was the site of seventy-six sterilizations.[184]

Georgia did not enact a sterilization law until 1937, the last American state to do so. There, too, psychiatrists and other physicians were the leading propagandists. As early as 1901 a psychiatrist at the only state mental health institution had written that strict marriage laws would prevent many cases of mental illness.[185] Over the next three decades the Medical Association of Georgia set the tempo for eugenic campaigning, but the sterilization movement only caught fire in the 1930s when a group of civic-minded women interested in birth control and children's health joined forces with mental health care reformers. In 1935 a compulsory sterilization bill passed the state house of representatives and senate, only to be vetoed by Eugene Talmadge, the populist governor. Two years later the Progressive E. D. Rivers became governor, triggering a flood of New Deal legislation that included a new sterilization bill.

183. C. D. Mitchell, "Report of the Superintendent," in Mississippi State Hospital, *Forty-Second Biennial Report*, in *Biennial Report of Eleemosynary Institutions* (1933–35) (Jackson: Turner, 1935), p. 13. Cited in Larson, *Sex, Race, and Science*, p. 122; see also pp. 119–24.
184. Larson, *Sex, Race, and Science*, pp. 124–31.
185. T. O. Powell, "Marriage, Heredity, and Its Relations to Insanity and Allied Morbid Conditions," *Transactions of the Medical Association of Georgia* 52 (1901): 273–85.

With state government controled by the pro-Roosevelt wing of the Democratic party, there was no veto and the bill became law on 24 February 1937. Thus Georgia too adopted sterilization because physicians and psychiatrists agitated for its introduction, with Progressive notions serving as catalysts.[186] Without a political culture that accorded weight to the advice of psychiatrists, they probably could not have changed the minds of legislators on such sensitive topics.

The relations between U.S. psychiatrists and the campaign for segregation, sterilization, and marriage laws occurred in two stages. The first was the swelling of interest among psychiatrists nationally before the First World War. The wartime experiences of many leading psychiatrists then caused attention to shift from the quotidian concerns of hospital psychiatrists to dynamic models of the mind, psychological methods of therapy, child guidance, and less punitive forms of preventive mental health care. This change of focus ushered in the second stage, which featured a transfer of psychiatric interest in eugenics from the national to the state level. The gap between national and regional interests widened as the occupational conditions surrounding most state hospital psychiatric practice became increasingly less relevant to growing numbers of psychiatrists. Paradoxically, then, eugenics gradually lost its attraction for psychiatrists generally just as eugenicist psychiatrists were scoring some important legislative successes, especially in the Deep South. In some states, psychiatric interest in eugenic measures never seriously abated until the Second World War. But by the 1930s it was clear that eugenic theory carried less and less currency, as some psychiatrists (Meyer, White, Blumer, Meyerson) publicly voiced their opposition to negative eugenic policies, and others (Goddard, Fernald) retracted their earlier views. Important organizations discouraged support for sterilization. Thus U.S. psychiatrists may have lobbied for eugenic measures, but they were also some of the first defectors from the movement.

In retrospect, there were painfully few good reasons for psychiatrists to have supported the eugenic crusade. It must be remembered, however, that in early twentieth-century America the seminal question was not who endorsed eugenics but who did not. Among educated and professional men and women who prided themselves on having a social conscience, there were few who entirely rejected the observations and recommendations of eugenicists, and psychiatrists were no different. In

186. Edward J. Larson, "Belated Progress: The Enactment of Eugenic Legislation in Georgia," *Journal of the History of Medicine and Allied Sciences* 46 (1991): 44–64, 59.

fact if any group had reasons for supporting these policies it was they—particularly those mired in the problems of state hospitals. Every working day they faced what they thought were the intractable casualties of irresponsible policy making in the field of public mental health. They encountered outside interference, overcrowding and underfunding of their facilities, and mounting numbers of chronically ill patients. At the same time, other branches of medicine were making impressive progress. The mystery is not why some U.S. psychiatrists endorsed eugenics but why all of them were not seduced by its alarmist language and terms of reference. The same holds true for Canadian psychiatrists.

KEEPING THIS YOUNG COUNTRY SANE:
C. K. CLARKE, EUGENICS, AND
CANADIAN PSYCHIATRY, 1890–1940

A s the debate over eugenics among U.S. psychiatrists was peaking around the outbreak of the First World War, a small group of Canadian psychiatrists was helping to lay the groundwork for eugenics in Canada by doggedly preaching the need to control fertility. Like their U.S. counterparts, Canadian eugenicists argued that there were two chief reasons why the country was at a biologic crossroads. The first was the influx of immigrants beginning in the 1890s, a phenomenon that tended to dominate debates over Canadian eugenics into the 1920s. Some Canadian psychiatrists were convinced that the federal government had to ensure that mentally and physically handicapped immigrants could not enter the country and take undue advantage of Canada's charitable institutions and organizations, and a few of them—most prominently C. K. Clarke—struggled mightily if not always successfully to alert federal officials to this ostensible crisis. The second reason was concern about the mentally ill and feebleminded elements of Canadian society. The fear that the feebleminded were not only uncommonly promiscuous but also dangerous because of their hereditary traits prompted psychiatrists to campaign for tighter controls over their reproduction. These efforts, primarily during the interwar period, led to the two Canadian sterilization laws: Alberta's (1928) and British Columbia's (1933). Thus the views of psychiatrists on the custodial treatment of the mentally disabled had a distinct impact on Canadian social policy.

The traditional Canadian reliance on government to take the initiative in public charity helps explain why psychiatrists in Canada were more heavily in favor of sterilization than were those in the United States. While psychiatrists in both countries were advocating the segregation of the mentally ill and feebleminded, Canadian psychiatrists were supporting sterilization and eugenic immigration restriction as essential to the public health movement. Unlike many U.S. psychiatrists—particularly those of the NCMH—who mostly depended on private philanthropy for financial support, Canadian mental hygienists usually found themselves forced to rely on government funding, a fact that may also explain why eugenicists tended to monopolize the discourse on public health in Canada but not necessarily in the United States. Put another way, there was nowhere near as much vocal opposition to eugenic measures by Canadian psychiatrists, and this was probably due to the greater emphasis in Canadian political culture on the necessity for governments to intervene in health and welfare. Canadian psychiatrists expected government to supply them with the resources and power to meet their public health objectives. When resources were not forthcoming, psychiatrists and other eugenicists simply lobbied harder, more publicly, and more loudly, which helps to explain why psychiatrists' eugenic theories persisted in Canada long after they were being robustly challenged in the United States. Thus White, Meyer, Myerson, and Blumer had few counterparts in Canada when it came to questioning the need for segregation, sterilization, marriage laws, and immigration restriction. The history of Canadian social policy explains why U.S. psychiatric support for eugenics tended to be strongest at the state level: wherever government and mental health physicians functioned in close proximity, eugenic measures enjoyed considerable psychiatric approval.

I

Like U.S. progressives, many educated Canadians in the early twentieth century thought their country faced a crisis. They worried about the impact of urbanization and industrialization on the institutions and morals of the young nation. They argued that traditional Canadian ideas, values, and attitudes along with the peculiar qualities of agrarian life seemed to be disappearing and leaving nothing in their place. Some concerned Canadians threw themselves into reform, taking on such problems as prostitution, alcoholism, delinquency, immigration, disease, and unsafe living and working conditions. Though reformers came from various walks of life, religious backgrounds, and parts of the country, they were united on the urgency of these problems and the need to improve the quality of life. Some Canadian reformers argued that the starting point should be a regeneration in morals. Relying on what they considered the unique and venerable values of Anglo-Saxon imperial culture, they looked to an elite of educated and ethical Canadians to teach the country how to resist the corruptive temptations of "commercialism" and the modern city. Once people were taught that love, charity, and self-sacrifice were better than greed, competition, and materialism, these reformers contended, Canadians would be happier, healthier, and more virtuous. Other reformers favored expanded governmental intervention in social services, welfare, and industry. They sincerely believed that the state could mitigate the severity of the natural laws that governed the social and economic relations of Canadians and thereby enhance the nation's wealth and prosperity dramatically.[1]

Much of Canadian social reform centered on public health, and cities were the particular targets. Between 1890 and 1920, Montreal and Toronto, Canada's two biggest and most industrialized cities, almost tripled in population, both surpassing the half-million mark. Municipal authorities encountered staggering problems in the face of this growth, and by the first decade of the new century, Torontonians believed they were in the midst of a public health crisis. People pouring into Canadian cities by the thousands made it harder and harder to ensure housing, garbage removal, sewage control, inspection of schoolchildren, clean water and milk, and safe streets and working conditions. Mortality rates, especially among children, were depressingly high and compared unfavorably with those in some U.S. cities.[2] Canadian officials responded by expanding federal, provincial, and municipal public health bureaucracies, and this expansion was a major departure for Canadian government.[3]

In Toronto the physicians Peter Bryce, Charles Hodgetts, J. W. S. McCullough, Helen MacMurchy, and Charles Hastings were the chief

1. S. E. D. Shortt, *The Search for an Ideal: Six Canadian Intellectuals and Their Convictions in an Age of Transition, 1890–1930* (Toronto: University of Toronto Press, 1976). See also R. C. Brown and Ramsey Cook, *Canada, 1896–1921: A Nation Transformed* (Toronto: McClelland and Stewart), 1974.
2. W. G. Smith, *A Study in Canadian Immigration* (Toronto: Ryerson, 1920), p. 35. See also Angus McLaren, *Our Own Master Race: Eugenics in Canada, 1885–1945* (Toronto: McClelland and Stewart, 1990), p. 31.
3. Paul Adolphus Bator, " 'Saving Lives on the Wholesale Plan': Public Health Reform in the City of Toronto, 1900–1930" (Ph.D. diss., University of Toronto, 1979), pp. 12, 98.

crusaders. In their struggle to have government take more responsibility for public health they encountered considerable resistance from both private practitioners and government officials. Many physicians distrusted preventive medicine because they feared that it authorized substantial government intervention in medical practice. An orientation toward prevention might, some private, fee-for-service practitioners feared, overshadow the efforts of curative medicine and reduce the flow of patients into physicians' offices. General practitioners' incomes were low at the time, so this perceived threat to income, contrasted with the fixed salaries of public health doctors, sparked resentment. As Hodgetts claimed in 1912, the expanding role of the Ontario Provincial Board of Health (founded in 1882) "was and is still considered by many as a usurpation of the functions of the physician by the state."[4] On occasion politicians and government officials also proved recalcitrant when it came to state initiatives. But undaunted physician reformers campaigned to augment the power of the Provincial Board of Health and municipal medical officers. Medical reformers also tried to rid public health of political interference, and their efforts led in Toronto to doctors and politicians vying over which were better qualified to protect public health.[5]

Medical reformers found strong support for their crusade among Canada's elite. Above all, they discovered that when they targeted immigrants, both as victims and as the source of poor public health conditions, many native-born Canadians paid close attention. In the years before the First World War, Torontonians became increasingly uneasy about the growing numbers of immigrants. Thanks in large part to federal government advertising, immigration to Canada had jumped from 21,716 in 1897 to a prewar peak of 400,870 by 1913. Between 1910 and 1918, immigrants to Canada averaged 214,775 per year, roughly the entire population of Montreal as recently as 1891. Although the majority were from the United States or the British Isles, out of a total of 1,244,597 newcomers to Canada between 1900 and 1909, 315,151 came from Continental Europe. The impact on a city like Toronto was pronounced. Between the turn of the century and 1911 the number of Toronto's non-English-speaking citizens more than quadrupled, from fewer than 6,000 to more than 30,000.[6] Many Torontonians and public health officials charged that immigrants tended to be ignorant

4. Charles Hodgetts, "Relationship of the Medical Practitioner to Public Health," *Public Health Journal* 3 (1912): 249. Cited in Bator, " 'Saving Lives on the Wholesale Plan,' " p. 24.
5. Bator, " 'Saving Lives on the Wholesale Plan,' " pp. 65, 113.
6. Bator, " 'Saving Lives on the Wholesale Plan,' " pp. 67, 96, 115.

about the most fundamental sanitary and hygienic procedures and therefore needed to be educated about the health hazards they inadvertently created for themselves and others. Some took pity on immigrants having difficulty trying to adapt to Canadian society, but a sinister view persisted that a high percentage of newcomers were carriers of hereditary weaknesses that made them prone to crime, dependence, and physical and mental disabilities.

Concern about immigration dovetailed with growing anxiety among native English-speaking Canadians about the future of the British Empire. Just as English Victorians and Edwardians expressed worries about the high fertility rates of the poor urban classes of the British Isles and other races around the world, so many English-speaking Canadians shared the fears that Anglo-Saxons were being outbred by inferior human groups. When poverty-stricken men, women, and children from central and eastern Europe and the slums of British cities had begun disembarking in the late 1890s, Canadians' fears about "race suicide" had escalated. The steady arrival of such immigrants over the years led to warnings about their low quality and triggered campaigns to assimilate newcomers by training them to be law-abiding, productive, healthy, and self-reliant citizens.

Women's reform groups played a particularly large role in this endeavor. They emphasized that to build a great nation and empire priority had to be given to making the home—in the words of the 1912 Montreal Child Welfare Exhibition handbook—the "cornerstone of a morally sound society." Groups such as the local suffrage associations, the National Council of Women, the Women's Christian Temperance Union, and the Young Women's Christian Association directed their energies toward transforming women—whether immigrant or not—into better mothers. Women must become "mothers of the race"; for the stakes were high: "If we are to become a great nation, the well-being of our children must be our first care," as the exhibition handbook proclaimed.[7] The citizenship and the very nature of Canadian women were defined largely in terms of their maternal and reproductive duties and capabilities. According to Helen MacMurchy, "The dearest wish of a true woman is to be a mother."[8] With sentiments like these, eugenics was

7. Child Welfare Exhibition, *Souvenir Handbook*, 8–22 October 1912. Cited in Carol Bacchi, "Race Regeneration and Social Purity: A Study of the Social Attitudes of Canada's English-Speaking Suffragists," *Histoire Sociale/Social History* 11 (1978): 460–74, 467.
8. Helen MacMurchy, *The Canadian Mother's Book* (Ottawa: Queen's Printer, 1927), pp. 8–9. Cited in Veronica Strong-Boag, "Canada's Women Doctors: Feminism Constrained," in

never far from reformers' minds. It fit comfortably into the discourse on reform because it suggested preventive measures that could be used to monitor reproductive practices. Thus, imperialism, eugenics, and maternal feminism frequently intersected.[9]

Canadian psychiatrists quickly became a vitally interested party in this debate. Echoing their U.S. counterparts, one of their leading complaints by the end of the nineteenth century had been that their asylums were overcrowded with hopeless cases. Soon they began alleging that foreign-born patients were disproportionately represented in public asylums and that this was due principally to immigrants' hereditary defectiveness. Moreover, they asserted that in their roles as expert witnesses in criminal trials they were seeing growing numbers of disturbed immigrants charged with violent crimes. No Canadian physician publicized these views more vociferously and persistently than Charles K. Clarke. He stands out because his career—spanning his service both in Ontario mental hospitals and in the Canadian public health movement—vividly demonstrates the appeal of eugenics both to psychiatrists who were state asylum physicians and to those who were mental hygienists. Even before he left the Rockwood Asylum in Kingston to take over the head psychiatrist's post at the Toronto Asylum in 1905, Clarke had shown a mounting interest in the subject of heredity and immigration. Like provincial psychiatric colleagues such as R. M. Bucke, Daniel Clark, and James Russell, he had begun emphasizing the role of heredity in the incidence of insanity in the 1890s.[10] Except for one interlude later in his career, Clarke remained Canada's most consistent medical proponent of immigration restriction until his death in early 1924. What initially compelled him to turn to hereditarianism and eugenics was a combination of his passionate identification with the professional fortunes of psychiatry and Canada's late nineteenth-century cultural climate, which stressed race, empire, reproduction, child welfare, and public health reform.

Clarke's immersion in eugenics, like Blumer's, took time and was due in large measure to the declining prospects in asylum psychiatry. As late

S. E. D. Shortt, ed., *Medicine in Canadian Society: Historical Perspectives* (Montreal: McGill-Queen's University Press, 1981), p. 225.

9. See Kathleen Janet McConnachie, "Science and Ideology: The Mental Hygiene and Eugenics Movements in the Inter-War Years, 1919–1939" (Ph.D. diss., University of Toronto, 1987), p. 217; and Barbara Roberts, " 'A Work of Empire': Canadian Reformers and British Female Immigration," in *A Not Unreasonable Claim: Women and Reform in Canada, 1880s–1920s*, ed. Linda Kealey (Toronto: Women's Press, 1979), pp. 185–201. See also Cynthia R. Comacchio, *"Nations are Built of Babies": Saving Ontario's Mothers and Children, 1900–1940* (Montreal: McGill-Queen's University Press, 1993), pp. 18–20.

10. Rainer K. Baehre, "The Ill-Regulated Mind: A Study in the Making of Psychiatry in Ontario, 1830–1921" (Ph.D. diss., York University, 1985), pp. 410–12.

as 1894 he had claimed that environment and nurture indisputably affected the incidence of insanity. "Fortunately it is nature's custom," he wrote, "when given half a chance not to perpetuate the ills of the human race, and although tendencies may be transmitted, if people can supply themselves with healthy occupations and live good lives no harm will come." This view was consistent with his confidence that patients' health improved from hospitalization in a psychiatric asylum. As an asylum physician in the mid 1890s he had not yet rejected the theory of "moral treatment." Nor did he yet believe that involuntary measures were needed to reduce the rate of hereditary illness. So in stark contrast to his later fondness for eugenic laws governing immigration and the segregation of the mentally ill, he wrote: "Those who hope to find a cure for the evil [of hereditary disease] in legislation will meet with bitter disappointment."[11]

But Clarke's views were about to change abruptly, as a result of his 1895 experience as an expert medical witness in the Valentine Shortis murder trial. As there was no doubt that Shortis had actually committed the crime, his lawyers entered a plea of not guilty on the basis of insanity. They even dispatched a commission to Ireland to trace his ancestry and obtain evidence of his hereditary degeneracy. After interviewing Shortis for three hours Clarke labeled him a "moral imbecile with homicidal mania, paranoid class." But his efforts to prove Shortis's insanity were in vain; for on 4 November 1895 Shortis was condemned to be executed (although the death sentence was later commuted to life imprisonment).[12]

The effect on Clarke was profound. His sense of justice was grievously offended by the spectacle of a government that would do virtually nothing to prevent immigrants like Shortis from entering the country and then condemn to death these same unfortunates for committing crimes for which they were not responsible, at least in the eyes of physicians like Clarke. As an asylum psychiatrist he also asked how long would it be before asylums became flooded with similar immigrants who, though perhaps not guilty of capital crimes, were nonetheless disposed to violence and other criminal actions? How many were like William Metcalf's murderer, lunatics capable of unpredictable behavior? Questions like

11. ARK, 1894, pp. 71–72.
12. Cyril Greenland, "L'affaire Shortis and the Valleyfield Murders," Canadian Psychiatric Association Journal 7 (1962): 261–71. In 1907, Clarke again interviewed Shortis and concluded that his earlier diagnosis had been correct. Shortis, he asserted, was a dangerous paranoid schizophrenic who was afflicted with delusions of persecution. But in the 1920s two other Canadian psychiatrists were so impressed with Shortis's condition that they recommended his release. Martin L. Friedland, "The Case of Valentine Shortis: A Study of Crime and Politics in Canada" (Ph.D. diss., University of Toronto, Faculty of Law, 1985), pp. 87–95, 322, 369.

these must have run through his mind at the time of the Shortis trial. They insistently drew his attention to Canada's immigration policy.

Within one year of the Shortis trial, Clarke had become a convert to degeneracy theory and the notion that there are hereditarily defective men, women, and children who present a grave danger to public health as well as law and order. In 1896 he joined the Canadian National Council of Women (NCW) and the medical superintendents of the London and Hamilton asylums in calling for an inquiry into the question of child immigration, a controversial issue by the 1890s thanks mainly to "Doctor" Thomas J. Barnardo and the heads of other programs designed to send British slum children to Canada. In 1870, Barnardo had founded a home for destitute children in London, England, the first of many that would ultimately form the largest child rescue agency in Great Britain. He was responsible for dispatching thirty thousand of the roughly eighty thousand children who were to emigrate to Canada before the federal government ceased subsidizing the program in 1925. Complaints about these youngsters were rife. Canadians from various organizations and interest groups alleged that they drove down wages by flooding the labor market; corrupted the morals of young Canadians; and bore a "hereditary taint" that turned them bad once they hit the streets of their new country. Native-born Canadians were increasingly convinced that slum children simply returned to their perverse habits after coming to Canada and eventually turned up in the nation's reformatories, jails, penitentiaries, and asylums.[13] Clarke and his fellow psychiatrists were particularly interested in the effect of child immigrants on asylum admission rates, and this primarily explains their emphatic support of the NCW report of 1896. As Clarke told an NCW representative, child immigrants "presented all of the characteristics of degeneracy" including vice and criminality. He warned that the defective heredity of most of these children would have an baneful impact "on the race as a whole." "When we remember that fully fifty per cent. of the admissions to our asylums are the outcome of a bad heredity," he concluded, "we naturally pause when we endeavor to prophesy the result of the importation of a large number of degenerate children."[14]

13. Joy Parr, *Laboring Children: British Immigrant Apprentices to Canada, 1869–1924* (Montreal: McGill-Queen's University Press, 1980). See also Neil Sutherland, *Children in English-Canadian Society: Framing the Twentieth-Century Consensus* (Toronto: University of Toronto Press, 1976), pp. 28–34.
14. Clarke to Mrs. Talbot MacBeth, 2 May 1896, NCW, *Yearbook* (1896), pp. 472–75. Richard M. Bucke, from the London Asylum, was equally strident, asserting that child immigrants had a tendency "to be vicious, immoral, and even criminal." He noted that over twenty years at the London Asylum, "quite a number of young men and women who have been imported

Another measure of the impact of the Shortis trial and child immigration on Clarke's thinking was his unpublished novel "The Amiable Morons," a thinly disguised fictional account of Shortis's life and trial which Clarke wrote in later years. Referring to supposedly "defective" people like Shortis, he lamented "the general apathy in regard to those irresponsible victims of a bad heredity."[15] By "apathy" Clarke chiefly meant the attitudes of those in the federal government who determined and enforced immigration policy. Up through 1891 the Department of Agriculture had responsibility for immigration; thereafter it became the responsibility of the Department of the Interior, which, not coincidentally, also dealt with land settlement. In 1893 a separate Immigration Branch was set up within the Department of Interior. The independent Department of Immigration and Colonization was established in 1917 and survived until 1936, after which it became a branch of the Department of Mines and Resources.[16]

Canadian immigration in the mid-1890s was still governed by the terms of the 1869 Immigration Act, which contained provisions barring the entry of insane, destitute, and disabled immigrants. From 1889 to 1902 the federal government followed a policy of sending back unwanted immigrants to their country of origin in what amounted to an informal system of deportation; yet virtually no medical inspections were performed on immigrants disembarking at Canadian ports or crossing the U.S.-Canadian border. Municipalities objected to the arrival of immigrants carrying loathsome or contagious diseases such as smallpox, tuberculosis, and scarlet fever. Quarantining such immigrants was expensive and inconvenient. Canadians began calling for the federal Immigration Branch to prevent immigrants from landing in the first place. Critics charged that federal officials all too frequently ignored demands for discriminating inspection of aliens in order to admit immigrants to settle Canada's farmlands and work Canada's factories.[17]

as children . . . have come under my care as epileptic maniacs, lunatics, and more or less insane imbeciles. I have found such patients, I may say always, congenitally defective and incurable, and as long as they live they will have to be supported by the State."

15. C. K. Clarke, "The Amiable Morons," CKCA, Unpublished MS, IIg.2.

16. This arrangement lasted until 1950, when the Department of Citizenship and Immigration was formed.

17. On deportation and immigration policy in Canadian history, see Barbara Roberts, *Whence They Came: Deportation from Canada, 1900–1935* (Ottawa: University of Ottawa Press, 1988). For the role of doctors in deportation and the inspection of immigrants, see Zlata Godler, "Doctors and the New Immigrants," *Canadian Ethnic Studies* 9 (1977): 6–17; and Barbara Roberts, "Doctors and Deports: The Role of the Medical Profession in Canadian Deportation, 1900–1920," ibid. 18 (1986): 17–36. See also Valerie Knowles, *Strangers at Our Gates: Canadian Immigration and Immigration Policy* (Toronto: Dundurn, 1992); and Gerald Tulchin-

Clarke's initial pleas for medical inspection of insane immigrants came at roughly this time; in fact he was one of the first Canadians to protest specifically against the unregulated arrival of insane or feebleminded immigrants. In 1902 he wrote, "We are prone to underestimate the part heredity plays in the evolution of insanity."[18] One year later he predicted that the country would soon be flooded by an "enormous current of alien degenerates," particularly "the most degenerate peoples in Central and Southern Europe." He described these people as "defectives," men, women, and children with pronounced criminal or pathological tendencies, in stark contrast to "the sturdy agriculturalists of the British Isles." Whether a "defective immigrant" ultimately became mentally ill or committed a crime, Clarke argued, the result was the same: "He becomes a burden upon the State which owes him nothing." He recommended "A far more rigid system of inspection than that in use at present" as well as a deportation policy for "the indigent classes of immigrants who show marked evidence of mental disease or defect, or criminal tendency."[19]

Clarke's experience as medical superintendent of the Kingston Asylum convinced him that unregulated immigration constituted a serious drain on the public purse and a severe imposition on asylum psychiatry. As he admitted in 1903, Kingston was "the centre of a long settled district, unaffected to any great extent by immigration,"[20] but over the previous ten years the provincial government had, nonetheless, committed sixty-three immigrant patients to his care. To Clarke's mind, their family histories proved that they were hereditary defectives. He then calculated the total cost to the province for the maintenance of these immigrants as $72,875.83. "If that is already the case in one small institution comparatively remote from the direct effects of immigration, what must be the total amount for the whole Dominion?" he asked.[21]

Clarke's frustration had as much to do with the chronic violent and criminal nature of some foreign-born patients as it did with their racial and national background. As in the United States, asylums in Ontario were being exploited by countless families as places to send their senile and severely handicapped relatives, and curing these patients was an impossibility, which, Clarke lamented, accounted for "the smallness of our

sky, ed., *Immigration in Canada: Historical Perspectives* (Mississauga, Ont.: Copp Clark Longman, 1994).
18. ARK, 1902, p. 56.
19. ARK, 1903, pp. 56–59.
20. ARK, 1903, p. 58.
21. ARK, 1903, pp. 54–59.

discharge list."[22] But "the insane of the criminal class" caused him even more trouble. These patients made his job harder by poisoning the atmosphere in the asylum with their "shocking" language, "degrading ideas," and frankly "homicidal" behavior. Clarke urged the provincial government to remove these "degenerates" from Rockwood so he could go back to doing what he did best: treating his patients.[23] This conflation of immigration, degeneracy, and criminality quickly became a reflex response of North American psychiatrists confronted with the challenges of treating foreign-born patients in the early twentieth century.

Another episode in Clarke's pre-1903 career helped to draw his attention to the topic of immigration. In 1901 he served as a royal commissioner investigating the Provincial Asylum for the Insane at New Westminster, British Columbia. While there, he wrote two years later, he was struck by the large number of Chinese patients.[24] Although he was on the West Coast at a time of heightened nativist and anti-Asian sentiment,[25] it is not at all clear that he drew nativist or racially bigoted conclusions while in New Westminster. His report contained no references to immigrants, Chinese or otherwise, and he confined his remarks to the many improvements in hospital conditions he believed were long overdue at the New Westminster asylum.[26] If indeed he was appalled by the presence of foreign inmates there, it is curious that he said nothing about them in his report. It was only later, after he returned to Kingston, that he reflected on his West Coast visit and what he had seen in New Westminster.

What punctuated this process of reflection was Clarke's growing awareness of immigration to New York State and its consequences for psychiatric practice there. New York City was the main U.S. port of entry, and about one-quarter of all insane immigrants were hospitalized in New York State. As we shall see in the next chapter, these circumstances triggered a good many complaints from U.S. physicians. According to public health officials' statistics, immigrants were steadily filling up not only the state's asylums but its prisons, hospitals, and jails. Clarke

22. ARK, 1897, p. 94. See also ARK, 1898, p. 118.
23. ARK, 1899, pp. 101–3.
24. ARK, 1899, p. 58.
25. Patricia E. Roy, *A White Man's Province: British Columbia Politicians and Chinese and Japanese Immigrants, 1858–1914* (Vancouver: University of British Columbia Press, 1989); W. Peter Ward, *White Canada Forever: Popular Attitudes and Public Policy toward Orientals in British Columbia* (Montreal: McGill-Queen's University Press, 1990).
26. British Columbia, *Royal Commission of Inquiry on the Hospital for the Insane in New Westminster* (Victoria: Queen's Printer, 1901).

kept a close eye on these developments thanks in part to his collegial relations with Blumer and other Empire State psychiatrists. He was fully aware of their dissatisfaction with politicians' reluctance to tighten inspection and deportation laws, which according to some psychiatrists and state charity officials had facilitated the turning of state hospitals into massive custodial institutions for the violently and incurably ill. Exploiting the conventional theory that immigrants were prone to crime, depravity, and disease, N.Y. psychiatrists championed immigration restriction not only to reduce the number of patients in public asylums but also to shift attention from their own therapeutic futility.

Clarke, already impatient with Ontario's political inaction on reform of provincial mental institutions, and starting to see the effects of immigration on his own asylum, sympathized with his New York colleagues, and like them, he began to view the federal government as responsible for many of his own problems. He knew that some immigrants to the United States made their way north to Canada and that it was only a matter of time before Canada would experience its own immigration crisis. In fact xenophobic Canadians were already disturbed by the increasing number of immigrants, particularly those of non-British and non-American origins. By 1903 the total number of immigrants had mushroomed to 138,660, with about a third from non-Anglo sources.[27] Thus, Clarke had good reason to look to New York to understand the potential effects of immigration on Canadian psychiatry.[28] His own mounting difficulties as a provincial hospital psychiatrist, his professional ties to U.S. asylum physicians, and the increasingly anxious Canadian debate over immigration combined to foster in Clarke what was to become one of the fiercest obsessions of his entire career.

Clarke's 1903 comments on immigrants caught the attention of other Canadian public health physicians. The most important early admirer of these views was Peter Bryce (1853–1932). As a young man Bryce had developed a passionate interest in preventive medicine and public health reform. From 1882 to 1904 he served as first secretary of

27. Knowles, *Strangers at Our Gates*, p. 72.
28. Knowles, *Strangers at Our Gates*, p. 72. In his 1903 remarks about Canadian immigrants Clarke cited H. E. Allison's paper at the May 1903 AMPA meeting in Washington, D.C. See H. E. Allison, "Hospital Provision for the Insane Criminal," *PAMPA* 10 (1903): 241–64; and "Discussion," ibid., pp. 264–67. For statistics on New York State insane immigrants, see Henry Hurd, ed., *The Institutional Care of the Insane in the United States and Canada*, 4 Vols. (Baltimore: Johns Hopkins University Press, 1916–17), 1:362–68. The topic of New York State's disproportionate fiscal responsibilities to dependent U.S. immigrants surfaced so often in the psychiatric literature of the era that it is impossible to cite everything published; but for more on this phenomenon, see the next chapter.

the Ontario Board of Health and quickly acquired a continental reputation as an expert in public health. He was one of the few Canadians
elected president of the American Public Health Association. He was,
then, a natural choice as the first chief medical officer of the Immigration Branch of the Department of the Interior, a position he was to
hold until 1921. The post of chief medical officer had materialized because of the 1902 amendments to the 1869 Immigration Act. Not only
did these revisions expand the list of diseases that could disqualify an
immigrant from entering Canada, but they also permitted the medical
profession to cooperate with immigration officials in the inspection of
newcomers. In 1903 the Immigration Branch began medical inspections by hiring doctors on a fee-for-service basis to inspect immigrants
and detain diseased newcomers either for deportation or further treatment and admission. The same year Bryce was asked to investigate the
existing state of medical inspection facilities and procedures. It was on
the basis of his report that the government offered him the position of
chief medical officer.[29]

Bryce subscribed to some strong though fairly conventional theories
about immigration, reproduction, and fertility. He shared the fears of
many Canadians of British descent that falling birthrates of native Canadians signaled degeneracy and race suicide. He also warily eyed the
rising numbers of immigrants, suspecting that all too many entered the
country with certifiable mental and physical disabilities. In his attempt
to professionalize the medical inspection of immigrants Bryce found an
early ally and friend in Clarke.[30] Bryce quoted Clarke's remarks about
immigrant "criminals of hereditary instinct" and "sturdy agriculturalists
of the British Isles"; for he too made the invidious distinction between
immigrants of the "northern races" and central and eastern European
"non-agriculturalists" who came from

> the poor quarters of large continental cities, and who have neither the de-
> sire, physical capacity, or individual moral qualities or training necessary to
> make them face the difficulties incident to rural life in a new country. Such
> become city dwellers and only reproduce in America the life of civic nomads
> to the injury of the native born artisan and to the degradation of the morals
> of our cities by creating ghettos therein with their customs and morals but
> transferred from their former habitats.

29. Roberts, "Doctors and Deports," pp. 19–21.
30. Clarke to Bryce, 26 February 1904, PAC, RG (record group) 76, vol. 268, file 228124,
pt. 4.

Bryce concluded by agreeing with Clarke that Canada had to "prevent the defective and parasitic classes from becoming a burden to the country."[31]

Clearly Bryce and Clarke were of one mind. Thanks to Bryce's position, Clarke seemingly had the ear of influential Immigration Branch officials, and he looked to be on the verge of his own career as expert adviser to the federal government on immigration matters. These factors probably played a role in his appointment to the post of Toronto Asylum medical superintendent in 1905. Provincial and municipal authorities knew full well by then that the Toronto Asylum, a major public charitable institution in a city undergoing substantial public health reform, would be the focal point of much public and official attention. Moreover, as Clarke learned soon after his move to the Queen City, the Toronto Asylum was admitting ever more immigrant patients. It was far from coincidental, then, that Clarke, a physician believed to possess specialized knowledge about the relations between immigration and public mental health, should get the post.[32]

II

With his arrival in Toronto, Clarke appeared to have reached a major career milestone. As he remarked to Blumer shortly after his appointment was announced, the new Conservative provincial government had hinted that a new psychiatric institution with psychopathic outpatient wards and modern facilities for diagnosis, research, teaching, and treatment was a distinct possibility in the near future.[33] To Clarke such a hospital symbolized his release from asylum practice and a grand opportunity to treat patients suffering from curable and recently acquired illnesses. He justified the construction of a psychiatric institute by claiming that it would save money because incipient cases of mental disease could

31. Peter Bryce, "Report on Immigration Inspection Services at Atlantic Seaports," 28 September 1903, PAC, RG 76, vol. 268, file 228124, pt. 4. See also McLaren, *Our Own Master Race*, pp. 52–56.

32. There may also have been a political reason for Clarke's appointment. The new Conservative Party, fresh from its provincial victory, was rewarding favorites; the transfer of Clarke to Toronto made room for the appointment of Edward Ryan—whom Clarke dubbed a "political hireling"—as medical superintendent of Rockwood. It was appointments like Ryan's that persuaded Clarke that political patronage ruled provincial policy on the operation of Ontario's asylums. Cyril Greenland, "The Origins of the Toronto Psychiatric Hospital," in "TPH: History and Memories of the Toronto Psychiatric Hospital," ed. Edward Shorter, QSMHC, Unpublished MSS, 1993, p. 32.

33. Clarke to Blumer, 11 September 1905, BP, box 30.

he treated early and thus prevented from reaching a chronic stage at which indefinite hospitalization was the only alternative. Above all, he insisted that a psychiatric institute be placed under his supervision and not that of the physicians affiliated with Toronto General Hospital (TGH).[34] Thus Clarke was poised, by 1906, to create a professional empire in Toronto for himself and Canadian psychiatry.

But in the meantime he unquestionably faced some daunting challenges at the Toronto Asylum. The facility had become a largely custodial institution with falling cure rates. Clarke laid much of the blame on immigrants and immigration policy. "It is to be regretted that so many defectives from the old world have found their way to our wards."[35] He criticized both the quality of medical inspection of immigrants and the deportation law. Earlier in 1906 the Canadian government had made deportations legal for the first time. Immigrants who within two years of their arrival in Canada ended up in a publicly funded charitable institution—such as an insane asylum—were eligible for deportation.[36] To Clarke, the two-years' residence rule was simply too short. Many immigrants, he contended, arrived with dementia praecox, an incurable mental disease of very long duration which was often not detected by medical inspectors at Canada's ports of entry. Immigrants with this disease could go undetected until the moment their symptoms became florid and they had to be institutionalized; becoming virtually permanent public charges until the day they died. This left Ontario, where many immigrants eventually settled, with the responsibility to support them. As Clarke put it in 1907, failure to inspect the mental health of immigrants meant Canadians—and particularly Ontarians—"have unwittingly taxed ourselves unfairly."[37]

In his crusade to end the immigration of mentally ill persons, Clarke did something that was to characterize his entire career. By helping to spark an acrimonious jurisdictional feud between two levels of government he demonstrated his intense devotion to principle and his utter lack of diplomacy. In the process he also lost a friend and ally in Peter Bryce.

Clarke began his stay in Toronto enjoying the support of S. A. Armstrong, Ontario's inspector of prisons and public charities. Armstrong too

---

34. ART, 1906, p. 6.
35. Thomas E. Brown, " 'Living with God's Afflicted': A History of the Provincial Lunatic Asylum at Toronto, 1830–1911" (Ph.D. diss., Queen's University, 1980), p. 355. ART, 1906, p. 6.
36. Costs for deportation and removal to the port whence they came were borne either by the immigrants themselves or the municipality that requested the deportation. Roberts, *Whence They Came*, pp. 12–13.
37. ART, 1906, p. 3; 1907, p. 8.

protested that Ontario had to shoulder an unfair burden because of Ottawa's negligence. Like Clarke, he believed that "the system of inspection maintained by the Federal Government at the port of landing is totally inadequate to the demands made upon it by the large immigration of the past few years." Armstrong also objected to the deportation process as defined by the federal regulations. To deport an insane dependent, the municipal and provincial authorities had to provide the immigration officials with a detailed transportation record of the immigrant, including the name of the ship and the date of landing—information often impossible to determine. Language barriers were notoriously difficult to surmount. Some patients, Armstrong alleged, deliberately lied to delay deportation. Others were too psychotic to provide any reliable information. Armstrong strenuously urged the federal authorities to introduce a card catalog system registering all vital data for every immigrant who arrived in Canada. "Lastly," he concluded, "a more detailed medical examination of the immigrant should be made, either on arrival or when on board the steamer in transit, by men who are skilled in mental diseases." Clarke concurred, arguing that the example of New York State and the problems with Canada's new deportation law showed that "defectives should be weeded out as far as possible at the port of sailing. This would save untold misery and expense both to the patients, the steamship companies and the country."[38] Unfortunately for Clarke and Canadian psychiatrists this specific reform would not be introduced until 1928.

As Armstrong's and Clarke's 1907 comments indicate, there was still a great deal of dissatisfaction at provincial and municipal levels with the functioning of national immigration laws. A glimpse at the records of the Immigration Branch—in particular those dealing with deportation proceedings—reveals highly uneasy relations between federal and provincial authorities over the implementation of immigration policy. Armstrong and Clarke were quick to conclude that federal officials and civil servants were less than enthusiastic about enforcing the law. Clarke imagined that the Immigration Branch was beholden to interest groups such as the steamship companies, who made sizable profits from bringing in immigrants; the Canadian Manufacturers' Association, which wanted unrestricted immigration to flood the pool of available labor and bring down wages; and immigrant organizations, which wanted deportation and immigration laws relaxed. Clarke was not wrong to believe that all

38. ART, 1907, pp. xviii–xix.

these constituencies exploited their political contacts to influence policy, but he erred in taking matters into his own hands and going to the Canadian press to publicize what he thought were the failures of federal action. As a result he was to fall out with both Peter Bryce and provincial officials and retreat from the field of immigration policy between 1910 and 1916. His experience trying to cooperate with the federal and provincial governments between 1906 and 1910 reinforced the lesson that politics and effective mental health care did not mix; it also belies the popular notion that doctors, politicians, and bureaucrats formed a unified front conspiratorially dedicated to the xenophobic subordination of immigrants.[39]

Beginning in 1906, then, Clarke found himself enmeshed in a complex organizational structure that stretched from the Toronto Asylum at the bottom to the Canadian prime minister's office at the top. He and Armstrong were determined to defend what they thought were the interests of psychiatry and Ontario respectively. They began pressuring federal immigration officials to deport patients, but they discovered that federal bureaucrats insisted on following the law to the letter. Some immigrant patients had, for example, already been discharged from Clarke's Toronto Asylum while still under the two-year limit. Fearing that these foreigners would eventually have to be readmitted, Armstrong and Clarke argued that they ought to be deported. But the Immigration Branch informed them that there was nothing the federal government could do if they were not presently hospitalized dependents. This triggered a testy exchange of letters between Armstrong and William Duncan Scott, superintendent of immigration and Bryce's immediate superior.

Born in 1861, William "Big Bill" Scott had become superintendent of immigration in 1903 and was to continue in that capacity until 1919. His real views are difficult to determine from Immigration Branch records,[40] but it is clear that he did not see eye to eye with provincial public charity officials like Clarke and Armstrong. They in turn thought Scott at best a tiresome bureaucrat, at worst a corrupt public servant catering to the interests of big business and powerful immigrant lobbies. Peter Bryce found himself caught in the middle. At once a physician and a federal

---

39. For versions of this theory, see Roberts, *Whence They Came*; McLaren, *Our Own Master Race*.

40. Harold Martin Troper, *Only Farmers Need Apply: Official Canadian Government Encouragement of Immigration from the United States, 1896–1911* (Toronto: Griffin House, 1972), pp. 12, 19, 20, 28, 44, 121, 140. See also Knowles, *Strangers at Our Gates*, pp. 84–85.

civil servant, his loyalties were divided between his profession and his supervisor, Scott, with whom he had a decidedly uneasy relationship.[41] In the end, though, he sided with Scott and the Immigration Branch.

Matters came to a head during the economic recession of 1907–8. Armstrong, prodded behind the scenes by Clarke and others, continually petitioned the Immigration Branch to deport foreign-born patients in Ontario's asylums. Federal officials were reluctant to authorize deportation for fear that immigrants homesick and down on their luck would exploit deportation as an inexpensive means of return to their homelands. Furthermore, the more deportations, the more attention would focus on the failures of the department's inspectors at Canada's ports of entry. In addition, immigration officials worried that the federal government might be vulnerable to legal action if deportation proceedings were not properly conducted; thus inspectors had to fill out departmental deportation forms in exacting detail.[42]

Another reason officials like Scott insisted on psychiatrists supplying as much information as possible on deportable immigrants was the fact that shipping companies were required under law to retransport deportees. These companies demanded proof that immigrants had in fact been brought to Canada on their ships and transported inland by their railways. As Scott acknowledged, failure to provide proof gave the companies a pretext to delay and hamper deportations.[43] Thus, federal officials were far more sensitive than provincial officials to the wishes of the transportation companies, which for obvious reasons did not want to incur the costs of sending immigrants back.

41. See, e.g., Peter Bryce to Wilfred Laurier, 28 May 1906, PAC, RG 76, vol. 414, file 110484, where he complained to the prime minister of Canada that Scott had tried to usurp his authority as chief medical officer of the Immigration Branch by demanding that all correspondence from medical inspectors be sent first to Scott, and not Bryce.

42. Peter Bryce to J. Obed Smith, 1 August 1906, PAC, RG 76, vol. 376, file 518766. See also William Scott to Thomas Southworth, 7 November 1906, PAC, vol. 393, file 563236, pt. 1. Bryce repeated this cautionary advice in 1914. See Peter Bryce, "Instructions for the Medical Inspection of Immigrants," *Canadian Journal of Medicine and Surgery* 36 (1914): 116–36; esp. pp. 124–29 and his thoughts on the "Examination for Suspected Mentally Defective Immigrants."

43. See, e.g., Robert Kerr to William Scott, 28 March 1908, and Scott to Kerr, 16 April 1908, PAC, RG 76, vol. 393, file 563236, pt. 1. Another example of the alleged lack of cooperation provided by the transportation companies in cases of deportation was the attempt on the part of the companies' ship doctors to hamstring the efforts of immigration officers to return deportees under safe and healthy conditions. See J. Bruce Walker to Scott, 22 January 1908, PAC, RG 76, vol. 393, file 563236, pt. 1. On 17 March 1908, Walker again warned Scott "that deportation proceedings are being scrutinized more and more closely by the transportation companies concerned, and too much care cannot therefore be exercised" to see that each case conformed to the provisions of the Immigration Act. Ibid.

Historians have largely ignored the relations between Canadian politicians, bureaucrats, and immigration officers on the one hand and large business and immigrant organizations on the other. Some politicians did indeed meddle frequently in the administration of Canadian medical inspection and deportation. Sir Wilfred Laurier, Canada's prime minister from 1896 to 1911, took a keen interest in the awarding of contracts to and staffing of the Quebec medical inspection posts at Quebec City and Montreal.[44] Officials like Scott may have been susceptible to influence from these sources.[45] At least one physician was fired by the government for taking bribes from a steamship booking agent in return for illegally approving immigrants, although there is no proof of his complicity.[46] There was, then, at least some truth to Clarke's allegations of influence exercised by political and mercantile elements.

How much is another matter, however. What Clarke and his Ontario associates encountered most often was bureaucratic impartiality—sprinkled with a generous dose of inertia. A major cause of friction between Ontario and the Immigration Branch in 1907–8 was Clarke's wish to deport foreign-born patients who had taken up residence in Canada *before* the 1906 act. When immigration officials pointed out that this was illegal, it only made Clarke angrier; for it reminded him of what he thought to be the inadequacy of the country's immigration laws and the inefficiency of its port inspection. Clarke reacted by bombarding Armstrong with letters of protest, some of which were forwarded to Scott. Clarke repeatedly cited the poor family histories of many of his foreign-born patients and warned the Immigration Branch that unless reforms were made in the medical inspection of newcomers, Canada would be host to a growing number of degenerate families like the Jukes of New York State.[47]

44. See esp. correspondence between J. D. Pagé, medical inspector at Quebec City, and Prime Minister Laurier. PAC, Wilfred Laurier Papers, MG (MS group) 26, particularly files 107982, 115541, and 120667. The relationship between Laurier and Pagé may have dated back to much earlier days in the Province of Quebec and led to controversies over Pagé's alleged preferential treatment at the hands of the Department of the Interior.
45. Bryce's older brother certainly thought so. In 1906 he wrote to Laurier that Scott was "a politician first and is apt to subordinate public [interests?] to more temporary considerations. I have known instances of this." George Bryce to Wilfrid Laurier, 12 May 1906, PAC, MG 26, 110298. For evidence of immigrant organizations trying to affect deportation decisions, see A. Goldstein of the Baron de Hirsch Institute and Hebrew Benevolent Society to Peter Bryce, 26 January 1905, PAC, RG 76, vol. 270, file 228124.
46. PAC, RG 76, file 366144. Cited in Roberts, "Doctors and Deports," p. 22.
47. For Clarke's involvement in the deportation of immigrant patients from the Toronto Asylum see PAO, RG 63, A-6, Deportations Actions—Jails and Asylums, boxes 694–700, esp. box 697, cases 8458 and 8474. A particularly strongly worded memorandum that Armstrong

At some point in 1908, Clarke, feeling that neither federal nor provincial officials were acting quickly enough, went public with his dissatisfaction. First he capitalized on the publicity surrounding a gruesome murder trial. A twenty-seven-year-old British immigrant was convicted of shooting and killing an eighty-year-old farmer on Christmas Day 1907. The jury, afraid that if found insane he would get off with a light sentence, found the defendant guilty. Before dismissing the jury the judge admitted that Clarke had briefed him regarding the criminal menace immigrants posed to the country. "The immigration question," the chief justice declared, "at present is a matter of the greatest importance to the people of this country. There seems to be a unanimity of opinion that people such as are being dumped into this country are of a different character and will not blend well with the people of this country." Showing all the signs of having been tutored by Clarke, the judge then admonished both provincial and federal officials to "redouble their efforts" to deport and keep out defective newcomers.[48]

Clarke did not stop there. For the balance of the year and into the next, he published a series of articles on immigration which attracted press attention.[49] "We are beginning to be able to sympathize with the trials gone through by the United States and we should profit by the experience of New York, and apply even more rigorous methods than those adopted by that State in the suppression of undesirable immigration," Clarke argued. He alleged that England and other countries were deliberately sending their orphans and asylum inmates to Canada simply "to get rid of them." How these individuals made it past the port medical inspectors remained a mystery to Clarke.[50]

The widespread publication of Clarke's opinions coincided with an explosion of interest in immigration in the Canadian medical press. Although editorials occasionally defended the Immigration Branch, most criticized it and its work.[51] *Canada Lancet* quoted Clarke as saying: "Rudyard Kipling told us that Canada's greatest need was to be supplied by pumping in the population. Even those who are believers in his remedy

forwarded to Scott was Clarke's letter to Armstrong of 11 May 1907, PAC, RG 76, vol. 393, file 563236.

48. *Ottawa Free Press*, 8 April 1908. See also PAC, RG 76, vol. 393, file 563236, pt. 2.

49. C. K. Clarke, "The Defective and Insane Immigrant," *BOHI* 2 (1908): 3–22; also published in *University (Toronto) Monthly* 8 (1908): 273–78; "Canada and Defective Immigration," *AJI* 65 (1908): 186–88; and "Immigration of Defectives," *BOHI* 2 (1909): 47–50.

50. See, e.g., PAO, RG 63, A-6, box 697, case 8474; box 698, case 8530.

51. See, e.g., "Physically Unfit Immigrants," *Canada Lancet* 41 (1908): 944–45; "The Undesirable Immigrant," *Canadian Practitioner and Review* 33 (1908): 477–78; "Undesirable Immigrants," ibid. 35 (1910): 660–61; and "Why Is the Immigration Act not Enforced?" *Canadian Journal of Medicine and Surgery* 25 (1909): 251–53.

for ills, real or supposed, would, we feel certain, add to his alliterative phrase the suggestion that the supply should not be allowed to tap streams reeking with insanity, crime, and degeneracy."[52] Immigration Branch protests that its officers were simply doing their job and "were most willing to facilitate the operation of the [immigration] law" seemed to fall on deaf ears inside the Canadian medical community.[53]

In the neighboring province of Quebec many of the same complaints were being voiced, chiefly by Clarke's counterpart, Thomas Burgess.[54] The similarities between Clarke's and Burgess's views on immigration were understandable. First, Burgess was the godson of Joseph Workman and had served under him at the Toronto Asylum as an assistant physician in the 1870s. Burgess, like Clarke, regarded Workman as a giant among nineteenth-century psychiatrists and shared Workman's jaundiced views about the effects of politics on psychiatry. Second, Burgess's Verdun Protestant Asylum patient population was rising steadily. In the first ten years of the twentieth century it was to go from 354 to 610 patients, and reach 700 by 1916. Echoing other psychiatrists, Burgess blamed the congestion in his wards on immigration.[55] To him, as to Clarke, there were many foreign-born patients in Canadian asylums who could legitimately be said to have "broken down mentally after they had earned a residence" in the country. But the "proportion who should never have been brought to our shores" betokened the scandalous failure of the federal government to prevent Canada from becoming what Burgess called "a 'dumping ground' for the degenerates of Europe."[56] Burgess insisted that "all persons should be rigidly examined by liberally salaried medical officers appointed by the Dominion Government, before being allowed to embark, and should furnish proof that they have never been insane or epileptic, and that their parents have never been affected with such diseases."[57] Like Clarke, he believed that all too often non-

52. Editorial, "The Defective and Insane Immigrant," *Canada Lancet* 42 (1908): 61–62.
53. William Scott to Dr. Hoolahan, 26 December 1907, PAC, RG 76, vol. 393, file 563236, pt. 1.
54. Burgess was named president of the AMPA in 1905 and later collaborated with Blumer, Brush, Richard Dewey, and Henry Hurd on the publication in 1916–17 of a four-volume history of the institutional care of the insane in the United States and Canada. See Hurd, *Institutional Care of the Insane*.
55. Peter Keating, *La science du mal: L'institution de la psychiatrie au Québec, 1800–1914* (Montreal: Boréal, 1993), p. 132. See also Guy Grenier, "L'implantation et les applications de la doctrine de la dégénérescence dans le champ de la médecine et de l'hygiène mentale au Québec entre 1885 et 1930" (MA thesis, University of Montreal, 1990), pp. 128–30. For Burgess's history of Verdun's early years, see Hurd, *Institutional Care of the Insane*, 4:293–326.
56. T. J. W. Burgess, "Presidential Address: The Insane in Canada," *PAMPA* 12 (1905): 87–122, 105, 107.
57. Cited in Clarke, "Defective and Insane Immigrant," p. 19.

medical considerations shaped immigration policy. Even after the Immigration Law was amended in 1910 to extend the eligibility period for deportation from two to five years, Burgess told the AMPA: "I will say that in my own hospital to-day over one-third of my population are foreigners and ten per cent are of the Jewish race. We are crying out and for years past we have been crying out against the Immigration Department. The trouble is we have too much politics. Time and again I have reported patients for deportation; friends of the patients have a government pull and the government will not deport them."[58] Thus Burgess's perception of his role as a tireless medical warrior against corrupt political elements was highly congruent with Clarke's own self-image.

Burgess's interpretation of the immigration issue was colored by a fierce sense of Christian duty. To early twentieth-century reformers, Canada's immigration policy was based—inexplicably—on quantity rather than quality, on admitting as many immigrants as possible without any regard for the capacity of newcomers to adapt to their new country, its laws, customs, values, and institutions. "To welcome aliens simply because they can grow wheat and devour groceries is to give ourselves over to the grossest materialism," an affront to "the doctrine of Christ," one Canadian restrictionist had argued in 1900.[59] Burgess too believed that eugenic immigration restriction was an aspect of what another Quebec psychiatrist called "the noble cause of Social Welfare," which in turn was based on the Christian virtues of "charity" and "brotherhood."[60] The Christian duty of the psychiatrist lay in his or her willingness to fight to improve the medical conditions of hospitalized patients. The crowding of a psychiatrist's wards with "degenerate" immigrants—who by definition were immoral and disreputable—was not just an inconvenience, according to Burgess; it was a violation of God's will. Burgess was hardly unique in his disposition to couch mental health reform in terms of a Christian calling. Countless other Canadians—including a good

58. T. J. W. Burgess, "Discussion," *PAMPA* 19 (1912): 195.
59. J. R. Conn, "Immigration," *Queen's Quarterly* 8 (1900): 120–21.
60. A. H. Desloges, "Immigration," *Public Health Journal* 10 (1919): 1–5, 1–2. For Burgess's religious definition of the vocation of medicine, see T. J. W. Burgess, "Valedictory Address to the Graduates in Medicine at McGill University," *Montreal Medical Journal* 29 (1900): 400–401. As he told the McGill medical graduates, "The privilege of relieving suffering humanity, . . . of endeavoring to imitate the example of Him who went about doing good, is indeed reward above all monetary considerations. No more Christlike emblem can be found than the physician braving the dangers of pestilence in the wretched hovels of the poor, . . . without hope of earthly reward, but feeling amply recompensed in the conscientious discharge of his merciful calling. One day of such an opportunity to render service to God and man is worth a whole life spent in the acquisition of a science which confers such power upon its possessor."

many suffragists and women physicians—felt the same way.[61] Little wonder that he and other Canadian psychiatrists practically demonized the Immigration Branch.

The readiness of psychiatrists like Burgess and Clarke to publicize the shortcomings and question the moral motives of the Immigration Branch predictably irked William Scott and Peter Bryce. Scott had always advised that deportations be conducted with as little fanfare as possible. He resented people pointing out the mistakes made by medical inspectors and hinting that immigration officials were hostage to immigrant or business organizations.[62] But what seemed to poison relations fatally was Ontario's decision in 1908 to resort to its own deportations when it could secure the consent of the deportees and arrange for relatives and friends to support them when they arrived in their home countries. The problem was that this measure was a violation of the provisions of the Immigration Act.[63] Scott reacted by ordering Bryce to investigate Ontario's charges that the province's charity institutions were "overflowing with immigrants." Ontario officials maliciously denied Bryce access to the records. Scott then told Bryce to prepare his report anyway.[64]

Bryce's report, published in 1910, constituted the federal salvo in what had become an escalating bureaucratic war between Ottawa and Toronto. Unsurprisingly, Bryce concluded that medical inspection of immigrants was in fact highly efficient as reflected in the data regarding the statistical relationship between immigrants and disease. Bryce denied that immigrants made up a disproportionately large group in Ontario asylums, showing that their rate of admission actually declined relative to the rise in the number of immigrants among the general populations of Toronto and the province at large. Trying to disprove what he called "a too popular opinion," Bryce insisted that there was

61. Strong-Boag, "Canada's Women Doctors," pp. 219–20.
62. As Scott wrote, New York State experience had "shown that the speculative lawyer may by Habeus Corpus proceedings give a great deal of trouble before the case has been gotten out of the country." Scott to Thomas Southworth, 7 November 1906, PAC, RG 76, vol. 393, file 563236, pt. 1. The bad feelings between Clarke and Scott were still alive in 1919 when Scott challenged Clarke to reveal the names of the immigrant organizations alleged to have brought in defective children under the guise of philanthropy. Clarke never did divulge this information or release the relevant files into Ottawa's hands. See McConnachie, "Science and Ideology," pp. 100–102.
63. As the Ottawa *Free Press* reported on 30 December 1908, one of the deportees had been in Canada for twenty-one years, and her deportation epitomized "the height of cruelty."
64. The documents relating to this battle between Ottawa and Ontario's Queen's Park are in PAC, RG 76, vol. 537, file 803777. See esp. Bryce to Scott, 15 January 1909, where Bryce recounts his difficulties with Armstrong, who allegedly told him Ottawa's immigration policy was "infernal."

"a remarkable freedom from disease in the immigrants arriving in Canada." Indeed he defied much professional opinion in U.S.-Canadian psychiatry by arguing that there was a "notable absence of mental defectives amongst the peoples from southern countries," that is, peoples not from Great Britain, Northern Europe, and the United States.[65] The difference between his 1910 opinions and those he expressed in 1904 on becoming the Immigration Branch's chief medical officer could not have been greater.

Bryce probably overestimated the competence of Canada's medical inspectors. Immigrants were supposedly examined at their port of departure by the ships' doctors, but Immigration Branch officials understandably took a dim view of their credentials and honesty. Too, accounts consistently stressed the hurried nature of the process once immigrants arrived in Canada—what Clarke called "the gigantic task of inspecting a large number of people in a short time."[66] The steamship companies liked to time their ships' landings for late in the day so the medical inspectors would be too harried to do a thorough examination of the disembarking hordes.[67] Typically physicians had to inspect two or three hundred immigrants an hour once the ships landed. As one physician described the ordeal in 1912, in a matter of seconds the medical inspector "beg[an] at the alien's feet, when he [was] about ten feet away and marching toward the examiner, and end[ed] by the turning of the eyelids, exposing the superior cul-de-sac and the examination of his scalp."[68] Nighttime inspections were particularly difficult. Without adequate light it was hard to detect the hue of the immigrant's skin or perform an eye examination, and it was almost impossible to determine the mental state of children dull from sleepiness. Even the Binet-Simon intelligence tests in use starting in 1920 were frequently inexact; many who were rejected were later found to have normal intelligence and vice versa.[69] The medical training of the inspectors left much to be desired, according to psychiatrist J. D. Pagé, who told Bryce: "you have not in the whole service a single man advanced enough in nervous disorders"

65. P. H. Bryce, "Report of the Chief Medical Officer," *Sessional Papers of Canada* 44, no. 25, (1910): 99–110, 108, 110.
66. Clarke, "Defective and Insane Immigrant," p. 21.
67. J. D. Pagé, "Medical Aspects of Immigration," *Public Health Journal* 19 (1928): 366–73, 367.
68. Charles A. Bailey, "The Medical Inspection of Immigrants," *Public Health Journal* 3 (1912): 433–39, 435. See also Bryce, "Medical Inspection of Immigrants," p. 127.
69. Janice Dickin McGinnis, "From Health to Welfare: Federal Government Policies regarding Standards of Public Health for Canadians, 1918–1945" (Ph.D. diss., University of Alberta, 1980), pp. 50–51.

with the knowledge to answer the questions on the form required for each insane immigrant's medical report.[70]

Nonetheless, Bryce's data showed that no matter how inefficient the system, there was no reason for grave alarm. To Bryce, Clarke's views were based on little more than impressionistic and anecdotal evidence.[71] Probably Bryce's and Clarke's opinions had diverged so sharply because Bryce had come to believe that the 1906 Immigration Act had addressed the major faults of the medical inspection system. But also at issue was the question of bureaucratic partisanship. Once the conflict between Ottawa and Ontario had come to a head, Bryce found himself in the position of having to defend the Immigration Branch, and defend it he did. In the process he not only severed relations with his old friend Clarke but shed much-needed light on a debate increasingly monopolized by restrictionist physicians.

The results of this showdown, coming just when Clarke saw his dream of a psychiatric institute fading, strengthened his belief that he could trust hardly anyone. Indeed the timing of the immigration and the psychiatric institute controversies is suggestive. Clarke had not limited his criticisms to the Immigration Branch. As he undiplomatically wrote Armstrong in 1907, "I am surprised and distressed to find that your Department does not seem to wake up to its responsibilities in connection with these deportations."[72] Not for the last time in his career, Clarke's blunt, lecturing style cost him friends and allies and probably alienated some of his most ardent supporters at Queen's Park. This did little to help his campaigns for a psychiatric institute and immigration reform.

In Clarke's opinion, he had been deserted by former friends and psychiatric colleagues. His reaction was to withdraw abruptly from the public debate over immigration after 1909. With his acceptance of the post of medical superintendent of the TGH and his departure from the ranks of provincial psychiatry in 1911, after more than thirty years of public service, Clarke set his sights on achieving his aim of practicing curative psychiatry by other means. Only when fresh obstacles to the realization of this goal arose in later years did his attention shift

70. J. D. Pagé to Bryce, 29 July 1914, PAC, RG 76, vol. 376, file 518766.
71. Bryce was probably correct when, in a direct reference to Clarke himself, he patronizingly wrote, in 1910, "It is perhaps natural that [the writer of the Report for 1907 of the Toronto Hospital for the Insane] should draw general conclusions from the results of his own individual experience." Peter Bryce, "Notes on Admissions to Asylums of Ontario 1900 to May 1908 Based on Returns Supplied Directly from Asylum Reports," 22 January 1910, PAC, RG 76, vol. 537, file 803777, p. 7.
72. Clarke to Armstrong, 11 May 1907, PAC, RG 76, vol. 393, file 563236 A.1.

back to the immigration question, underlining once again the links between professional disappointment and psychiatric enthusiasm for eugenic measures.

III

The provincial government's decision not to erect a psychiatric institute left Clarke crestfallen but not defeated. Even before he left the provincial mental health care system in 1911 he had resolved to establish a psychiatric clinic on his own. In December 1909 he had set up Canada's first outpatient clinic devoted to the early detection and treatment of mental illness. Housed in a small building on the TGH grounds close to the city core, the new clinic was intended to attract individuals and families reluctant to seek medical help at an asylum. The purpose of the clinic was to treat people with early signs of mental and nervous disease before their conditions worsened. These patients, Clarke hoped, would be easier to deal with and more socially reputable than the population at the Toronto Asylum. The reality proved somewhat different: poor people formed the clinic's main clientele.[73]

To staff his new clinic Clarke had offered the post of medical director to Ernest Jones, Sigmund Freud's disciple. From 1908 to 1913, Jones held part-time posts as a pathologist at Clarke's Toronto Asylum and as an associate professor of psychiatry at the University of Toronto. These were five years of controversy and conflict for Jones, who frequently complained about the resistance to psychoanalysis in Toronto and throughout its medical community. Jones quickly became a pariah in Toronto, and his departure in May 1913 with his live-in mistress was largely unmourned by the city's physicians and respectable citizens.[74]

Whereas Clarke himself attended seventy-four times during the ten months after the clinic opened in December 1909, Jones never performed any clinical work there.[75] He was extremely busy with his other posts as well as his proselytizing for psychoanalysis. Surprisingly, he held Clarke, who had little sympathy for psychoanalysis, in high regard, and Clarke

---

73. C. K. Clarke, "A Clinic for Nervous and Mental Diseases," *BOHI* 4 (1911): 73–77.
74. Thomas E. Brown, "Dr. Ernest Jones, Psychoanalysis, and the Canadian Medical Profession, 1908–1913," in Shortt, *Medicine in Canadian Society*, pp. 315–60, 353.
75. One reason Jones felt little interest in the clinic may have been the shortage of equipment and lack of furnishings. Even Clarke admitted "there was no quiet room available and not even an examining couch." John D. Griffin, "Ernest Jones: Director of Canada's First Psychiatric Clinic," QSMHC, Unpublished MSS, 1994. Cited with permission from the author. See also Clarke, "Clinic for Nervous and Mental Diseases," p. 76.

reciprocated.[76] These two intellectually dissimilar characters were able to work together because of a common self-perception: each saw himself as someone swimming against the tide of human ignorance, prejudice, inertia, and self-interest in a battle to improve both the understanding and the treatment of emotional disorders.

In the event, Clarke's clinic closed in 1913 with the rebuilding of the TGH. The next year he reopened it as a department of the new hospital. The new clinic was part of a significant re-organization and reconstruction, a project that included Clarke's own appointment as TGH medical superintendent in 1911.[77] One of Clarke's less admirable reforms at the TGH was his decision to close down its "nervous ward" run by D. Campbell Meyers, a neurologist who treated patients suffering from the "functional neuroses"—hysteria, neurasthenia, and obsessional disorders. Clarke's termination of Meyers's ward showed that, his eagerness to improve the quality of care for the mentally ill notwithstanding, professional motives weighed heavily, sometimes to the point of compromising his laudable mission. Meyers, a product of the growing specialization occurring in late nineteenth-century hospital practice, had in 1906 opened Canada's first psychiatric general hospital unit. Once Clarke had begun campaigning for a psychiatric institute administratively separate from general hospitals, he and Meyers had become mortal enemies. Foreseeing that Clarke's Kraepelinian agenda would mean the closure of his TGH ward, Meyers had argued with justification that treating patients suffering from the "functional neuroses" on the same ward as those suffering from psychotic diseases would be a big mistake. The two categories of patients

76. For Clarke's hostile views on psychoanalysis, see Brown, "Dr. Ernest Jones," pp. 334–35. Jones called Clarke his "protector" in a 1911 letter to Freud and traced Clarke's resignation from the Toronto Asylum to "the unfavourable conditions in the [provincial] service." Jones to Freud, 22 May 1911, in R. Andrew Paskauskas, ed., *The Complete Correspondence of Sigmund Freud and Ernest Jones, 1908–1939* (Cambridge: Harvard University Press, 1993), p. 104. Jones later recalled Clarke "as a man of parts, an excellent Canadian type. He was a very kind and humane person. . . . He possessed little scientific knowledge, but his heart was set right in this respect and his ambition was to develop it in his sphere to the best of his abilities." Ernest Jones, *Free Associations: Memories of a Psycho-Analyst* (New York: Basic Books, 1959), p. 178. In 1915, in an obvious allusion to Jones, Clarke talked about "one of my assistants who would have been an ornament to Psychiatry and who had before him the most brilliant possibilities. He understood how thoroughly collaboration between the clinical and laboratory sides of Psychiatry should be if any advance is to be made, and yet when he stood up for his ideals was bitterly condemned." Jones, Clarke believed, like other public hospital psychiatrists, left the Ontario provincial service "simply because they could not conscientiously exist under conditions forced upon them by the laymen who, while honest and conscientious, but without scientific knowledge, yet, to a great extent, control the policy of Hospitals for the Insane." C. K. Clarke, "The Need of a Psychiatric Clinic," *BOHI* 8 (1915): 103–8.
77. For Clarke's own optimism and enthusiasm about the new TGH, see his *A History of the Toronto General Hospital* (Toronto: William Briggs, 1913), esp. pp. 117–37.

should be kept separate, not mixed together in the same ward as called for in Clarke's clinic.[78] In what quickly became a territorial struggle between neurology and psychiatry for therapeutic responsibility for marginally disturbed patients, Clarke won. In the process he terminated something that already did much of what he wanted to accomplish with his psychiatric clinic, but that mattered little to him. The end of the "nervous ward" left him free to inaugurate his own clinic for the early treatment of nervous and mentally ill persons and to lay claim to a clientele of relatively desirable patients formerly monopolized by Meyers.[79]

Thus Clarke had by 1914 managed to reverse some of the defeats he had sustained in the provincial service. He was the medical superintendent of a recently rebuilt modern general hospital with a mandate to improve both the diagnosis and treatment of mental illness and the formal education of clinical psychiatrists. In many respects he had achieved what he had hoped to accomplish when he went to Toronto in 1905. He had his psychiatric institute independent of general hospitals. He soon discovered, though, that his tantalizing dream of reforming psychiatry was as elusive as ever, a realization that would lead him to launch a new offensive against those in charge of Canada's immigration policy.

In 1916, when he broke his silence on immigration, something besides that was clearly worrying him. After all, it was during his silence that the annual rate of newcomers was peaking, increasing from 173,694 in 1909 to 400,870 in 1913. Then, the beginning of the war had slowed immigration to a trickle. These facts did not keep him from declaring in 1916 that his earlier warnings about immigration were as germane as ever:

A few years ago I was foolhardy enough to write a series of articles on the Defective and Insane Immigrant, and soon found myself in the centre of an unpleasant controversy, as the facts and figures presented did not appeal to practical politicians who were anxious to cultivate the vote of the new immigrant who had recently arrived. That was not a new experience, as the

78. See Campbell Meyers, "Some Notes on the Functional Neuroses," CKCA, Campbell Meyers Papers, Va.14.
79. Robert Pos, J. Allan Walters, and Frank G. Sommers, "D. Campbell Meyers, M.D., 1863–1927: Pioneer of Canadian Hospital Psychiatry," *Canadian Psychiatric Association Journal* 20 (1975): 393–402. See also Brown, " 'Living With God's Afflicted,' " p. 370. J. D. Griffin has referred to the "classical Clarke-ian position of 'no psychiatric units in general hospital.' " J. D. Griffin to Robert Pos, 23 July 1974, QSMHC, Robert Pos Collection. According to Griffin, who heard the story from Clare Hincks, Clarke's 1914 clinic was unpopular with the TGH medical staff, making it all the easier for Clarke to affiliate it with Toronto's social services. Interview with J. D. Griffin, 17 May 1996.

average politician is generally apt to consider the advantage of the moment, rather than the future welfare of the community.[80]

Plainly Clarke was responding to the mounting concern in Canada for how casualty rates might impair reproductive fitness after the war, especially if, as he expected, Europe dumped its diseased classes on Canadian soil. To him medical inspection was the key to meeting Canada's dysgenic war crisis and the eugenic problems of a postwar world.[81]

But the main reason he defended the restrictionist position for the first time since 1909 was probably the 1914 opening of his new clinic and the way that had caused his attention to shift decisively to the question of feeblemindedness. Clarke's previous clinical experience with mental disorders had been confined to the mainly psychotic and severely disabled patients at the Kingston and Toronto asylums. In 1914, however, he and his staff had encountered a category of men, women, and children whose mental and behavioral symptoms were often less conspicuous than those of insane asylum patients. He claimed to have become aware of these so-called feebleminded defectives because the Toronto schools, Juvenile Court, Public Health Department, and various social agencies referred cases to him at the TGH for psychiatric examination. In his own words, these persons were "not easily detected except by those who are familiar and experienced in psychiatric and psychological methods." This, he asserted, made them dangerous; for they often roamed the streets and provided the material out of which criminals, prostitutes, juvenile delinquents, and dependent single mothers were created. Not only were the feebleminded antisocial but they "invariably" mated with "mental weaklings of their own class as partners, thus perpetuating the race of defectives." The crux of the problem to him was that many of these

80. C. K. Clarke, "The Defective Immigrant," *Public Health Journal* 7 (1916): 462–65.

81. For the Canadian debate over the war's dysgenic impact, see McConnachie, "Science and Ideology," pp. 23–24. Although there is no evidence that he had anything to do with an abortive private member's sterilization bill introduced in the Ontario legislature in 1912, Clarke may have decided that its withdrawal in response to public opinion meant that the segregation of the mentally unfit and immigration regulation through medical inspection were the only eugenic measures with any chance of public or official approval for the time being. See also McLaren, *Our Own Master Race*, pp. 42–43. This consideration probably accounts for the fact that pre-war medical opinion in Canada was, at most, divided over sterilization. As the noted Canadian J. S. Woodsworth said in 1916: "Sterilization has been proposed. But general sentiment is so strong against such a radical measure that its adoption is not practicable." Winnipeg *Free Press*, 15 November 1916, p. 11. Cited in McLaren, ibid., p. 43. See also Robert R. Rentoul, "Proposed Sterilization of Certain Degenerate States," *Canadian Practitioner and Review* 35 (1910): 569–76 (Rentoul was a British physician); J. P. Downey, "Heredity as a Cause of Mental Defectiveness," *BOHI* 6 (1912): 25–33; Editorial, "Eugenics," *Canada Lancet* 47 (1913): 2–3; and L. R. Yealland, "Heredity vs. Asexualization," *BOHI* 7 (1914): 256–62.

chronic, "incorrigible" defectives were immigrants who should have been weeded out at Canadian or foreign ports or deported.[82] Thus, despite promising developments between 1911 and 1915, Clarke's occupational position had reverted in certain respects to that of his years in the provincial public service. Once again it appeared as if defective immigrants were preventing him from making psychiatry a curative form of medicine. For a second time, he concluded, cynical politicians and indifferent civil servants were subverting his attempt to place psychiatry on a more efficacious and reputable footing.

Clarke's interest in the feebleminded was right in step with the broader movement sweeping North America as the eugenic campaign gained momentum. Largely because of the growing use of intelligence tests and the influx of youngsters into the public schools thanks to compulsory attendance laws, more and more officials were becoming alarmed at what they perceived as rising numbers of defective or retarded children. They insisted that after the task of diagnosing the feebleminded was accomplished, there were only two practical ways of dealing with these persons: institutional segregation or sterilization.

Helen MacMurchy (1862–1940) probably did more than anyone to try to convince Canadians that the feebleminded were a menace. She had a long and eventful life, which included a brief but passionate love affair in 1909 with the British birth control activist Marie Stopes, then half MacMurchy's age. Although not among the pathbreaking wave of Canadian women to gain admission to medical school, MacMurchy was one of the first to carve a highly successful career for herself in a profession generally unreceptive to female physicians. Indeed few Canadians had a more distinguished and influential career in public health. Educated at Women's Medical College and the University of Toronto, where she received her M.D. degree in 1901, she was the first woman accepted to the Johns Hopkins University for postgraduate study in medicine and the first woman appointed to the resident staff of the TGH's Department of Obstetrics and Gynaecology, with a cross-appointment as lecturer at the University of Toronto. After briefly trying private practice she switched to public service. From 1906 to 1916 she prepared annual re-

82. C. K. Clarke, "A Study of 5600 Cases Passing through the Psychiatric Clinic of the Toronto General Hospital," *CJMH* 3 (1921–22): 11–24, 16; "The Work of the Psychiatric Clinic of the Toronto General Hospital," *The Public Health Journal* 9 (1918): 97–98; and "The Story of the Toronto General Hospital Psychiatric Clinic," *CJMH* 1 (1919): 30–37. See also Jennifer Stephen, "The 'Incorrigible,' the 'Bad,' and the 'Immoral': Toronto's 'Factory Girls' and the Work of the Toronto Psychiatric Clinic," in *Law, Society, and the State: Essays in Modern Legal History*, ed. Louis A. Knafla and Susan W. S. Binnie (Toronto: University of Toronto Press, 1995), pp. 405–39.

Helen MacMurchy. Courtesy of the Canadian Museum of Health and Medicine at The Toronto Hospital, Canada.

ports on the feebleminded for the Ontario government. In 1915, one year after she officially became Ontario inspector of the feebleminded, she obtained the post of inspector of special education classes for Ontario's Department of Education. From 1920 to 1934 she worked for the federal government's newly created Department of Health.[83] Per-

83. Kathleen Janet McConnachie, "Methodology in the Study of Women in History: A Case Study of Helen MacMurchy," *Ontario History* 75 (1983): 61–70. See also McLaren, *Our Own Master Race*, pp. 28–45; and Comacchio, *"Nations Are Built of Babies,"* pp. 19, 70–71, 73–74,

haps no physician played a larger role in the history of Canadian eugenics.[84]

MacMurchy was a good example of the early twentieth-century reformers who combined in a single career pioneering efforts on behalf of women, profoundly sincere interests in improving the mental and physical health of disadvantaged Canadians, and an equally passionate advocacy of punitive state policies such as sterilization and immigration restriction. Like eugenic physicians in the United States, she believed that feebleminded women had much higher birthrates. As early as 1908 she argued that although segregation of the mentally handicapped would ultimately eliminate most of these persons, the quickest and most cost-effective way to solve the problem was sterilization.[85] Despite the retractions of U.S. physicians such as Henry Goddard and Walter Fernald by the 1920s, MacMurchy clung tenaciously to her views about the fecundity and sexual promiscuity of the feebleminded. She forged close ties with the National Council of Women, which under the medical leadership of Dr. Elizabeth Smith Shortt endorsed sterilization, segregation, and immigration restriction as weapons in the fight against "the rapid increase of the feebleminded" until the late 1920s.[86] MacMurchy crowned her career at retirement in 1934 with the publication of a book urging sterilization as the latest in a series of modern measures provided by medical science to reduce the number of unfit babies. She rejected birth control as a means of regulating reproduction, calling it "unnatural" and "contrary to one's higher instincts." What needed to be addressed, according to her, was "the burden of the good citizen"—the costs of supporting the children of Canada's mental defectives. These "troublers" were not numerous, she stated—barely ten out of every thousand—but their offspring were "increasing much faster than the progeny of the nine hun-

---

76–78, 82–83, 95–96, 120–21, 149, 162, 170. Harvey G. Simmons, *From Asylum to Welfare* (Downsview, Ont.: National Institute on Mental Retardation, 1982), pp. 67–71. For the experiences of earlier women doctors in Canada, see Strong-Boag, "Canada's Women Doctors," pp. 109–29.

84. MacMurchy may have been even more influential as a eugenicist than Clarke, who was on record as opposed to gynecologic surgery for women patients. See C. K. Clarke to Robert Christie, 1 February 1899, PAO, Correspondence of the Inspector of Prisons and Public Charities, RG 10, 2–A-1. Cited in S. E. D. Shortt, *Victorian Lunacy: Richard M. Bucke and the Practice of Late Nineteenth-Century Psychiatry* (Cambridge: Cambridge University Press, 1986), p. 154. See also C. K. Clarke, "Insanity and Surgical Operations," *Albany Medical Annals* 20 (1899): 1–6. Clarke argued that for those patients at Kingston's asylum who submitted to pelvic surgery, "the effect on the mental condition [is] generally disappointing and in some instances harmful" (p. 1).

85. Helen MacMurchy, *The Feebleminded in Ontario: Second Report* (Toronto: Provincial Secretary, 1908), p. 15. Cited in McLaren, *Our Own Master Race*, p. 42.

86. NCW, *Yearbook*, 1926, pp. 74–76. See also McConnachie, "Science and Ideology," p. 217.

dred and ninety good and capable citizens."[87] MacMurchy hastened to say that sterilization should be performed only on those institutionalized patients who could be discharged into the community. She also advised that sterilization laws should not contain any "element of compulsion." But she endorsed the province of Alberta's sterilization legislation of 1928 even though it authorized involuntary sterilization of defectives with the consent of a guardian and the recommendation of a eugenics board.[88] Thus MacMurchy remained a convert to the sterilization cause and most medical theories about the feebleminded long after they had been shown to be groundless.

But for MacMurchy, sterilization was only one component of a much more ambitious public health reform program. She came to eugenics through her consuming concern about the health and welfare of the "race," an interest that also dovetailed with her studies of infant and maternal mortality. She was fairly representative of early twentieth-century Canadian women who entered public life either individually or through organizations such as the NCW. Unmarried and childless herself, she was convinced, like many other activist and reformist Canadian women of her time, that most social ills could be traced to mothers' ignorance of elementary rules of diet, nutrition, sanitation, reproduction, and personal cleanliness. As one Canadian suffragist argued in 1912, Canada would pay a severe price if it left alcoholic mothers "free to fill cradles with degenerate babies."[89] MacMurchy's own solution was simple: strict reliance on medical advice and the technical intervention of licensed doctors. Like Clarke she fully expected to be heeded when she devoted her considerable energies to the study of a specific social problem.[90] She most likely also shared with him a self-image as an inspired and enlightened outsider fated to combat entrenched interests. As a woman struggling to succeed professionally and be taken seriously as an medical expert, MacMurchy felt even more alienated and ostracized than Clarke. He himself was no freethinker when it came to issues of sex, class, or race, but the similarities between his and MacMurchy's careers could hardly have escaped his attention.

87. Helen MacMurchy, *Sterilization? Birth Control? A Book for Family Welfare and Safety* (Toronto: Macmillan, 1934), p. 5.
88. MacMurchy, *Sterilization?* pp. 79–84. In 1937 the Alberta government removed the consent provision from the 1928 Act. McLaren, *Our Own Master Race*, p. 100. According to Kathleen McConnachie, MacMurchy's prosterilization thinking was "atypical" by the late 1920s. McConnachie, "Science and Ideology," p. 224.
89. NCW, *Annual Report*, 1912, p. 29. Cited in Bacchi, "Race Regeneration and Social Purity," p. 464.
90. McLaren, *Our Own Master Race*, pp. 34–35.

Naturally, then, the two physicians joined forces from 1914 to 1920 to campaign for improved and expanded facilities for the mentally retarded. MacMurchy won Clarke's collaboration in the campaign to secure provincial funding for classes for backward children; a register for all mental defectives in Toronto; and a new custodial, farmlike institution for mentally handicapped children. Clarke credited MacMurchy with the idea of "resurrect[ing]" his psychiatric clinic that had closed down in 1913.[91] Her efforts also paved the way for the formation in 1912 of the Provincial Association for the Care of the Feebleminded (PACFM), an Ontario organization whose president Clarke was later to become. As a leading member, Clarke reencountered the political forces that had disappointed him seven years earlier. In trying to convince the provincial secretary that Ontario needed a major new facility for the feebleminded to augment the existing institution at Orillia, Clarke and MacMurchy rarely gave the same estimates of the percentage of the population that was mentally subnormal. Provincial government officials knew this. More important, they feared the political repercussions of the tax rate hike required to pay for the open-ended commitment PACFM desired. This governmental hesitation drew a predictable response from Clarke, by now a feisty PACFM crusader. When a motion condemning the Conservative government policy governing the feebleminded was defeated, he wrote in his inimitably candid style to the leader of the Liberal opposition in 1916:

> The whole thing is most amusing and shows the curse of political control in public institutions. It seems to me that you have remarkable texts from which to preach your sermon, as no better illustration of the absurdity of our present system could be furnished than that of Mr. Downey and his institution for the feebleminded at Orillia. No one objects particularly to Mr. Downey, but his reign at Orillia has been little better than a joke. He is ignorant of his subject, is utterly opposed to all scientific advancement, and his institution does not offer one thing better than simple custodial care of a number of idiots and imbeciles. He does not even attempt to reach the class in which we are particularly interested; that is, the class which is such a menace to the community—namely, the high-grade imbecile.[92]

But there were reasons for renewed hope just as Clarke penned this blunt letter. That year the Conservative provincial government appointed its

91. Clarke, "Toronto General Hospital Psychiatric Clinic," p. 30.
92. Clarke to N. W. Rowell, 27 April 1916, CKCA, Ik.6.

one-man Royal Commission on the Care and Control of the Mentally Defective and Feebleminded in Ontario. But by the time he commission's report appeared in 1919, the economic climate had changed. Financial constraints compelled the government to ignore most of its recommendations, including the crucial one that a new custodial provincial institution for the feebleminded be erected.[93] The next year MacMurchy left for Ottawa, and her post of inspector of the feebleminded was abolished, bringing an end to an era of concerted provincial activism.[94] Simultaneously Ontario eugenicists were dealt another serious blow. The provincial government's refusal to build an up-to-date institution for the feebleminded meant that custodial segregation could not be relied upon to prevent the reproduction of the supposedly unfit. That set the stage for a new offensive in favor of medical inspection of immigrants, engineered by Clarke and his allies, to be followed in turn by a campaign in the post-Clarke era to introduce legislation calling for the sterilization of the mentally deficient.

IV

With the demise of PACFM becoming steadily more likely, Ontario mental health care reformers banded together in 1918 to form the Canadian National Committee for Mental Hygiene.[95] In one sense, the CNCMH was simply PACFM under another name. Of the thirty-seven Toronto members of the CNCMH in 1920, seventeen had been PACFM members, including Clarke, who was named the CNCMH's first medical director.[96] Mainly because of his stature and clout in the mental health reform movement, the CNCMH devoted much of its resources and energy up until his death in 1924 to the immigration issue. Like PACFM, the CNCMH also lobbied for reform of mental retardation policy, but what it said and did about that issue while Clarke was alive was tied

---

93. Ontario Legislative Assembly, *Report on the Care and Control of the Mentally Defective and Feebleminded in Ontario by the Honorable Frank Egerton Hodgins* (Toronto: King's Printer, 1919). See also "The Mentally Deficient in Ontario: Mr. Justice Hodgins' Recommendations," *Public Health Journal* 11 (1920): 126–34.

94. Simmons, *From Asylum to Welfare*, pp. 65–109.

95. McConnachie, "Science and Ideology"; Theresa R. Richardson, *The Century of the Child: The Mental Hygiene Movement and Social Policy in the United States and Canada* (Albany: State University of New York Press, 1989), pp. 59–74; Sutherland, *Children in English-Canadian Society*, pp. 71–78. See also David MacLennan, "Beyond the Asylum: Professionalization and the Mental Hygiene Movement in Canada, 1914–1928," *Canadian Bulletin of Medical History* 4 (1987): 7–23.

96. Simmons, *From Asylum to Welfare*, p. 100.

Clarence Hincks. Courtesy of the American
Psychiatric Association.

consistently and concretely to medical inspection of immigrants. Only
after his death did the CNCMH's principal point of eugenic interest
became sterilization, testimony to Clarke's powerful impact on the committee in its fledgling stage.

Although Clarke's role in the early years was significant, the organization really owed its origins to Clarence Hincks (1885–1964), a young
Canadian psychiatrist and Clarke's clinical assistant. Hincks, who became
CNCMH general director in 1924, was the only child of a schoolteacher
mother and a clergyman father fourteen years younger than his wife.
They proceeded, in Hincks's own words, to "spoil" their only son "utterly," an experience, he wrote in his autobiography, that gave him "a
feeling of absolute confidence and security." At an early age Hincks discovered he was an expert at "promotion and the selling of things," which
came in handy for the CNCMH in later years.[97]

As a psychiatrist Hincks was neither a superb nor a well-trained cli-
nician, but he was an exceptionally hard and inspired worker. Intellec-

97. C. M. Hincks, "Prospecting for Mental Health: The Autobiography of Clare Hincks,"
QSMHC, Unpublished MSS, 1962, pp. 1–4.

tually he was interested in almost every new idea he encountered during his career, including psychoanalysis, but he saved his loyalty for just one cause: mental hygiene and, through it, the prevention of psychological illness. Hincks was ready to support any theory or measure as long as he thought it could advance mental hygiene. He also was a very good fund-raiser, which made him an enormous asset.[98] It was probably no coincidence that Hincks and Clifford Beers, the founder of the NCMH (1909), suffered from emotional problems. Beers attempted suicide and was hospitalized as a mental patient; Hincks had his first nervous breakdown in college at the age of sixteen and had similar bouts of depression until his retirement in 1959. Both oscillated in life between depression and bursts of "sometimes frenzied" energy.[99] They met for the first time in 1917 and after that worked closely together. Their collaboration included Hincks's stint as general director of the NCMH from 1930 to 1938.[100]

Like so many who joined the mental hygiene movement, Hincks had fared poorly in private practice after graduating in 1907. He drifted into psychiatry after being named district medical inspector for schools in West Toronto. Faced with a large number of students with behavioral, emotional, and learning problems, he became interested in intelligence testing and in 1913–14 was the first to use the Binet-Simon tests in Canada. On MacMurchy's suggestion, he went "for a chat" with Clarke, to see if he could find further work along those lines. It just so happened that his visit occurred on the eve of the opening of Clarke's clinic. Clarke was impressed with Hincks and invited him to become part of the clinic's team. Hincks accepted and quickly developed a profound respect for the older psychiatrist. In his autobiography he called Clarke "my father in psychiatry" and made no effort to conceal his admiration for Clarke's medical expertise and clinical intuition.[101]

98. Charles G. Roland, *Clarence Hincks: Mental Health Crusader* (Toronto: Hannah Institute for the History of Medicine and Dundurn, 1990), pp. 9, 90–92.

99. John D. Griffin, "The Amazing Careers of Hincks and Beers," *Canadian Journal of Psychiatry* 27 (1982): 668–71, 668. For the life and career of Beers, see Norman Dain, *Clifford W. Beers: Advocate for the Insane* (Pittsburgh: University of Pittsburgh Press, 1980). According to Hincks, his "attacks" were due to a neurosis, not a psychosis, a mental condition that proved to be his "greatest asset in life—opening up an intriguing world of adventure and human service." Hincks, "Prospecting for Mental Health," pp. 12–14.

100. Hincks continued part-time as CNCMH general director while serving the NCMH. In 1913, Hincks and Beers had actually attended the same conference on mental health in Buffalo. Hincks covered the conference for the *Toronto Star*, and in its 26 August 1913 issue he mentioned Beers. But in his autobiography Hincks claimed never to have heard of Beers before 1917. Roland, *Clarence Hincks*, p. 31.

101. See John D. Griffin, *In Search of Sanity: A Chronicle of the Canadian Mental Health Association* (London, Ont.: Third Eye, 1989). For Hincks's memories of Clarke, see Hincks, "Prospecting for Mental Health," pp. 27–29, 39–40, 49–50.

After just two years at Clarke's clinic, Hincks was "restless" and bored. In 1917 he asked Clarke:

What are we doing to re-organize our asylums that in many instances are a disgrace to our civilization? What are we doing to stimulate adequate facilities for mental defectives? What are we doing to stimulate the mental hygiene training of physicians, nurses, social workers and other groups throughout Canada? What are we doing to provide psychiatric screening for the thousands of immigrants who are flowing into this country? What are we doing to secure the partnership of our people and of governments in providing adequate facilities in our field and in promoting necessary research?

Hincks told Clarke that he wanted "to pioneer a new deal for the insane and mental defectives throughout Canada." He promptly set off on a fact-finding mission to the United States to talk to Beers and other mental hygienists. This trip "turned out to be a major milestone in my professional life," he later wrote; for he returned to Canada committed to forming the Canadian equivalent of the NCMH.[102]

After his return in early 1918, Hincks almost single-handedly gathered together a group of potential donors and members, arranged to have Beers speak to them in Toronto, and later that year launched the CNCMH. Once the committee was formed, Hincks and Clarke swung into action. Fund raising was an immediate concern, though it was made easier by the fact that in the postwar period the CNCMH was to enjoy the support of many of Canada's social, economic, professional, and academic elite. The committee also targeted government as a source of financial support. The overall goal was to forge a powerful and cohesive organization capable of working with government and voluntary agencies to improve public mental health.

Like the NCMH, the CNCMH was organized around the belief that the existing resources for treating mental illness were inadequate; that mental disease and feeblemindedness were much more serious and widespread than most Canadians imagined; and that through the scientific study of emotional and cognitive disorders physicians could learn how to prevent and treat these conditions. One of the first tasks for the CNCMH, mental hygienists argued, was to conduct surveys, featuring diagnostic testing and examinations, to determine the exact extent of mental defectiveness and the full range of intelligence, particularly

102. Hincks, "Prospecting for Mental Health," p. 29.

among the young in schools and custodial institutions. At the same time, psychiatrists and psychologists drawn to the organization saw it as a vehicle for improving training for experts in public mental health and upgrading the quality of professional teaching in universities.[103] Perhaps the biggest attraction to psychiatrists was that the committee and its vision of mental hygiene offered an escape route into society for physicians laboring in public mental hospitals. In Clarke's words, "The psychiatrist of the future," imbued with the spirit of mental hygiene, would no longer be confined necessarily to institutions; instead he or she would be "found in everyday life, ready to apply the ounce of prevention in preference to the pound of cure."[104]

The attention that war-related psychiatric issues such as shell shock received between 1914 and 1918 probably made Canadians more receptive to an organization such as the CNCMH. As Hincks noted in 1921, the well-publicized psychiatric case load in the Canadian army during the First World War had compelled "Canadians . . . to realize that mental disabilities are prevalent [throughout the country], and as much in need of skilled attention as physical diseases."[105] Thus, whereas some U.S. mental hygienists drew the conclusion from shell-shock studies that psychological disorders were fugacious and could be acquired easily and independently of inherited predisposition, Clarke, Hincks, and the CNCMH argued the opposite: that the rate of psychiatric war casualties indicated that hereditary weakness had infected even the most robust of Canadian men. The data from their school surveys, completed in the postwar period, appeared to confirm their allegations. All too often, they complained, they discovered a high percentage of immigrant children among the youngsters they diagnosed as delinquent, immoral, or subnormal. To Clarke, all psychiatric issues seemed to come back to the problem of immigration. With the formation of the CNCMH, he now saw another opportunity for striking at the immigration roots of the nation's eugenic crisis.

Thanks chiefly to Clarke, in the years immediately after the cessation

103. Richardson, *Century of the Child*, pp. 59–74; Griffin, *In Search of Sanity*, pp. 78–79.
104. C. K. Clarke, "The Fourth Maudsley Lecture," *Journal of Mental Science* 69 (1923): 279–96, 296.
105. C. M. Hincks, "Recent Progress of the Mental Hygiene Movement in Canada," *Canadian Medical Association Journal* 11 (1921): 823. Cited in Thomas E. Brown, "Shell Shock in the Canadian Expeditionary Force, 1914–1918: Canadian Psychiatry in the Great War," in *Health, Disease and Medicine: Essays in Canadian History*, ed. Charles G. Roland (Toronto: Hannah Institute for the History of Medicine, 1984), pp. 308–32, 323. See also C. K. Clarke and C. B. Farrar, "One Thousand Cases from the Canadian Army," *CJMH* 1 (1919–20): 313–17, 315.

of hostilities in Europe, immigration inspection became a prime interest of the CNCMH. To devote his energies to the CNCMH, he gave up his appointment as medical superintendent of the TGH in 1918 and his deanship at the University of Toronto's Faculty of Medicine in 1920. Not that Clarke was alone in emphasizing immigration; as one CNCMH psychiatrist observed in 1919; "When a year or more ago, it was proposed to organize in Canada a committee for Mental Hygiene, of the various reasons advanced to justify the *'raison d'être'* of such a body the one which, above all, appealed to me most, was the work that could be undertaken by the committee in connection with immigration."[106] To Clarke, alerting the country to the dangers of unrestricted immigration was the pivotal challenge facing the CNCMH. In 1920 he wrote, "The Canadian National Committee for Mental Hygiene has been attacked time and again because it has combatted the idea that a free country and improved hygienic conditions will make the defective child mentally competent and the insane person sane. This is all very well in theory, but we know by experience acquired in various clinics that the impossible never happens, and the number of weaklings of vicious and anti-social type imposed on Canada by this sort of immigration is large."[107] With the formation of the CNCMH, Clarke felt he finally belonged to an organization that stood a good chance of taking on the entrenched self-interests that he imagined hamstrung national immigration policy making.

Another reason immigration loomed large on the CNCMH's agenda was the "Red Scare" of 1918–20. Clarke knew that the post-war period was a propitious time to win overdue federal support for his and the CNCMH's position on immigration. In 1918 and 1919 a series of labor

---

106. J. D. Pagé, "Immigration and the Canadian National Committee for Mental Hygiene," *CJMH* 1 (1919): 58–61, 58. See also the CNCMH's October 1920 issue of the *Mental Hygiene Bulletin* devoted entirely to immigration. Much of it consisted of highly selective excerpts from W. G. Smith's *Study in Canadian Immigration*, quotations that painted a dismal picture of foreign-born Canadians. Smith's book, though it contained a forward by Clarke, was actually a moderate analysis of immigration. Smith concluded that the statistical case against certain nationalities of immigrants was "unproved, though not unprovable." He also cautioned that "British justice" demanded that until such proof was available, immigrants—like all people—were innocent of the charge of disproportionate defectiveness. W. G. Smith, "Immigration and Defectives," *CJMH* 2 (1920): 73–86. For a sympathetic account of the plight of Jewish immigrants to Canada, see David H. Frauman, "The Social Service Problems of the Jewish Immigrant," *CJMH* 1 (1919): 323–27. Frauman contended that the "highly nervous" reputation of Jewish immigrants to the New World was due more to "environment" than heredity. These views signify that within the Canadian mental hygiene movement there was perhaps less consensus over what caused immigrants' emotional and physical problems than some have alleged.

107. C. K. Clarke, "Foreword" to Smith, *Study in Canadian Immigration*, p. 12.

strikes swept the country. The most serious and violent confrontation was the Winnipeg Strike of June 1919, which ended with one dead, one wounded, and scores of arrests. A common fear expressed by civic, political, and business leaders was that the Winnipeg Strike was an attempt to establish a Bolshevik state. Official anxiety centered on the Industrial Workers of the World, or "Wobblies." Many Canadians hostile toward organized labor were convinced that most of the workers behind the strike were foreign-born IWW members, and this perception naturally caused attention to shift to the responsibilities of federal immigration authorities to monitor the arrival of newcomers.

Clarke wasted little time in highlighting the link between immigration and social deviance. In 1919 he circulated among members of the federal cabinet in Ottawa his unpublished novel "The Amiable Morons" in order to demonstrate the ties between immigration and criminality. He argued that the majority of Canada's British immigrants were slum dwellers and largely responsible for "the unrest which is disturbing Canada at the present moment." "The centres of unrest and discontent," he wrote,

are in the cities and no matter where the blame for the chaotic state of affairs in Canada to-day is to be placed, it is only too evident to students of sociology that undesirable immigration is one of the most potent causes of the disturbances. Bolshevism is not a new world disease, but merely a hot house product imported from the slum centres of Europe, where degeneracy has produced its inevitable results. The specimens of advocates of their doctrines we have met should never have been admitted to this country, as their influence for evil is difficult to estimate, although it is undoubtedly great. Certainly the ideals which have counted so much in the past in keeping this young country sane, and an example of virility, are in danger as a result of the type of immigration that has been fostered of late years. We have been nursing a reptile that may easily prove our undoing when it is fully developed.[108]

Thus strikes and labor agitation were the product of defective brains, which, Clarke reassured Canadians, could be detected by a properly trained psychiatrist. In certain respects his message had changed little since he had first spoken out against unrestricted immigration. What was new was the warning that undesirable immigrants were not just biologically prolific, expensive to care for, and prone to crime but politically dangerous as well.

108. C. K. Clarke, "Immigration," *Public Health Journal* 10 (1919): 441–44, 443.

Clarke wrote these words with the intention of influencing government policy, and in that respect he was successful. Before June 1919 it was illegal to deport an immigrant solely because of membership in a labor organization, but in the wake of the Winnipeg Strike, Parliament passed amendments to the Criminal Code and the Immigration Act to make it possible to deport or refuse admission to newcomers who could be shown to have an interest in overthrowing government, destroying property, or promoting riots or other public disorders. As well, a literacy test for immigrants over the age of fifteen was approved, and the list of "undesirables" was lengthened to include conditions such as "constitutional psychopathic inferiority," a favorite label for the feebleminded.[109] Although the number of specifically politically motivated postwar deportations was not large, the 1919 amendments had been prompted by the labor strife in Winnipeg and other Canadian centers;[110] so too the 1919 transfer of all medical inspectors from the Department of the Interior to the newly created Department of Health in what—initially at least—seemed a salutary development. All these changes bore the stamp of Clarke's ideas and testified to the lobbying clout of the CNCMH in the altered Canadian political, cultural, social, and economic atmosphere after the war.

By tying Bolshevism to the issue of mental defectiveness Clarke had pointed to the possibility that politically suspicious aliens could be either deported or denied entry for medical reasons, making the job of deporting or excluding them all the easier. He had also given notice that the CNCMH was willing to collaborate in the serious task of postwar national reconstruction, an enterprise that stressed the mending of the country's divisions and a new affirmation of national solidarity. Once the Armistice was signed, much of the Canadian wartime unity began to unravel, and the familiar regional, ethnic, religious, linguistic, and class discontent resurfaced with vigor. Agrarian, labor, and sectional protests spread throughout the country, leading Canadians to long for a rebirth of citizenship and new leadership to help bring it about.[111] Clarke pat-

109. Roberts, *Whence They Came*, p. 19. In this respect, Canadian legislators were following the example set by the 1917 U.S. Immigration Act, which introduced a literacy test for newcomers and added the category of "constitutional psychopathic inferiority" to the list of excludable classes. See Chapter 4 in this book for the psychiatric dimensions of the U.S. debate over immigration restriction.

110. Donald Avery, *"Dangerous Foreigners": European Immigrant Workers and Labor Radicalism in Canada, 1896–1932* (Toronto: McClelland and Stewart, 1979). See also Roberts, *Whence They Came*, pp. 71–98; and Knowles, *Strangers at Our Gates*, pp. 98–101.

111. J. S. Woodsworth, "Nation Building," *University Magazine* 16 (1917): 99. Cited in Robert Craig Brown and Ramsey Cook, *Canada, 1896–1921: A Nation Transformed* (Toronto: McClelland and Stewart, 1974), p. 321.

ently hoped that his offer of the CNCMH's good offices for this purpose would convince federal politicians to fund the commitee. It was a classical case of pitching a message to suit the aims of a potential donor. Clarke's efforts were rewarded; despite initial resistance, Ottawa decided to spend money on the new organization.[112]

But Clarke had reasons other than fund raising for publicizing the dangers of lax medical inspection after 1919. It quickly became obvious that the medical inspectors in the Department of Health did not enjoy even their limited pre-1919 influence and professional freedom, especially in deportation. They served in a merely advisory capacity, empowered only to fill out the department's inspection forms and rely on civil officials to make the admission decisions. All too often, civil agents chose to overlook entry regulations when ordered to do so by departmental authorities. Moreover, to many psychiatrists, the problem of defective immigrants would never be solved until inspection at foreign ports of embarkation was also carried out by Canadian physicians, something the Canadian government was not to begin until 1928.[113] If physicians had lamented the constraints on medical inspectors before the war, they had even more cause after 1919. To Clarke, this decline in medical authority over the inspection of immigrants meant the situation in the early 1920s remained critical.

This professional factor in Clarke's thinking stands out graphically in the context of Canada's postwar immigration policy. Thanks to the 1919 revisions, culture and ideology became crucial considerations when evaluating immigrants, which led to a decisive shift in both attitudes and practices. Officially, immigrants from the white Commonwealth countries, the United States, and northwestern European nations were favored. As a federal member of Parliament said in 1923, "We need immigrants of the right class, and I would say that immigrants should be preferably of British stock and that they should be sound physically and mentally."[114] Yet, at the same time, Clarke continued to decry the quality of British immigrants, particularly the children who were still being

112. For Clarke's correspondence with Sir Thomas White, federal minister of finance, regarding grants for the CNCMH from Ottawa, see C. M. Hincks, "General Correspondence 1918–1922," QSMHC, box 1, no. 3. According to John D. Griffin, the first federal grant, worth $10,000, was awarded in 1919. In 1928 that amount was increased to $20,000. Annual federal grants have increased since that time and continue to this very day. Griffin, *In Search of Sanity*, pp. 62–63.
113. Roberts, "Doctors and Deports," p. 31. See also Pagé, "Medical Aspects of Immigration," p. 368.
114. Canada, House of Commons, *Debates*, 17 May 1923, p. 2844. Cited in Knowles, *Strangers at Our Gates*, p. 101.

brought to Canada by organizations such as the Barnardo Homes and the Salvation Army. In a confidential memo of 1922 to the Canadian High Commissioner in Great Britain he also complained about "a great deal of the Central European stuff [which] is not only undesirable but actually harmful." He blamed their admission to Canada on what he called the "pull" enjoyed by Jewish immigrant groups. Yet his discontent derived not from a belief that these immigrants were in general any worse than British newcomers but from the fact that a clause in the Immigration Act permitted the minister of immigration "to override any decision by the medical officers."[115] Thus what irked him most was the impunity with which politicians could ignore a physician's diagnosis and in the process endanger the nation's health. To someone who described himself as being "somewhat strenuous on this subject" for more than twenty years, the events of the early 1920s added up to little overall progress. Despite the legislative reforms of 1919, it still appeared to Clarke that many of the systemic problems persisted. Politics still had a marked effect on the medical inspection of immigrants.

These thoughts were clearly plaguing Clarke when on 24 May 1923 the Medico-Psychological Association of Great Britain and Ireland invited him to deliver the fourth Maudsley Lecture in London. Typically frank, he did not paint a platitudinously bright picture of psychiatry's future for his Anglo-Irish audience. Wasting no time getting to the topic he considered most important, he told his audience that immigration had pushed Canada to the brink of crisis. The country was being "bled white" by emigration to the United States and pumped full of defective and "mentally diseased" immigrants, many of whom were British. Psychiatry, too, was at a crossroads, he declared. Psychiatrists had "to produce a new order of things" and break free of the inertial forces of a past dominated by the "institutional monarchs" of asylum medicine. The psychiatrist's "kingdom [was] slipping from him and passing into hands far less competent to deal with the problems of prevention and cure than he."[116] Nothing, he stressed, illustrated this dilemma more emphatically than the psychiatric inspection of immigrants. His contemporaries might look forward to a future brimming with professional promise, but he was far from sanguine. Hailed as one of the finest Anglo-American psychiatrists of his day, he overflowed with the bitterness and pessimism built up over forty years of

115. C. K. Clarke to P. C. Larkin, "Confidential Report on Immigration," 2 March 1922, CKCA, IIa.6. See also McConnachie, "Science and Ideology," pp. 100–102, 114.
116. Clarke, "Fourth Maudsley Lecture," pp. 281–82, 292.

psychiatry. He had fought politicians and public servants far too long to change his expectations at age sixty-six.

One other event that seemed to vindicate his life's work took place on 12 October 1923. On that day Clarke took part in laying the cornerstone of the Toronto Psychiatric Hospital, a facility that today carries his name and for which he had been campaigning since 1905. But Clarke's voice was soon to be silenced forever. In late 1923 he fell seriously ill, and in January 1924, Clarke, by then perhaps Canada's most famous psychiatrist, died of a stroke.

Was the knowledge that his career-long dream of a psychiatric institute would be fulfilled a source of gratification in his remaining days? Possibly; but the likelihood is that the emotional toll exacted by his life's work was too great for him to forgive, forget, or rejoice. Clarke was a committed reformer who lived in an era of reform, yet curiously he was also a man very much in conflict with his own times. As a physician interested in the campaign to prevent mental disease, update psychiatric diagnosis, modernize treatment, and improve the conditions of the care of the mentally ill in Canada, he was in the forefront of change. But the resistance he encountered suggests that even when it appeared that Canadians favored strikingly new public policies toward vulnerable and disadvantaged groups, reform was far from easy. Clarke discovered a dismaying fact of life in early twentieth-century Canada: though he was a member of an influential elite whose reputation for expertise was gradually growing, he—like his U.S. counterparts—continued to be hampered by public and private masters.[117] When these masters—primarily those in government—failed to follow his advice, Clarke reacted with bitter pugnacity, imagining that his hands were being tied by more powerful people with different agendas. To him it came down to a struggle between the venality of politicians and self interested groups and the disinterested humanitarianism and patriotism of modern psychiatry. His thinking mirrored that of other frustrated professionals entrusted with a public responsibility to disadvantaged men, women, and children, yet still accountable to officials whose behavior suggested that their real commitment was to fiscal restraint and political expediency. When he left the provincial psychiatric service intending to free himself of these circumstances, he only found the same forces arrayed against him and his new strategies for transforming the practice of psychiatry.

His career, then, illustrated how a brilliant and talented physician

117. Arthur S. Link and Richard L. McCormick, *Progressivism* (Arlington Heights, Ill.: Davidson, 1983), p. 95.

could choose to devote so much time and energy to the eugenic cause of immigration restriction. As an asylum superintendent Clarke noted the impact of immigration on the size of his patient population, his therapeutic options, and the living conditions in his institution. As an expert witness in criminal trials he watched as Canada tried to execute what he believed to be insane aliens after indiscriminately permitting their admission to the country. When trying to save these unfortunates from the gallows, he and other psychiatrists were not only humiliated and derided during cross-examination but also subjected to petty inconveniences and hostile press attacks. Those offenders spared received long prison sentences, not the treatment in special institutions for the criminally insane which psychiatrists recommended. No wonder Clarke and others had hopes for eugenic measures. Eugenics explained why the world was manifestly not the way psychiatrists wanted it to be. Clarke genuinely believed the time had come for Canadians to defer to selfless and knowledgeable psychiatrists to save the country from dire consequences and the practice of psychiatry from floundering. His misfortune was that many early twentieth-century Canadians failed to share his sense of urgency.

V

Eugenics in Canada began what in some respects was a steady decline with the death of Clarke in 1924. Once medical officers were assigned to inspect prospective immigrants in England and Europe in 1928, medical alarm over immigration started to subside. In 1930–31, with the depression well under way, the federal government suspended immigration, permitting only a few exceptions for British subjects and American citizens. Immigration dropped from 1,166,000 between 1921 and 1931 to 140,000 between 1931 and 1941. European immigration to Canada came to a virtual standstill. Though these measures were enacted mainly because of Canadians' suspicions that foreigners were stealing jobs from native-born residents, they were also hailed by the nation's racist groups, such as the Ku Klux Klan.[118] For those in the medical profession who for decades had been calling for close medical monitoring of the flood of immigrants, the issue was now moot.

In the meantime Canadian interest in sterilization was accelerating. Whereas before the war even the tiny minority of Canadians who sup-

118. Knowles, *Strangers at Our Gates*, pp. 108–9.

ported sterilization as a public health measure had believed it far too controversial an issue to promote seriously, in the 1920s more and more influential Canadians became receptive to it, possibly out of impatience with the slowness of eugenically inspired reform of immigration policy. The ground had been prepared by figures such as Clarke and Mac-Murchy who stressed the hereditary nature of feeblemindedness. The upsurge in U.S. sterilization laws beginning in 1923 and the *Buck v. Bell* U.S. Supreme Court ruling of 1927 emboldened prosterilization Canadian eugenicists. Numerous organizations, many of them women's groups such as the NCW, endorsed sterilization as part of a broader campaign to address the health needs of children and mothers. In this climate, it is not surprising that countless prominent Canadians were ready to accept the theory that the feebleminded posed a hereditary threat to the country. The provinces of Alberta and British Columbia responded by passing sterilization laws. Everywhere else in Canada the efforts of sterilization advocates fell short, and by the the Second World War the momentum had dissipated. Some CNCMH members may indeed have been "ambivalent" about sterilization laws in the 1920s.[119] Still, as a whole the CNCMH was more aggressive than the NCMH in promoting sterilization as a mental hygiene measure.

Just as the NCMH had carried out surveys in the Deep South to determine the extent of feeblemindedness, so Hincks and the CNCMH conducted similar ones in Alberta and British Columbia between 1918 and 1922. In British Columbia the committee investigated not only homes for the feebleminded and insane but orphanages, industrial schools, public schools, and detention homes. Their findings resembled those from their Alberta surveys: the rate of feeblemindedness was alarmingly high and much of it was due to immigration. Echoing Clarke's stress on "quality" rather than "volume" of immigration, Hincks reported that "it is particularly desirable to reject the insane and mentally deficient because they often prove a greater menace than any other group." But as Alberta could do little about a federal matter like immigration, Hincks hinted that sterilization was one measure the province could use "to prevent an increase of its abnormal population."[120]

119. McConnachie, "Science and Ideology," pp. 214, 223.
120. "Mental Hygiene Survey of the Province of Alberta," 1921, pp. 4, 42. Cited in Timothy J. Christian, "The Mentally Ill and Human Rights in Alberta: A Study of the Alberta Sexual Sterilization Act," QSMHC, unpublished paper, University of Alberta, n.d., pp. 2–7. Christian's study shows in fact that between 1928 and 1971, eastern European–born patients were disproportionately represented among those sterilized under the Alberta law, evidence that the link between immigration and mental deficiency existed in the minds of far more people than simply the CNCMH. See also Terry Chapman, "The Early Eugenics Movement in

These conclusions were quickly taken up by Alberta women's groups, including the United Farmers of Alberta, the United Farm Women of Alberta, the Imperial Order of Daughters of the Empire, and the Women's Christian Temperance Union. Influenced by the mental hygiene survey and resolutions passed at the 1922 annual convention of the UFA, in 1923 the Alberta minister of health suggested sterilization as an alternative to segregation in mental institutions. Four years later the provincial health minister George Hoadley brought before the Alberta legislature the Sexual Sterilization Act, which provided for the sterilization of mental defectives based on the recommendation of a four-person board and the consent of a parent or guardian. The bill passed on 7 March 1928, but not before Hincks took direct action to ensure its success. He managed to get at least one U.S. authority on feeblemindedness to write Hoadley in defense of the legislation, evidence that the health minister used in the provincial legislature's debate on the bill. As Hincks wrote after the bill passed, "Our National Committee will co-operate with governments in making sterilization laws that are enacted effective. We will attempt to carry the main body of public opinion with us through educational campaigns." The CNCMH applauded Hoadley "for the courageous manner in which such a controversial matter has been so successfully handled."[121]

Hincks's intervention in the passage of the Alberta act notwithstanding, his attitude toward sterilization in the 1920s is best described as vacillating.[122] From the beginning his approach to the debate over the feebleminded had been linked to his frustration over the failure of government—especially Ontario's—to respond to his, PACFM's, and the CNCMH's recommendations. As he complained in 1919,

> Deputations have gone to the Provincial Parliament Buildings annually for about twenty years. I, myself, have made the journey five or more times. We have told our story to the Cabinet. What has been our reception? Invariably during the last five years at least, a most courteous one. What has been the attitude of members of the Cabinet? As a rule a sympathetic

Western Canada," *Alberta History* 25 (1977): 14–16. Kathleen McConnachie has argued that sterilization legislation in Canada's West was "a distinct by-product of prairie fundamentalism and reform traditions of the women's institutes" and therefore "a unique Western study." McConnachie, "Science and Ideology," pp. 3–4.
121. C. M. Hincks to George Wallace, n.d. [ca. 1928]; Wallace to Hincks, 24 February 1928, and Hincks to Wallace, 2 April 1928, QSMHC, C. M. Hincks, General Correspondence, box 2, no. 25. See also "Sterilization in Canada," *Mental Hygiene Bulletin* 3, nos. 2 and 3 (1928): 3.
122. McConnachie, "Science and Ideology," p. 224.

understanding of our problem from the Premier down. Then why haven't we got results? Because I take it that reforms would cost money, and because the governments have received no special mandate from the electors to spend money for such reforms. . . . What then must we do in Ontario and other provinces of the Dominion? We must make the feebleminded problem an election issue.[123]

Try as it might, though, the CNCMH never successfully made the feebleminded "an election issue." This failure, combined with the fact that the Ontario government never did "elaborate a coherent mental retardation policy," produced a change in Hincks's strategy and the tactics of many other CNCMH reformers. By 1925, Hincks himself had admitted that he and the CNCMH were at a crossroads, having stressed research, surveys, and the education of mental health workers during the Clarke years.[124] Obviously feeling that it was time to assert his leadership and shift the CNCMH's priorities, he went in late 1925 to Europe for six months, presumably to pick up ideas for a new strategy for the organization.

Before his departure for Europe he had questioned many of the stock assumptions about the feebleminded, including his own high estimates of the percentage of mentally retarded persons who came from "unsound stock" (in 1919 he had claimed it was 80 percent). Willing to endorse sterilization "under careful safeguards" if physicians could determine precisely who would pass on their feeblemindedness to their children, he nonetheless conceded that "we know less than we thought we knew" about the link between heredity and feeblemindedness. Drawing on Walter Fernald's studies he added that those diagnosed with mental deficiency were neither excessively promiscuous, nor threats to the community, nor lazy and unproductive workers. Finally, he qualified his earlier enthusiasm for IQ testing when he said that it alone could not predict how competent someone would be outside an institution.[125]

123. C. M. Hincks, "Governments and the Feebleminded," a speech to the Social Welfare Congress, 14 January 1919. Mental Health Canada Archives. Cited in Simmons, *From Asylum to Welfare*, p. 101.
124. Roland, *Clarence Hincks*, pp. 89–90.
125. C. M. Hincks, "Recent Additions to Our Knowledge of Mental Deficiency," *Social Welfare* 7 (1925): 91–93. In 1926 the *Mental Hygiene Bulletin* echoed Hincks's thoughts: "It is obvious that our ideas with regard to the feebleminded have undergone somewhat of a revolution within the last few years." Or, in the words of the assistant medical director of the CNCMH, Canada ought to praise "restless men of science" brave enough to challenge the "legend" that "*all* the feebleminded inherited their defect, *all* were potential criminals, *all* were utterly unfitted for self-supporting community existence, and that *all* should be completely and permanently segregated in institutions." *Mental Hygiene Bulletin* 4 (1926): 1–2. His emphasis.

After his return from Europe Hincks's thinking about sterilization had changed yet again. By 1927 he was doing his best to convince Albertans that they needed sterilization legislation. He was still championing sterilization as late as 1946, long after it stood any chances of becoming official government policy in either Canada or the United States.[126] What was Hincks's real position? The probable answer is that he, like so many others, believed sterilization was an effective public health weapon that would never be accepted as long as it was justified by the standard eugenic and social Darwinist theories that had proved persuasive before the First World War. Hincks and the CNCMH worried that some sterilization advocates were so radical as to force moderate supporters into opposition. The CNCMH supported sterilization as a purely practical solution to the problem of paroling and discharging inmates from overcrowded institutions. The challenge was to strip sterilization advocacy of its flamboyant eugenic overtones, thereby making it palatable to a wider audience and to the CNCMH's university-based researchers, who were increasingly defining mental hygiene in terms of environmental factors.[127] From the CNCMH's perspective, sterilization was the moderate policy of choice for "hard-headed men and women who have to deal with concrete problems each day [and who] were not inclined to look upon sterilization as a panacea; but they were willing to concede it a place in a well-rounded scheme in which education and supervision should play the major roles."[128] To the minds of many superintendents and officials, sterilization made it safe to release patients into the community (where they manifestly could not afford to have children), opening up beds and allowing for new admissions. In other words, sterilization as a birth control measure was possibly the key to a policy of deinstitutionalization which

126. C. M. Hincks, "Sterilize the Unfit," *Maclean's*, 15 February 1946, pp. 39–40. See also Griffin, *In Search of Sanity*, p. 56.
127. McConnachie, "Science and Ideology," p. 225. In fact Clifford Beers warned the CNCMH in 1934 about going on the record about controversial issues such as sterilization for fear of damaging the entire mental hygiene movement. *Montreal Gazette*, 8 December 1934, University of Toronto, Rare Book Room, William Blatz Papers, box 15. Cited in ibid., p. 227.
128. *Mental Hygiene Bulletin* 4, nos. 3 and 4 (1929): 1 and 4. The CNCMH, under Hincks's guidance, looked beyond Canada's borders for signs of interest in sterilization and did its best to publicize this evidence. See ibid. 4, no. 2 (1929): 3, where it republished a letter to the London *Daily Mail* of 21 February 1929 from British physicians, clergymen, and "other distinguished persons" in favor of sterilization. When it came to prosterilization, hard-line eugenicists such as E. S. Gosney of Pasadena, California, who stressed the importance of heredity over environment, the CNCMH did its best to rehabilitate their reputations rather than alienate a potentially powerful ally. "There is little doubt," the CNCMH newsletter declared in 1930, "that the world owes a very great debt to enthusiasts, or in other words, 'cranks' " like Gosney." "The Good 'Cranks' Do," ibid. 5, no. 1 (1930): 3.

might solve the chronic problems of overcrowding and underfunding. But its benefits did not end there, according to Hincks. As he said in 1927, "I find myself favoring sterilization, not on eugenical grounds alone, but on euthenical as well. I am convinced that [the mentally deficient] should not be given an opportunity to thwart and stifle healthy child development."[129] A eugenic rationale was no longer the only plinth on which a prosterilization position had to rest.[130]

Hincks clearly imagined that these subtle wrinkles in prosterilization thinking would revitalize the CNCMH when it was stagnating dangerously. Perhaps he believed he had been successful and was ready for new challenges; for in 1930 he accepted the position of general director of the NCMH, making him in effect the head of the mental hygiene movement in both Canada and the United States. Though in hindsight the Canadian sterilization campaign was actually beginning its decline in the early 1930s, Hincks's efforts did pave the way for further Canadian legislative initiatives, including British Columbia's July 1933 sterilization law.[131] By the early 1930s, eugenicists had been able to forge broader coalitions with other public interest groups on the basis of support for sterilization.

The CNCMH's role in the Canadian eugenics movement was reduced considerably, however, when the Eugenics Society of Canada (ESC) was formed in 1930 and Hincks began juggling the directorships of both the CNCMH and the NCMH. The Ontario-centered ESC actually had a limited regional power base, but its membership list was very impressive, with physicians constituting the biggest single group. The ESC included such prominent Canadians as Hincks; Madge Thurlow Macklin, Canada's leading geneticist; Dr. H. A. Bruce, lieutenant-governor of Ontario; Dr. F. J. Conboy, who would be Toronto mayor from 1942 to 1944; and psychiatrist Clarence B. Farrar, head of the Toronto Psychiatric Hos-

129. Province of Alberta Eugenics Board Correspondence File. Cited in Christian, "Human Rights in Alberta," p. 7.
130. For similar trends in the United States, see James W. Trent, *Investigating the Feeble Mind: A History of Mental Retardation in the United States* (Berkeley: University of California Press, 1994), pp. 192–224.
131. As McLaren states, the 1933 victory for eugenicists in British Columbia coincided with the defeat of a similar bill in the province of Manitoba. McLaren, *Our Own Master Race*, p. 91. For the history of the campaign to pass the British Columbia law, see ibid. pp. 89–99, 101–6. Although Hincks, Clarke, and the CNCMH conducted surveys in British Columbia in 1918–19 drawing attention to the scope of feeblemindedness in that province, according to McLaren, it was women's groups that were "the earliest and most vigorous proponents of sterilization" in that province. Ibid., pp. 93–94. See also M. Stewart, "Some Aspects of Eugenical Sterilization in British Columbia with Special Reference to Patients Sterilized from Essondale Provincial Mental Hospital since 1945," 17 August 1945, QSMHC.

Clarence B. Farrar. Courtesy of the American Psychiatric Association.

pital.[132] From the ESC's vantage point, Farrar's membership was a distinct coup; for by then he was one of the brightest luminaries in U.S.-Canadian psychiatry. Born in upper New York State in 1874, Farrar died in Toronto at the age of ninety-five. Trained under William Osler at Johns Hopkins and Emil Kraepelin at Heidelberg, he served under Edward Brush at the Sheppard-Pratt Hospital. From 1923 to 1925 he was superintendent of the private Homewood Retreat in Guelph, Ontario. Clarke had long since noted his promise and had used his influence to ensure that Farrar had no trouble getting a license to practice medicine in Ontario so he could take the Homewood job.[133] There is every indication that Clarke wanted Farrar to succeed him when and if a psychiatric

132. See McLaren, *Our Own Master Race*, pp. 202–3 n. 34, for a list of the ESC's members. See also McConnachie, "Science and Ideology," p. 213.
133. In 1919, Clarke and Farrar had collaborated on a study of western Canadian facilities for hospitalized ex-soldiers. C. K. Clarke and C. B. Farrar, "One Thousand Cases from the Canadian Army," *CJMH* 1 (1920): 313–17. For correspondence between Clarke and Farrar in 1918–19, see CKCA, Ih. 8–10.

institute should be built,[134] and indeed Farrar was named the first head of the Toronto Psychiatric Hospital in 1925. Farrar's connections to Blumer and Brush were similarly strong. In 1931 he succeeded Brush as editor of the *AJP*.[135] Farrar was part of that venerable tradition of U.S.-Canadian medical journalism that stretched back to the days of John Gray in the mid-nineteenth century.

Farrar's long medical career was noteworthy chiefly because his thinking closely followed the rhythms of psychiatry between the early 1900s and his retirement in 1947. Hardly an innovator when it came to treatment, he believed in the virtues of combining systematic clinical observation and laboratory medicine. Early in his career he agreed with the reigning theory that psychiatric disorders were biologic phenomena and largely inherited; and these views persisted into the interwar period, predisposing him to look favorably on eugenic measures such as sterilization.[136] He praised western Canadian interest in sterilization legislation while denouncing any opposition—particularly from Catholics—as either hypocritical or obscurantist. In 1931, despite the accumulating evidence that the hereditary component to feeblemindedness was smaller than earlier imagined, he estimated it at somewhere between 33 and 65 percent. Like so many psychiatrists he must have known that the eugenic argument for sterilization was becoming decreasingly plausible, which would explain the fact that in the early 1930s he tended to justify sterilization for other reasons: it provided a form of birth control for people who putatively had no self-control over their reproduction.[137] Thus it is hard not to conclude that Farrar, like Hincks, crafted his eugenic message for depression-era politicians concerned about public spending. With so many of his peers at the time, he could see that sterilization could address the grave economic problems facing most states and provinces. As another Canadian psychiatrist said in 1931, it was "impossible to procure sufficient funds . . . to adequately meet our requirements in caring for" the feebleminded. "What more ready and feasible plan," he asked, "could then be adopted to aid us in the matter than selective or eugenic sterilization?—a safe and effective treatment and one that does not deprive

134. Edward Shorter, "C. B. Farrar: A Life," in Shorter, "TPH," pp. 111–17.
135. It was thanks largely to Farrar that the *AJP* published a tribute to Blumer in 1932. See "Notes and Comment," *AJP* 12 (1932): 374–88. For Farrar's preparations for this tribute, see APA, RG Clarence B. Farrar, esp. folders 42–46.
136. See, e.g., his speech to the Children's Aid Society in Toronto. Toronto *Telegram*, 19 May 1926. Cited in Shorter, "C. B. Farrar," p. 120. See also ibid., p. 105.
137. C. B. Farrar, "Sterilization and Mental Hygiene," *Public Health Journal* 22 (1931): 92–94.

the individual of any organ, secretion or hormone, nor the indulgence of normal passions."[138]

Farrar's defense of sterilization coincided with a major ESC effort to persuade other provincial governments—particularly Ontario's—to follow Alberta's example. Under pressure from reform groups Ontario had established the Royal Commission on Public Welfare in 1929 to study the province's system of institutions for the mentally ill and deficient; and like the 1919 Royal Commission, this one also issued a report urging the government to expand institutional care for the mentally retarded. But unlike the earlier report, it recommended compulsory sterilization. The provincial government declined to follow the commission's recommendations on sterilization and limited its reforms to the administrative realm.[139] Nonetheless, the commission's endorsement of sterilization was taken as a signal by eugenic physicians that the time was right to persuade the country's largest province to pass a sterilization bill. The consensus among Ontario physicians—including psychiatrists—in favor of sterilization is little short of remarkable. In 1933 the Ontario Medical Association approved a resolution advocating voluntary sterilization for patients, whether hospital inmates or not. Seven years later it asked various local medical societies throughout the province their opinions on sterilization legislation for Ontario's feebleminded. Twelve societies approved of such legislation, three were noncommittal, and only one was opposed.[140] With this kind of medical support it is no wonder sterilization enjoyed so much publicity in Ontario in the years leading up to the Second World War.

Ontario eugenicists were hopeful. In 1935 a delegation from the ESC met with the premier of Ontario and was told the province was studying the question of sterilization. The next year the ESC passed a resolution urging all provinces to emulate Alberta and British Columbia. But already the campaign was showing symptoms of self-destruction. In its efforts to end government procrastination the ESC proposed in a 1938 confidential memo to the provincial minister of health an amendment to the Ontario Medical Act which would have freed surgeons from any liability for performing sterilizations as long as there was patient consent or the consent of a parent or guardian. So many unofficial sterilizations were being performed by Ontario physicians for therapeutic, eugenic,

138. Walter English, "Presidential Address: The Feebleminded Problem," *AJP* 11 (1931): 1–8, 4.
139. Simmons, *From Asylum to Welfare*, pp. 113–19.
140. W. L. Hutton, "News from Canada," *Eugenics Review* 32 (1940): 56.

and birth control purposes that the ESC thought it time to make them legal. If passage of this amendment were to be secured, the ESC advised, then a similar amendment to the province's Hospitals' Act authorizing institutional sterilizations would be politically feasible. In other words, the ESC's objective was to use the back door to dodge "fresh argument" and get the legislation it really wanted: legal sterilizations of inmates of mental hospitals.[141]

But William Hutton, representing the ESC, blundered when he observed approvingly that by abiding by this advice Ontario would be following the footsteps of Nazi Germany. As Hutton noted, "Germany is seeking to purify the German people of defective inherited characteristics by widespread compulsory sterilization and over 300,000 persons have been sterilized. In our country under the democratic form of government, we believe in trusting the good sense of our professional people and depending upon public education to achieve the same ends."[142] This and other favorable references to similar eugenic developments in Hitler's Germany sealed the ESC's fate when war broke out in 1939 and a wave of revulsion against National Socialist policies swept the country. Eugenic hopes remained high, though, as late as 1938 when the provincial government appointed the Royal Commission on the Operation of the Mental Health Act; for buried among its many recommendations was another endorsement of sterilization.[143] Ontario never introduced a sterilization bill and ignored most of the commission's conclusions. Defeat in Ontario signaled that the "golden age" of the Canadian eugenics movement was over. To a nation mobilizing for war against the very country the ESC had roundly praised, eugenics was not a popular topic.[144] The swift demise of Canadian eugenics brought the collapse of the ESC in 1940.

Besides the outbreak of war, there were other reasons for the defeat of the sterilization cause in Ontario and the rapid decline of the Canadian eugenics movement. One was the much larger body of Catholic voters in Ontario than in either Alberta or British Columbia. In accordance with Pope Pius XI's 1930 encyclical on marriage and traditional Vatican teaching, the Catholic Church throughout Canada never relented in its

141. McConnachie, "Science and Ideology," p. 237.
142. W. L. Hutton to Harold Kirby, 24 January 1938, "Confidential Copy," QSMHC, History of Eugenics File.
143. Harvey G. Simmons, *Unbalanced: Mental Health Policy in Ontario, 1930–1989* (Toronto: Wall and Thompson, 1990), pp. 8–10.
144. McLaren, *Our Own Master Race*, pp. 107–26, 158–59.

absolute condemnation of eugenics.[145] Another reason was the determined opposition to sterilization from within the Ontario government in the person of Dr. B. T. McGhie, the deputy minister of health. McGhie was yet another example of a physician who remained interested in eugenics but at the same time rejected its extremist elements. In fact he remained a member of the ESC while fighting it over sterilization legislation. A former medical superintendent of the Orillia institution for the feebleminded, McGhie was an eloquent defender of education rather than custodialism or sexual surgery in the treatment of the mentally retarded. Using documents such as Abraham Myerson's 1936 American Neurological Association committee report on sterilization, he publicly disputed the main allegations about the feebleminded, including the charge that they inherited their conditions from their parents and were a danger to the community. Given his views, naturally he rejected sterilization and formidably opposed ESC lobbying within the Ontario government.[146]

As Angus McLaren has shown conclusively, eugenics did not necessarily die out in Canada even after the Second World War.[147] Both the Alberta and the British Columbia sterilization laws continued to function until their repeal in 1972. Of the two, the Alberta law was wider in scope and more punitive. For example, in British Columbia only inmates of institutions were sterilized, whereas in Alberta, clinic outpatients were eligible. Alberta officially sterilized 2,822 provincial residents by 1971. The records of British Columbia's Board of Eugenics were lost or destroyed, so it is impossible to know the exact figures for that province. Besides it is clear that even before these two bills were put into practice (and probably since their repeal) sterilizations were performed in other medical settings and provinces without benefit of legislation. As a British Columbia provincial hospital psychiatrist said in 1933, what the British Columbia sterilization bill "has accomplished is to make legal what has been done for years, that is, sterilization where it was requested. . . . You and I know that sterilization and the removing of the ovaries has gone on in the gynaecological services, and no particular reports with regard to the subject have been kept. People do not seem to object to this at all but when sterilization for the males comes up there is quite a stir. The foreign influence rather than the more enlightened American opinion makes itself felt."[148] Thus the likelihood is that many more Canadian

---

145. McLaren, *Our Own Master Race*, pp. 122–23, 125–26, 149–54.
146. Simmons, *From Asylum to Welfare*, pp. 119–33.
147. McLaren, *Our Own Master Race*, pp. 146–64.
148. A. L. Crease to B. T. McGhie, 1 May 1933, Provincial Archives of British Columbia,

mental patients were sterilized than the official data indicate and that operations continued to be performed until very recently. Moreover, in Alberta at least, the Eugenics Board went against the advice of its own attorney general's department in order to apply the sterilization law in a punitive fashion. For example, a handful of castrations—not sterilizations—were performed on men and women whose cases went before the board—testimony that once eugenicists had the power they wanted, their zeal often carried them beyond the letter of the law.[149] In other words, though the reputation of eugenics was badly damaged by 1940, its effects in Canada would be felt long after it ceased to be an opinion-making movement.

Responsibility for this trend can be traced in large part to the ideas and behavior of a few psychiatrists, particularly C. K. Clarke during his respected career. Even after his death in 1924 his influence on Canadian eugenics remained strong thanks to the way he affected the careers of younger psychiatrists such as Hincks and Farrar. His confrontational style shaped the debate over social policy; for he drew the conclusion that to overcome bureaucratic inertia and tap the state's material resources, reformers needed to employ alarmist rhetoric mitigated by references to impartial medical science. It was this legacy that he passed on to his followers in the CNCMH. If there is a tragic note to Clarke's life in psychiatry it is that he genuinely believed in what he said about immigrants and the feebleminded, whereas mental hygienists such as Hincks were very likely more opportunistic and less dogmatic. What ties Clarke to other Canadian and U.S. psychiatrists of his generation is that his depth of conviction can be traced to his formative experiences as a public asylum psychiatrist. What sets him apart from someone like Blumer is that he never liberated himself from this mentality after leaving the provincial service. This experience, similar to Blumer's at Utica, bred in him a visceral taste for extreme policies which was nowhere near as developed in psychiatrists like Hincks and Farrar who spent less time practicing as state hospital physicians and who lived long enough to see

Provincial Secretary, Mental Health Services, GR 542, box 14, "Sterilization." Cited in McLaren, *Our Own Master Race*, pp. 162–63. A copy of this letter can be found in *QSMHC*, History of Eugenics File. Evidence that even in Ontario, sterilizations were being performed is the letter of 8 July 1937 from W. L. Hutton, president of the ESC, to F. W. Wegenast, another ESC member. It reports the cases of three "feebleminded women" sterilized by "French-Canadian doctors in a French-Canadian Ottawa Hospital." Ibid.

149. Christian, "Human Rights in Alberta," pp. 109–12. There is also evidence that some sterilizations were based on faulty IQ testing. For example, in 1995 an Alberta woman sought compensation from the Province of Alberta for being sterilized in 1957 at the age of thirteen on the basis of a single intelligence test score of 64. *Globe and Mail*, 13 June 1995; *Toronto Star*, 12 June 1995.

the opening of new and more hopeful occupational avenues for psychiatry. For their generation, liberation from asylum psychiatry was a realistic expectation. It was only late in his career that Clarke could share this vision, and by then it was too late to change the eugenic thinking of the leading psychiatrist in early twentieth-century Canadian history.

4

A QUESTION OF PUBLIC HEALTH: PSYCHIATRY, EUGENICS, AND IMMIGRATION IN THE UNITED STATES, 1880–1925

The medical inspection of newcomers was also of vital interest to many U.S. psychiatrists, particularly those in New York State. Washington's immigration laws seemingly placed an enormously unfair fiscal burden on the Empire State by expecting it to feed, clothe, house, and rehabilitate defective aliens. Indeed in the years before the United States entered the First World War in 1917, the eugenic dimension to immigration arguably interested psychiatrists from the northeastern United States more than other eugenic matters. During the first two decades of the twentieth century, immigration was a frequent topic of debate and discussion at annual AMPA meetings. The association struck committees to investigate immigration and to go to Washington to publicize psychiatric concern. Most U.S. psychiatrists agreed that the great waves of immigration posed an urgent public health danger. Some argued, like Clarke, that immigrants contributed more than their proportional share of admissions to the country's prisons, asylums, hospitals, reformatories, and training colonies for the feebleminded. The psychiatric consensus was that the laws governing medical inspection and deportation of immigrants had to be reformed and vigorously enforced if the country was to avert a crisis in state charity.

But the war changed U.S. psychiatrists' opinions about immigration just as it did their attitudes toward other aspects of eugenics, and debate among them over immigration waned, as did their efforts to persuade legislators to pass restrictive laws on admission and deportation. At the same time, however, restrictionist sentiment was actually beginning to swell among the general population, culminating in the xenophobic 1921 and 1924 immigration laws that particularly penalized newcomers from southern and eastern Europe and ended three centuries of open immigration to the United States. In other words, psychiatric concern over defective aliens declined just as nationwide alarm was mounting. An examination of the history of U.S. psychiatrists' attitudes toward immigration up to the mid-1920s reveals both that Canadian psychiatrists were far more persistent in their attempts to highlight the alleged eugenic consequences of immigration and that U.S. psychiatrists' theories of immigration must be carefully distinguished from the arguments of nativist Americans. In fact, psychiatrists' attitudes toward immigration are more accurately described as regulationist than restrictionist. Whatever blame U.S. psychiatrists must assume for their early support of immigration legislation, their enthusiasm soon cooled. Later their lack of involvement stood in stark contrast to the efforts of other opinion-making groups to introduce immigration laws based on discriminatory national quotas.

In 1903 when he delivered his eugenic presidential address to the American Medico-Psychological Association, G. Alder Blumer had much to say about immigration. In what was to be a common refrain among psychiatrists until the war, Blumer underlined the necessity "of keeping out insane and other defective immigrants by stringent federal statutes." This necessity, he asserted, carried "obvious" and "especial" importance with respect to the State of New York . . . , for while her foreign-born population is only twenty-five percent of the whole, fifty percent of the inmates of State hospitals are of foreign birth." He applauded Goodwin Brown, the ex-commissioner in lunacy, who in 1902 had appeared before a congressional committee as attorney to the New York State Commission in Lunacy to plead the state's case for tighter medical screening of immigrants. To Blumer it was a felicitous sign that Congress had responded with a new immigration act in March 1903 making it easier to exclude and deport aliens with mental defects. Although in his speech he made no explicit reference to the eugenic and hereditarian dimensions of immigration, it was clear from his other remarks that he believed the federal government bore the responsibility to take drastic legislative action to avert a eugenic disaster for both New York State and the country.[1]

Blumer made these comments just as his views on eugenics in general were beginning to change in response to his early experiences at Butler. Four years later he wrote that it was doubtful "that immigrants to a new country are composed very largely of the defective classes." Obviously mindful of the fact that he had once been an immigrant himself, he added that "mongrel men have doubtless been finding their way into the United States for centuries, but producing by cross breeding not bad results."[2] What was striking about Blumer's opinions about immigration by 1907, like his other eugenic opinions, was that they were evolving in diametrically different directions from those of the country and most of its psychiatrists. Around the turn of the century, Americans had begun to be aware of the influx of immigrants stretching back to the 1890s. Until the war, immigrants continued flocking into the country in numbers that astonished many Americans. In the quarter-century before 1914, eighteen million newcomers landed in the United States, and what caught the attention of native born Americans was their ethnic composition: 80 percent were from southern and eastern Europe. Between 1900 and 1910, roughly six million arrived from Austria-Hungary, Spain, Italy, and Russia. As recently as 1882 a third of the approximately 790,000 who reached Atlantic ports had hailed from Germany, only 32,000 from Italy, and 17,000 from Russia. In 1907, by comparison, Germany sent only 32,000, whereas Italy dispatched 285,000, Austria-Hungary 338,000, and the Russian Empire 250,000.[3]

This influx of aliens quickly drew attention to the country's immigration laws. Nineteenth-century U.S. prejudices against immigrants had festered for decades, but as late as the 1860s and 1870s, efforts to encourage immigration had outweighed attempts to restrict it, and there was no federal immigration law before 1882. Some states and city authorities, especially at busy ports of entry, had resorted to various measures intended to discourage the admission of newcomers who might

1. G. Alder Blumer, "Presidential Address," *AJI* 60 (1903): 1–18, 18.
2. G. Alder Blumer, "Are We Degenerating?" unpublished paper, 1907, BP, box 40. In 1925 Blumer told the APA that he too was "an immigrant who was fortunate enough to get by forty-seven years ago without any chalk mark at all." See "Discussion," *AJP* 4 (1925): 467. Blumer was referring to the standard procedure followed by public health officials at U.S. ports of entry of marking with chalk the shoulders of immigrants who were to be detained for further medical examination, and possibly exclusion. See Alan M. Kraut, *Silent Travelers: Germs, Genes, and the "Immigrant Menace"* (New York: Basic Books, 1994), esp. pp. 50–77.
3. John L. Thomas, "Nationalizing the Republic, 1877–1920," in *The Great Republic: A History of the American People,* ed. Bernard Bailyn et al., 3d ed. (Lexington, Mass: Heath, 1985), p. 627.

become public charges, but in 1876 the Supreme Court had ruled these laws unconstitutional. Despite opposition from steamship companies and business organizations, Congress passed the nation's first immigration law in 1882 shortly after New York threatened to close down its Castle Garden depot in protest over the absence of a federal statute. The new law excluded "any convict, lunatic, idiot, or any person unable to take care of himself or herself without becoming a public charge." Its chief disadvantages, according to public health officials, were its failures to provide either a definition of "lunacy" or a means of enforcement.[4] Accordingly, physicians began to speak out more and more about the impact of immigration on U.S. taxpayers and the incidence of mental illness.

This behavior was not unprecedented; for in the years leading up to the Civil War, psychiatrists had expressed similar misgivings about the benefits of immigration. The arrival of Catholic Irish in the 1830s and 1840s—roughly a million and a half of whom fled the ravages of the Great Famine of 1845–49—had had an almost immediate impact on recently constructed asylums such as Providence's Butler Hospital, where Irish patients flooded the wards. As psychiatrists had contended with these patients, they had complained that their different customs and bad habits—mainly intemperance—made them resistant to moral treatment and a malign influence in their asylums. Faced with Irish-born patients who seemed to defy curative attempts, psychiatrists had tended to blame the misfortunes of these patients on their defective heredity, stressing the links between heredity and immigration.[5] Religious and national bigotry clearly affected their views but were not the whole story. The widespread, anti–Old World belief that unscrupulous European governments were deliberately exporting their own troublemakers and dependents to the United States was also at work, refracted through a medical prism.[6]

Thanks to the efforts of Foster Pratt, a Michigan physician, the AMSAII was asked in 1884 to vote on a resolution urging Congress to do more than the 1882 law to exclude "defective classes" of newcomers. Pratt believed that since the 1850s there had been an increase in insanity rates owing primarily to immigration. Speaking before the AMSAII in

4. Kraut, *Silent Travelers*, p. 70. The 1882 law also imposed a head tax of fifty cents on every alien passenger arriving by boat. Maldwyn Allen Jones, *American Immigration* (Chicago: University of Chicago Press, 1960), pp. 250–51.
5. See Kraut, *Silent Travelers*, pp. 38–41. For psychiatrists and Irish patients in the antebellum era, see Gerald N. Grob, *Mental Institutions in America: Social Policy to 1875* (New York: Free Press, 1973), pp. 153–56, 230–41. See also David J. Rothman, *The Discovery of the Asylum: Social Order and Disorder in the New Republic* (Boston: Little, Brown, 1971), pp. 283, 285.
6. Jones, *American Immigration*, p. 152.

1884, 1886, and 1887, he contended that over the years European officials had carefully dispatched hereditarily tainted persons to the United States. These immigrants, he alleged, proceeded to intermarry with native-born white Americans, thereby spreading through reproduction their own mental disabilities. Utica's John Gray was far more optimistic about immigration than Pratt. He was confident that because life in the United States was better on the whole than aliens had experienced in their home countries, immigrants would be able to overcome their own deficiencies and other obstacles to assimilation. But Gray's more tolerant views may have been an echo of a past generation of psychiatrists; for in the end the AMSAII approved Pratt's resolution unanimously.[7]

These signals of mounting psychiatric concern about immigration indicate that psychiatrists were not immune to the xenophobia of other Americans, but coming at a time when most newcomers arrived from northern Europe, they also show that racism and religious bigotry were not necessarily the most potent ingredients in their attitudes. In 1882 an unprecedented 788,000 newcomers had arrived in the United States. Even if they had not brought with them a disproportionate share of mental illnesses, their arrival would still have been of grave concern to state charity administrators and physicians. These worries were borne out as early as the 1890s. The New York City Asylum for the Insane on Blackwell's Island had a patient population that was more than 80 percent immigrants. The Massachusetts public asylums at Worcester, Danvers, and Northampton had foreign-born patient rates close to 50 percent.[8] By 1904, New York State cared for roughly a quarter of the nation's foreign-born insane. In 1914 approximately 80 percent of all immigrants to the United States landed in New York State, and about 26 percent of all newcomers became residents there.[9] Asylum superintendents were hardly sympathetic toward a phenomenon that promised to make their jobs more difficult and their profession more vulnerable to criticism at a highly sensitive time in its history, when, above all, they wanted to dis-

7. Foster Pratt, "The Increase of Insanity in the United States: Its Causes and Sources," *JAMA* 1 (1883): 668–75. For Pratt's and Gray's remarks at the AMSAII, see "Proceedings of the Association of Medical Superintendents of American Institutions for the Insane," *AJI* 41 (1884): 62–77; and John P. Gray, "Heredity," ibid., pp. 1–21. See also J. Strong, "Education as a Factor in the Prevention of Insanity," *AJI* 42 (1885): 114–39; and H. M. Bannister and L. Hektoen, "Race and Insanity," *AJI* 44 (1888): 455–70.
8. David J. Rothman, *Conscience and Convenience: The Asylum and Its Alternatives in Progressive America* (Boston: Little, Brown, 1980), p. 24.
9. See "The Alien-Born in Relation to the Cost of the Insane," in *The Institutional Care of the Insane in the United States and Canada*, ed. Henry Hurd et al., 4 vols. (Baltimore: Johns Hopkins University Press, 1916–17), 1:362–68. See also James V. May, "Immigration as a Problem in the State Care of the Insane," *PAMPA* 19 (1912): 181–90.

spell the popular perception, inside and outside organized medicine, that psychiatrists were merely, in the words of James T. Searcy, "keepers of beneficiary institutions provided by the state."[10] Many drew the conclusion from these statistics that immigrants contributed more than their share of the nation's mentally ill persons.

Others contested this view. In 1898, Blumer's friend Franklin Sanborn maintained that "the question of immigration, in its social and sanitary aspects, is so complicated in the United States, that almost any general statement will involve local or historical contradictions. Both the quality and quantity of immigrants are continually varying while the change going on in American habits of life has been rapid and powerful with respect to insanity."[11] When statisticians in the early 1900s began to correct for age in compiling data on the relationship between insanity and immigration, they discovered that Sanborn was right: mere hospital admission figures were highly misleading, and the numerical gap between native-born and foreign-born patients was much narrower than many had believed.[12] But this finding was small consolation for state psychiatrists. Even if immigrants did not disproportionately increase asylum admissions, they were becoming a growing presence in institutions that were already full. State governments could have helped mitigate the overcrowding by building more mental hospitals, but those that were constructed were not nearly numerous or big enough to handle the surplus.[13]

Once the tide of largely southern and eastern European immigration began to swell, the restrictionist cause quickly gathered momentum. National leadership was assumed by the Immigration Restriction League, founded in 1894. Headed by a small group of New England Brahmins, including Prescott Hall, Charles Warren, and Robert DeCourcy Ward, the IRL made invidious distinctions between the "old" immigrants from northern Europe and the "new" ones from southern and eastern Europe. Drawing on fashionable ideas regarding the different characteristics of

10. James T. Searcy, "Have We a Specialty?" *AJI* 70 (1913): 263–72, 267.
11. Franklin Sanborn, "Insanity and Immigration," paper read at the meeting of the National Conference of Charities, New York, May 1898, BP, box 39. See also Sanborn to Blumer, 2 May 1898, BP, box 28. Sanborn believed that the anti-immigration argument was due to the fact that statisticians often ignored the difference between foreign-born immigrants and first generation newcomers with foreign parentage.
12. Gerald N. Grob, *Mental Illness and American Society, 1875–1940* (Princeton: Princeton University Press, 1983), pp. 169–70.
13. To ease the problem of overcrowding, some states experimented with boarding the chronically and harmlessly ill in households willing to take them in, though for a variety of reasons this program was rarely used. Gerald N. Grob, *Mad among Us: The History of the Care of America's Mentally Ill* (New York: Free Press, 1994), pp. 167–69.

races and nationalities, the IRL argued that Latin, Slavic, and Asiatic peoples had significantly high percentages of mental and physical diseases. The league championed a literacy test as the most effective way of detecting unwanted, defective foreigners. Acquiring considerable clout almost immediately, the IRL could take credit for the fact that in 1896 both houses of Congress passed a literacy bill sponsored by Senator Henry Cabot Lodge of Massachusetts. The bill provided for the exclusion of any immigrant unable to read forty words in some language. But President Grover Cleveland vetoed the bill, and similar bills were defeated in Congress in 1898, 1902, and 1906. When like measures next passed in Congress, in 1913 and 1915, they were vetoed by presidents William H. Taft and Woodrow Wilson respectively.[14]

Despite its setbacks, the campaign for a literacy test for immigrants drew considerable support from various sources. In 1902, William Williams, a progressive dedicated to ridding the public service of corruption and other forms of inefficiency, was appointed by President Theodore Roosevelt to be commissioner of immigration for the port of New York and its depot, Ellis Island. Williams served from 1902 to 1905, and again from 1909 to 1914. He observed that inasmuch as "the greatest number of illiterates come to-day from Southern Italy and from Austria, Poland, and Russia," a literacy test "would certainly bar out a large number, perhaps 150,000 to 175,000," and Prescott Hall agreed. After the literacy test's defeat in 1898, Hall's IRL had lapsed into three years of turpitude, only to revive in the fall of 1901 and, thanks to aggressive fund raising and lobbying, manage to have the test added as an amendment to the House of Representatives' immigration bill of 1902. Hall declared that the introduction of a literacy test would mean that immigrants from "southern and eastern countries of Europe and from Asia" would be "chiefly affected."[15] Thus, if at first glance a literacy test did not look

14. Jones, *American Immigration*, p. 260. See also John Higham, *Strangers in the Land: Patterns of American Nativism, 1860–1925*, 2d ed. (New York: Atheneum, 1967), pp. 102–5, 111–12, 128–29, 162–64, 189–93, 202–3.

15. U.S. Senate, *Report of the Committee on Immigration on the Bill (H.R. 12199) to Regulate the Immigration of Aliens into the United States*, 57th Cong., 2d sess., 1902, S. Doc. 62, pp. 4, 80 (hereafter cited as *Report*, 1902). See also Higham, *Strangers in the Land*, p. 112. That there were ulterior motives behind much support for a literacy test is apparent from the many cogent criticisms its opponents leveled against it. After all, some of the worst criminal aliens were literate. Then there was the question of how to administer such a test, not just for the many immigrants arriving by ship but also the scores of Canadians and Mexicans who crossed the border every day. And what happened if a father was literate, his family not? Would he be allowed to stay and his family be shipped home? See *Hearings before the Committee on Immigration and Naturalization, House of Representatives, 4, 7, 8 May 191, 1912*, 62d Cong., 2d sess., 1912.

like an effective means of achieving the eugenic goal of excluding specific national groups, in the eyes of some it was.

Psychiatrists and state mental health officials may have shared Williams's progressive view that the federal government should intervene in public health matters of national importance, especially the medical inspection and deportation of insane immigrants, but for somewhat different reasons. In 1902, Goodwin Brown looked to Washington for relief of New York State's financial burden of hospitalizing insane immigrants. Like many observers he was dissatisfied with the 1891 Immigration Act, which made immigration a wholly federal jurisdictional matter and forced steamship companies to return passengers rejected by U.S. inspectors.[16] Brown and others knew well that until Congress voted sufficient funds, officials could not effectively inspect the throngs arriving at border points. Moreover, the frontier between the United States and Canada was virtually unguarded, so that insane immigrants who could not gain access to the United States could always enter from Canada if they could escape the notice of Canadian inspectors.[17]

Brown had even more specific complaints about deportation, what observers called the nation's "second line of defense" against unfit immigrants. He argued that although there were provisions in the 1891 act for deporting an insane alien, the one-year period during which deportation was legal was far too short. In addition the law stipulated that aliens who became public charges within one year of admission could be deported only if it could be shown that their dependence was due to causes pertaining before landing. It was the responsibility of the overburdened federal immigration authorities to prove this, making the law effectively toothless, unlike the Canadian deportation law, which contained no reference to "causes existing prior to landing."[18] Thus, when Congress lengthened the period of eligibility for deportation from one to three years in the Immigration Acts of 1903 and 1907, it did not make it appreciably easier to deport. Brown might as well have been speaking for U.S. and Canadian psychiatrists when he said that he knew of

instance after instance—in fact there are thousands of them—where [immigrants] have been only a few months out of a hospital on the other side. They are sane when they are admitted here—that is, they will pass the

16. Higham, *Strangers in the Land*, pp. 99–100.
17. Jones, *American Immigration*, p. 262.
18. For a comparison between the Canadian and U.S. laws for deportation of insane immigrants, see U.S. Congress, Senate, *The Immigration Situation in Canada*, 61st Cong., 2d sess., 1910, S. Doc. 469, pp. 48–56 (hereafter cited as *Immigration Situation in Canada*).

ordinary inspection; they find difficulty in procuring employment; they get out of money; they are away from their friends, and, naturally, they soon go to pieces, and then they are recommitted. Now, when we find those cases under the existing statutes we have difficulty often times in securing their return.[19]

Impediments to the deportation of such cases made it extremely hard to ease overcrowding on asylum wards, and Brown and U.S. psychiatrists indeed had reason to be uneasy. Between 1907 and 1909 the United States deported a substantially smaller percentage of immigrants than did Canada.[20] The problem, in Brown's view, was that although "an alienist might be morally certain that the causes of such lunacy existed prior to departure, he would not, without absolute knowledge, be willing to certify to the fact."[21] The obvious solution, according to U.S. mental health experts, was to shift the onus of proof from the government to the immigrant. Brown and other psychiatrists wanted the law changed so that insane aliens who became "public charges" *after* landing had to demonstrate that their mental condition did not derive from causes *before* landing, but they knew they would encounter plenty of congressional opposition.[22]

Perhaps no U.S. physician played a more influential role in immigration policy than Thomas Salmon (1876–1927), born in Troy, New York. Lacking formal and clinical training in psychiatry, he nonetheless emerged as an expert on the psychiatric dimensions of immigration. The similarities among Salmon, Clarke, and Hincks are pronounced. Both Salmon and Clarke were highly interested in the mental health challenges posed by immigration and instrumental in launching the mental hygiene movement: Salmon as medical director of the NCMH; Clarke, of the CNCMH. Indeed, if "Clifford Beers founded the National Committee, put it on its feet, and kept it there; Thomas Salmon got it moving," according to Beers's biographer.[23] Salmon and Clarke loathed red tape and political interference in mental health care policy, and easily made enemies of bureaucrats and administrators. Like Hincks, Salmon was an indefatigable worker for the cause of preventive psychiatry. Sick-

19. *Report*, 1902, p. 236.
20. *Immigration Situation in Canada*, p. 55.
21. *Report*, 1902, p. 237.
22. For congressional criticism of this clause, see *Report*, 1902, pp. 254–55.
23. Norman Dain, *Clifford W. Beers: Advocate for the Insane* (Pittsburgh: University of Pittsburgh Press, 1980), p. 168. According to Adolf Meyer, Salmon "really was the mental hygienist in psychiatry." AFMH, Thomas Salmon Papers, box 1, folder 3.

Thomas Salmon. Courtesy of the Archives of Canadian Psychiatry and Mental Health Services.

ness and disability were common occurrences in Salmon's family, and Thomas, like Hincks, was no stranger to poor health. From an early age he suffered from migraines and as a young man recovered from tuberculosis. Perhaps because of their bouts with ill health Salmon and Hincks developed a fondness for athletics, the outdoors, and physical fitness.[24]

Salmon's first real taste of psychiatry was in his senior year as a medical student at Albany Medical College, where he avidly followed Blumer's lectures.[25] But upon graduation Salmon, soon to be married, decided to enter general practice. Like so many physicians ultimately drawn to the field of public health, he failed miserably in private practice in 1900–1901. With few prospects and a growing family, he was reintroduced to psychiatry through a stroke of good fortune that changed the course of his life. In October 1901 he investigated a diphtheria epidemic at the

24. Earl D. Bond, *Thomas W. Salmon: Psychiatrist* (New York: Norton, 1950), pp. 17–26. Salmon's love of the outdoors and recreation bordered on the reckless and led to his death by drowning while sailing in 1927 on Long Island Sound. For descriptions of Salmon's personality and views from other physicians who knew and worked with him, see AFMH, Thomas Salmon Papers, esp. box 1.
25. For the memories of one of Salmon's ex-classmates at Albany, see AFMH, Thomas Salmon Papers, box 1, folder 1.

Clarence Hincks, ca. 1913. Courtesy of the
Archives of Canadian Psychiatry and Mental
Health Services.

Willard State Hospital, and on the basis of his excellent work he was
appointed bacteriologist of all the New York State mental hospitals.
While at Willard he was able to indulge his fascination with psychiatry
when William Russell, a later ally in the mental hygiene movement,
invited him to attend psychiatric conferences. His confidence restored
and his interest in psychiatry rekindled, Salmon took the examinations
for the United States Public Health and Marine Hospital Service (short-
ened to the United States Public Health Service in 1912). In 1903 he
received his commission. The next year he was sent to the immigration
station at Ellis Island, "the gateway to a continent for many and for
Salmon the gateway to psychiatry,"[26] according to his biographer.

Salmon arrived at Ellis Island in 1904 in the midst of an official PHS

26. Bond, *Thomas W. Salmon*, p. 31.

campaign to improve the medical inspection of immigrants. The year before, Congress had shifted immigration from the Treasury Department to the newly created Department of Commerce and Labor. Under William Williams's progressive leadership the PHS was being pruned of many of its corrupt inspectors, those who clandestinely charged immigrants for bogus naturalization papers or accepted bribes from steamship companies to land immigrants known to have contagious diseases. Williams was adamant that PHS physicians be more vigilant in their inspections. Indeed he hoped that improved medical examinations would accomplish what politicians and policy makers seemed to want to avoid doing: overhauling the whole screening process. The 1903 Immigration Act included thirty-nine sections specifying grounds for exclusion, including medical reasons, and the 1907 act would give PHS surgeons the opportunity to note on an immigrant's medical certificate whether or not they thought the alien's infirmity would make him or her a "public charge."

But Williams discovered that translating legislation into practice was another matter. Conditions, like those at Canadian ports, dictated that inspection would be haphazard. In 1902 there were eight PHS physicians and one steward to inspect the 497,791 steerage and the 68,192 cabin passengers who landed at Ellis Island. Three years later there were only sixteen officers to conduct the medical examinations *and* run the island hospital for immigrants. By 1914 the number had risen to twenty-five, but even this increase was insufficient. The line examinations of steerage passengers were normally a hurried affair. Each immigrant, after climbing a flight of stairs and submitting to a quick glance from a PHS physician, had hands, eyes, and throat examined.[27] According to a woman journalist who was processed at Ellis Island while posing as an Irish immigrant, as late as 1920 these medical examinations were rough, "superficial," "very perfunctory," and "unnecessarily quick." She also alleged that she was sexually harassed during the quarantine inspections by PHS doctors on board ship and that even on Ellis Island young women could get better treatment in exchange for sexual favors. Otherwise, she stated, "all you got was to be yelled at."[28] This kind of evidence suggests that state hospital psychiatrists' complaints had some validity.

Other factors undermined Williams's attempt to turn Ellis Island into

27. Kraut, *Silent Travelers*, pp. 53–55, 57–58, 61.
28. *Hearings before a Subcommittee of the Committee on Immigration and Naturalization, House of Representatives, 20/21 December 1921*, 66th Cong., 2d sess., 1922, pp. 257–80.

a model progressive institution. Most medical officers resented the pressure he placed on them to identify more immigrants as defective. Similarly, the presence at Ellis Island of representatives from immigrant organizations was a nagging reminder that their work was being watched carefully by people suspicious of their motives. Groups such as the Hebrew Immigrant Aid Society and the Italian St. Raphael Society not only protested some PHS decisions but also hired physicians in appeal cases to perform their own diagnoses. Proud of their skills at conducting medical examinations under rushed conditions, inspectors congratulated themselves on their ability to know when to suspend judgment in borderline cases. Williams's goal of a smoothly functioning bureaucracy in which medical officers obediently followed inflexible orders from high-ranking officials was often at odds with the views and attitudes of the physicians working under him.[29]

Williams might have had more luck had his medical officers only had to diagnose physical infirmities like trachoma, the contagious eye disease that accounted for most medical exclusions; the diagnosis of insanity was far more troublesome, elusive, and inexact. Feeblemindedness, added in 1907 to mental illness and epilepsy as prohibited conditions, was no easier. As Salmon reminisced in 1924,

> During 1905, 1906, and 1907—in each of which years over one million immigrants arrived at the port of New York—I had the privilege of standing on the line as one of the medical inspectors and had the opportunity of noting all the insane and all the feebleminded who were coming in that great throng. It was a magnificent opportunity, but I lacked equipment. I had a little knowledge of psychiatry in my head, a little piece of chalk in my hand, and four seconds of time. I was supposed to take that little knowledge, that little piece of chalk and little time, and mark with the chalk an 'x' on the shoulder of every applicant I thought should be held for further mental examination. I was informed also that not more than a hundred a day could be so marked. Sometimes in the rush days, from nine o'clock in the morning until ten at night, 8000 people passed through that line. About 500 at the most were recommended for examination.[30]

29. Kraut, *Silent Travelers*, pp. 68–69, 75. Salmon had a low estimation of Williams. To Salmon, Williams "took a [purely] legal view" of his responsibility for Ellis Island aliens, too often leaving it up to the steamship companies to remedy the "misery" they created. Salmon to Caroline B. Alexander, 12 December 1913, Thomas Salmon Papers, AFMH, box 1, folder 8.
30. "Immigration and the Problem of the Alien Insane: Discussion," *AJP* 4 (1925): 465–66.

Or, as one former PHS doctor who served at Ellis Island noted, the psychiatric inspection of immigrants "was always haphazard. It couldn't be any other way because of the time given to pass the immigrants along the line."[31]

But to a physician like Salmon the challenge of practicing diagnostic psychiatry at Ellis Island was just the kind he enjoyed. He threw himself into his job, defining the signs PHS surgeons needed to recognize in order to detain suspicious looking immigrants for further testing. In 1905 he wrote:

> If the manner seems unduly animated, apathetic, supercilious or apprehensive, or if the expression is vacant or abstracted the immigrant is held and carefully examined. A tremor of the lips when the face is contorted during the eversion of the eyelids, a hint of negativism or retardation, an oddity of dress, unequal pupils, or an unusual decoration worn on the clothing—any is sufficient to arouse suspicion. The existence of well-marked stigmata of degeneration always serves to detain the immigrant for further inspection.[32]

To Salmon, Ellis Island needed to be reorganized from both the humanitarian and national interest perspectives. He urged that medical testing be done at the beginning of an immigrant's voyage to avoid the cruelty of deportation later and also recommended that better detention facilities be built to house those awaiting deportation. He conceded that some immigrants were disoriented by the experience of emigrating and landing in a new country and simply needed a little rest in proper surroundings to regain their mental composure. But above all, he insisted that medical inspection become a more thorough procedure because he, like so many psychiatrists, believed that many insane aliens were slipping past the guardians of the nation's borders.

To Salmon's dismay, this message antagonized his colleagues in the PHS. Careful examinations as well as more exclusions and deportations

---

31. Grover A. Kempf, transcript of unpublished interview, 1977, Office of the Statue of Liberty–Ellis Island Collaborative in New York City. Copy on file at the National Library of Medicine, Bethesda. Cited in Kraut, *Silent Travelers*, p. 71. In 1910 another mental health official testified that it was "difficult to make much of a diagnosis of these people when they land. Most of them wear their hats; they carry all their own baggage in their hands, and are often muffled with a shawl, and it is difficult to tell whether a mentally defective or a pervert is passed." See Sidney D. Wilgus, "The Problem of Immigration" and "Discussion," *New York State Hospitals Bulletin* 3 (1910): 117–37, 135.

32. Thomas W. Salmon, "The Diagnosis of Insanity in Immigrants," *Annual Report of the Surgeon General of the Public Health and Marine-Hospital Service*, 1905, p. 271. Cited in Kraut, *Silent Travelers*, p. 71.

meant extra paperwork.[33] So did the demand that physicians meticulously list the symptoms of those refused admission. Salmon's superiors also quickly grew tired of his persistent flouting of rules and orders and his criticism of regulations and existing facilities.[34] Indeed, Salmon was probably too progressive for even Williams's PHS. Predictably, Salmon was finally demoted from Ellis Island to the Boston Marine Hospital. His career was saved, though, because in the meantime he had won friends and admirers among New York State mental health care officials who shared his opinion that medical inspection of immigrants was inefficient. He was rewarded in 1911 when he was offered the position of chief medical examiner of the Board of Alienists in New York State.

Thus had Salmon channeled his impressive if somewhat inchoate energies into the debate over immigration. In the process, he revealed a mind and character similar to Clarke's. Both were ambitious and unreceptive to criticism when they thought they were right, which was most of the time. When they encountered resistance to their often well-intentioned plans, both men imagined that they were lonely but enlightened experts fighting the forces of inhumanity, obscurantism, and self-interest. Even Salmon's normally sympathetic biographer wondered if Salmon did not share "a certain temporary paranoia" characteristic of "all reformers." Like Clarke, Salmon's impatience was directed at the intelligent and powerful, those figures who "ought to have known better."[35] This is why harsh sentiments and genuine benevolence could coexist in their minds. It also explains why each psychiatrist resorted to extremism and exaggeration when he perceived that his teachings on immigration were at worst contested and at best ignored.

Another U.S. psychiatrist who gravitated toward the immigration issue in the early twentieth century was William A. White. But White soon tired of the topic, just as he eventually grew disenchanted with

33. According to one medical inspector of immigrants who worked with him at Ellis Island, Salmon "succeeded in having a great many more people detained. He pulled out a lot more than we were pulling." See testimony of Dr. Stimson, AFMH, Thomas Salmon Papers, box 1, folder 1.

34. In November 1906, Salmon was suspended for refusing to serve on "line duty" at Ellis Island. His excuse was that he had been needed more to examine immigrants detained for further observation. In the end he only received a reprimand. See Salmon to John McMullen, 8 November 1906, AFMH, Salmon Papers, box 1, folder 3. Salmon was also noticeably upset over the federal government's failure to furnish medical services for U.S. fisherman who fished off the Grand Banks. AFMH, box 3, folder 5. According to at least one of his medical coworkers, Salmon was intemperate in his criticism of PHS officers and should have known they were doing the best they could. AFMH, box 3, folder 1.

35. Bond, *Thomas W. Salmon*, p. 88.

most of eugenics. His temperament and mind were neither Clarke's nor Salmon's. Though he shared their desire to make mental medicine more reputable and scientifically up to date, White, thanks chiefly to his faith in psychoanalysis, was more eclectic, intellectually cosmopolitan, and optimistic about psychiatry's potential for curing mental disorders. He was uncomfortable with the awkward mixture of soaring expectations and therapeutic pessimism that frequently undergirded preventive psychiatry. Nonetheless, for most of the pre–First World War period, he supported efforts to improve medical inspection and facilitate deportations of insane aliens. Perhaps he felt that as medical superintendent of the country's only mental hospital run by the federal government he had an insider's access to those who formulated national policy, which would help to account for his activism between 1908 and 1910 when he served on an AMPA committee to lobby for a bill before Congress that would deport aliens who committed felonies in the United States. The link between criminality and insanity on the basis of the mental degeneracy of many immigrants was a theory to which most early twentieth-century psychiatrists subscribed, including the young White.[36] Legislation such as the 1903 act, which gave the states three years during which to deport alien insane or criminals, reinforced this association and consoled medical superintendents of state hospitals and institutions for the criminally insane; the former because ideally it reduced the number of insane criminals who might be committed to their asylums in the absence of an asylum for the criminally insane; and the latter because finally something was being done to ease over-crowding and enable physicians to pay more time to the challenges of rehabilitation and training.[37]

In 1908, Congressman William S. Bennet (N.Y.) introduced a bill that called for the deportation of *any* alien after serving his or her sentence for conviction of a felony. Bennet's bill finally passed both houses in 1910, much to the satisfaction of the AMPA. As White's committee wrote to Bennet in 1908, "If you can, by any possibility further the passage of a proper measure to secure the deportation of some of these undesirable people from our shores, I wish to assure you of the hearty co-operation of this committee. We will furnish you with any evidence

36. William A. White, "The Physical Basis of Insanity and the Insane Diathesis," *AJI* 50 (1894): 530–37; and "The Geographical Distribution of Insanity in the United States," *Journal of Nervous and Mental Disease* 30 (1903): 257–79.
37. See, e.g., H. E. Allison, "Hospital Provision for the Insane Criminal," *PAMPA* 10 (1903): 241–51, esp. 249–51. C. K. Clarke quoted from this paper in ARK, 1903, p. 57.

that we have at our disposal, and if necessary the several members will come to Washington and appear before the House Committee to which the bill is referred."[38] White was still interested in immigration in 1913 when he and S. E. Jelliffe invited Salmon to write a chapter on the mental health effects of immigration in their book on psychiatry, proof that these admirers of Freudian psychoanalysis respected Salmon's expertise and experience.[39]

White's remarks showed that the AMPA was firm in its endorsement of any means of both deporting and denying admission to a broad range of defective immigrants. At the same time, psychiatrists hoped to capitalize on the debate over immigration in order to establish national recognition of their alleged expertise in matters of public policy, thereby exerting an influence over law making. No matter how they might differ over the details of immigration policy, the AMPA's members were convinced that the time had come to "make ourselves felt in these great public issues which are now pressing upon the country," in the words of the 1908 president. The AMPA's psychiatrists were also afraid that unless they expressed their opinions openly and forcefully, decisions in the fields of health and public welfare would be made without them, possibly to their disadvantage.[40]

White's example also indicated that it was possible to support the medical regulation of immigration without necessarily converting to eugenics. As late as 1918 he still retained hopes that eugenic research might shed some light on the opaque subject of human genetics.[41] He was adamant however that the way to achieve eugenic goals was not through "legislation" nor "sumptuary" and "prohibitory laws." If, then, he pressed for immigration legislation it is likely that he did so not for eugenic reasons, but simply to screen immigrants for mental and physical disabilities.

38. William A. White, Owen Copp, and William Russell to William Bennet, 12 November 1908, WAW, box 3.

39. Thomas W. Salmon, "Immigration and the Mixture of Races in Relation to the Mental Health of the Nation," in *The Modern Treatment of Nervous and Mental Diseases*, ed. William A. White and S. E. Jelliffe, 2 vols. (Philadelphia: Lea and Febiger, 1913), 1:241–86.

40. For the AMPA's discussion of Bennet's bill, see *AJI* 65 (1908): 145–46; *AJI* 66 (1909): 160–62; *AJI* 67 (1910): 412–15. See also Charles P. Bancroft, "Presidential Address: Hopeful and Discouraging Aspects of the Psychiatric Outlook," *AJI* 65 (1908): 1–16, esp. 14–15; Albert Warren Ferris, "Italian Immigration and Insanity," *PAMPA* 15 (1908): 383–95, and "Discussion," pp. 395–400. In the words of the AMPA's 1913 president, psychiatrists were "being 'cross-fired' with urgent demands and inquiries, asking for reasons, why the insane are increasing faster than the population, and, not only that extreme grade, but why all milder grades of psychic defectiveness are also increasing." James T. Searcy, "Have We a Specialty?" *AJI* 70 (1913): 263–72, 268.

41. See White to H. H. Laughlin, 25 February 1918, WAW, box 17.

Other psychiatrists whose tastes ran in the same direction as White's probably endorsed the AMPA's position for that reason.[42]

The AMPA was not wrong in thinking that important legislative decisions regarding immigration were impending. In 1906 the IRL had made its renewed attempt to introduce a bill featuring a literacy test for immigrants, which had failed because the transportation companies and organizations such as the National Association of Manufacturers were opposed to any regulations that threatened to limit the flow of immigrants. The growing numbers of foreign-born Italian, Jewish, and Slavic voters also influenced the decisions of Washington legislators such as Speaker Joe Cannon, who did everything in his power to scuttle the literacy bill because, among other things, he saw it as a divisive issue that could split his own Republican Party.[43] President Theodore Roosevelt, though himself a eugenic restrictionist, shared Cannon's worries. He was also fearful that further restrictionist publicity surrounding the immigration question would jeopardize the sensitive negotiations he was conducting at the time with the Japanese, discussions that would lead in 1907 to the so-called Gentlemen's Agreement according to which the Japanese government voluntarily reduced its own emigration to the United States. The congressional and public debate over immigration culminated in the 1907 act, a defeat for the IRL and other supporters of a literacy test.[44] This act, despite its expansion of the list of excluded classes, was also little cause for rejoicing among psychiatrists. They resented nonmedical, political figures overruling the diagnoses of medical inspectors, viewing it as an insult to their specialty, and the act empowered the secretary of commerce with the discretionary authority to do just that: admit borderline cases in defiance of PHS physicians' opinions.

The 1907 act was not however a total disaster for restrictionists; for it ordered that each arriving alien would thenceforth pay a head tax of four dollars. It also provided for an investigative commission, headed by Senator William P. Dillingham of Vermont, to study the whole immigration question. The Dillingham Commission was the outgrowth of a compromise between restrictionists and antirestrictionists. The former hoped the commission would help to sustain public interest in immigration until national sentiments changed in favor of more exclusionary measures, and

42. For a clear statement of White's views on eugenic legislation, see White to Heber Butts, 21 May 1908, WAW, box 2.
43. In their effort to dodge the contentious restriction issue, the Republicans dropped it from their party platform between 1904 and 1912, after including it for more than a decade. Jones, *American Immigration*, pp. 261–62. See also Higham, *Strangers in the Land*, pp. 128–29.
44. Higham, *Strangers in the Land*, pp. 129–30.

the latter hoped its findings would settle the issue once and for all, indefinitely postponing a decision on the literacy test. The commission reflected the faith Roosevelt and many educated and influential Americans placed in the ability of experts to solve a problem that the country's politicians seemingly could not. Also, it offered politicians, including Roosevelt, the opportunity to dodge their responsibility to make decisions on highly sensitive and delicate issues by delegating them to a scientific and supposedly impartial committee.[45]

The commission took more than three years and spent roughly a million dollars to produce a report that ran to forty-two volumes. It held no public hearings and cross-examined no witnesses. The report was so long that it is doubtful that more than a handful of congressmen had the time to read it in its entirety. As might be expected, its findings included something to please every interested party. For restrictionists it stressed the qualitative differences between the "new," post-1880 immigration and the "old," pre-1880 immigration. The commission's broad conclusion was that the "new" immigrants posed an unprecedented assimilation problem. As the commission alleged, compared with the old immigrants, the new tended to come from European regions with weaker democratic traditions and institutions and vastly different cultural customs. New immigrants were said to be largely either farmers or unskilled laborers who clustered in established cities, whereas earlier immigrants with artisanal backgrounds supposedly spurred the growth of new industries and cities across the nation. As for the literacy test, the commission was strongly in favor of it, chiefly because its members insisted there was a link between illiteracy and poverty. Commission members viewed a literacy test as a means of screening out immigrants who stood a reasonable chance of becoming public charges after entry. But although the report provided ample fodder for the restrictionist cause, it did so less on racial or national than on economic grounds. A full twenty of the report's forty-two volumes were entirely devoted to the economic effects of immigration. The fact that the report paid scant attention to the biologic nature of immigrants greatly disappointed nativists, who considered race and eugenics to be the heart of the matter.

Thus the Dillingham Commission, though it contributed substantially to the national debate, was not the ammunition that eugenic restrictionists had hoped for. Its 1911 report may have been laden with unwarranted conclusions about differences among immigrant national groups, but it

45. Oscar Handlin, "Introduction," *Reports of the Immigration Commission: Abstracts of Reports of the Immigration Commission*, 2 vols. (New York: Arno and *New York Times*, 1970), 1:vi–vii.

did not spark a deluge of racially oriented legislation. It would be six years before a literacy test became law, and by then the United States would be on the verge of entering the war.[46] It is worth remembering that by 1911 myriad groups were agitating for further restriction, many with different solutions to the problem of selecting desirable immigrants. Psychiatrists, with their faith in medical inspection, were just one of these parties convinced that, in the words of one historian, "the regulatory system was not working, or at least not working efficiently or adequately. Every legal loophole could be closed by new legislation, but some parts of the body of immigration law simply were not enforceable. . . . Meanwhile the tide of immigration during these years [1911–13] was rising higher and higher." It is hardly surprising that Congress entertained the possibility of enacting more drastic measures.[47] One did not need to be a eugenicist to be concerned about immigration or support a literacy test.[48]

The ambiguous quality of the Dillingham Commission's conclusions was nowhere more evident than in its remarks about the link between immigration and insanity. The commission relied mainly on the national census for its statistical information and did no firsthand investigation of its own into the topic. Its report did concede, on the one hand, that "mentally unsound aliens in considerable numbers are admitted to the country in violation of the provisions of the immigration act" and did refer to "the inefficacy of the immigration law." It also sympathized with New York State's dilemma as the site of settlement for significant numbers of immigrants. The commission drew attention to the differences between Canadian and U.S. immigration and claimed both that Canadian inspectors enjoyed more authority over decisions regarding exclusion and that Canada's deportation law was sounder than Washington's. On the other hand, except for dropping the state's obligation to prove insanity

---

46. Jones, *American Immigration*, p. 269.
47. E. P. Hutchinson, *Legislative History of American Immigration Policy, 1798–1965* (Philadelphia: University of Pennsylvania Press, 1981), pp. 155–57. Hutchinson argues that the Dillingham Commission influenced legislation after 1911 "less through the report itself than through the personal influence and prestige of its members, esp. Dillingham and [Henry Cabot] Lodge in the Senate and [John L.] Burnett in the House, who played dominant roles in congressional work on immigration" (p. 156).
48. For example, see Samuel Gompers, *Seventy Years of Life and Labour*, 2 vols. (New York: Kelley, 1967), 2:151–73. Salmon was not far wrong in saying in 1912 that proponents of both unrestricted and highly restricted immigration concurred "that the tremendous problem of caring for our insane and defectives should not be rendered more difficult by the admission of insane and mentally defective immigrants." Thomas Salmon, "Some Medical Phases of Immigration," AFMH, Salmon Papers, box 1, folder 6.

owing to "causes prior to landing" in deportation cases, the report offered no concrete proposals for improving immigration laws. According to the report, "Under the conditions attending the disembarkation of immigrants at the ports of entry, an absolutely complete and errorless enforcement of the law is probably impossible. Nothing could possibly prevent the admission of some insane aliens except the obviously impossible requirement of detaining every arriving alien for observation for a considerable period." For those inclined to draw racist conclusions from the most recent data on immigration the commission's report was similarly disappointing. Not only did the commission warn that comparing the number of foreign-born inmates of mental hospitals with the number of native-born inmates without correcting for age was "manifestly unfair," it approvingly quoted the 1904 census report statement that "the distinction between native and foreign is rapidly losing significance as a means of gauging the real elements of population from which the insane are recruited most largely." From the nativist perspective perhaps the most shocking of the report's conclusions about insanity and immigration was that the incidence of mental disease was actually highest among "the nationalities furthest advanced in civilization"—for example, Scandinavians, Germans, Irish, and the Scots—rather than "the more backward races" of southern and eastern Europe.[49]

This finding did not prevent some psychiatrists from continuing to believe that the opposite was true. As with sterilization, a few intemperate psychiatrists called for extreme solutions to complex medical and social problems. Some, such as Carlos MacDonald, supported the IRL and its campaign for a literacy test in the years between 1911 and 1917. MacDonald's strong preference for a literacy test was echoed in a more blatantly racist vein by Charles Potts, a New Jersey psychiatrist. "From my observation," Potts wrote, "the southern Italian and Russian Jew are no more desirable (possibly less) than the Chinese." The ostensible link between psychiatry and the IRL's racially motivated crusade was strengthened by Hall's frequent reliance on the testimony of mental

49. "Immigration and Insanity," in U.S. Senate, *Reports of the Immigration Commission: Abstracts of Reports of the Immigration Commission with Conclusions and Recommendations and Views of the Minority*, 2 vols., 61st Cong., 3d sess., 1911, S. Doc. 747, 2:227–51; 235, 245, 251 (hereafter cited as *Abstracts*). For comparisons between the Canadian and the U.S. systems of immigration, see *Immigration Situation in Canada*, pp. 44–59; and Handlin, *Reports*, p. xxxvii. For another reference to the need to use statistics corrected for age when discussing the rates of mental illness among immigrants, see Edward Sandford to John L. Burnett, 18 May 1912, U.S. House of Representatives, *Hearings before the Committee on Immigration and Naturalization*, 62d Cong., 2d sess., 1912, pp. 218–21.

health care officials and physicians—particularly from New York State—regarding the contributions of immigration to mounting state hospital costs.[50]

Uncharitable opinions about specific national immigrant groups and their susceptibility to insanity, crime, and vice were, however, minority attitudes among U.S. psychiatrists. Most thought the real need was not new legislation but better enforcement of the old.[51] Like Canadian psychiatrists, their attitudes toward immigration arose largely if not wholly from their progressive sense of duty to combat the entrenched business "interests" allegedly profiting from unrestricted immigration. Political interference, in their view, only hamstrung the efficient operation of medical inspection and state hospitals, damaging the nation's public health and financial resources and inflicting incalculable suffering on the insane newcomers deported or denied admission. Psychiatrists' perceptions thus had more to do with progressive sentiments, occupational concerns, professional self-image, and humanitarian considerations than generalized prejudices. They supported whatever legal reforms promised to improve their working conditions and promote reliance on psychiatrists as public health experts. That translated into better screening of foreigners with a predisposition to mental illness, and if psychiatrists exaggerated the immigrant threat, it was for these reasons more than anything else.

These views were apparent at the AMPA's annual meetings as early as 1908. Albert Warren Ferris, then the president of the New York State Commission in Lunacy, argued that Italian immigrants who became insane in the United States were "recruited almost exclusively from the rosy, round, well-nourished vegetarian country people" of their home country. They fell victim to insanity, Ferris argued, largely because of the poor diet and hard working and living conditions they had to endure in the United States. Ferris's paper sparked a reaction from Charles Bancroft of the New Hampshire state hospital, who claimed to have watched Italian immigrants arrive at Ellis Island and observed that their faces bore "a lack of intelligence, ignorance" when compared with the faces of "the northern races." But when confronted with Ferris's evidence, Bancroft confessed that he had "received much enlightenment this evening" and

50. *Abstracts*, pp. 102–15; p. 115.
51. As Salmon contended in 1912, "Much can be done to prevent the admission of insane immigrants *without any changes in the immigration law*. It so often happens that when one law is ineffectively enforced new legislation is enacted, with no assurance that the new legislation will be enforced any better than that which is thought defective." Salmon to Homer Folks, 5 July 1912, AFMH, Salmon Papers, box 1, folder 6. His emphasis.

seemed sympathetic toward Ferris's point that "bad environment and poor hygienic conditions" were more responsible than constitutional, hereditary characteristics. Other AMPA psychiatrists indicated a general willingness to accept a documented case for either the sound mental health of southern European immigrants or the impact of environment on the incidence of insanity among newcomers.[52]

The same could be said about a 1910 meeting of New York State mental health care officials and physicians. If any forum were conducive to the airing of unfriendly opinions about immigrants this would have been it, given the anger of so many Empire State native-born residents over their state's seemingly disproportionate share of the costs of housing the nation's mentally ill aliens. Indeed at this meeting the chairman of the State Board of Alienists to the Lunacy Commission did contend that certain nationalities and religious groups were more disposed to crime and mental disease than others, calling Jewish immigrants in particular the "race" most likely to develop "nervous" or insane disorders. He then openly questioned whether "the psychology of all races" which entered the United States as immigrants would "allow them to go through the 'melting pot' and become conservative members of a republic." Nonetheless, his comments found few supporters. One psychiatrist agreed that "Russian Jews and Italians furnish a majority of our insane aliens." Yet he quickly cautioned that "We can not of course use the same standards or apply the same tests [to immigrants] that we use in estimating the mental calibre of native born patients. Moreover, the information concerning the early life, development and education of the alien is often very meagre; ignorance and illiteracy may be easily mistaken for true inferiority or degeneracy." Other data, he continued, suggested that immigrants showed no "unusual evidence of constitutional inferiority." Another psychiatrist reasoned that increased rates of insanity among immigrant groups were to be expected; after all, he said, think of what would happen if a large number of U.S. citizens were immediately whisked away to a foreign land with different language, customs, and institutions. Before jumping to unwarranted conclusions on the basis of "pure statistics," he summarized, Americans should consider the many

52. Ferris, "Italian Immigration and Insanity" and "Discussion." Bancroft's comments are on p. 400. See also H. M. Swift, "Insanity and Race," *AJI* 70 (1913): 143–54. As Swift wrote (pp. 143–44), "It cannot be assumed that the relative frequency of insanity among the races in America is necessarily a true indicator of relative race susceptibility in residents of the mother countries, because changes in environment may have had their modifying effects, so that in a given case it could hardly be said, without qualifications, whether such a patient might not have escaped insanity had he remained at home."

factors that undermine a primarily hereditarian theory of immigration.[53] A literacy test, these psychiatrists seemed to be saying, was an arbitrary criterion of selection that discriminated unfairly against individual immigrants; perhaps worse, its use would undercut support for trained and discerning medical inspectors.

Thus what united U.S. psychiatrists by the second decade of the twentieth century was the conviction that immigration legislation had to be improved both to stem the influx of defective aliens and to validate and capitalize on the expertise and diagnostic skills of physicians. Few disagreed that the system of inspection had to be overhauled. They insisted it was time to ensure that there be more physicians appointed as medical inspectors and that all inspectors be trained in hospitals for the mentally ill. A major step in this direction would be the erection of a mental hospital run by the Marine Hospital Service itself, an institution that would both house mentally ill aliens and serve as a training school for psychiatric inspectors. Otherwise, states such as New York would be left defenseless.[54]

Psychiatrists were equally convinced of the need to reform the deportation process. That the difficulties with it had not been eliminated after more than a decade of complaints was a source of bitter frustration for the AMPA. What made the situation offensive to psychiatrists was that the U.S. attorney general had upheld the Department of Commerce and Labor solicitor's ruling that a Bureau of Deportation recommendation to deport was "a mere matter of medical opinion" that had to be "substantiated by evidence showing that insanity actually existed before entry into the United States." Put another way, medical testimony about an immigrant's mental status was treated as little more than an "opinion" that could be—and often was—overruled. When the case in question was one of dementia praecox, state hospital officials saw ample potential for scandal. Dementia praecox—or what is now called schizophrenia—

---

53. Wilgus, "Problem of Immigration" and "Discussion," pp. 125, 127, 130. For rates of disease among Jewish immigrants in the twentieth century, see Kraut, *Silent Travelers*, pp. 136–65. Kraut describes the efforts of Dr. Maurice Fishberg, himself a Jewish immigrant from Russia and professor of clinical medicine at the New York University and Bellevue Medical College, who vigorously contested the nativist argument that Jewish immigrants had higher sickness and mortality rates than U.S.-born citizens. Kraut does not address the question of Jewish immigrants' rates of mental illness, however. According to historian Edward Shorter, "impressionistic" evidence from the history of medicine suggests the theory that hysteria and mental diseases such as manic-depressive illness "were commoner among Jews than non-Jews." He concedes that the evidence proves little, though it does "establish that this opinion was not just an anti-Semitic slander." See Edward Shorter, *From the Mind into the Body: The Cultural Origins of Psychosomatic Symptoms* (New York: Free Press, 1994), pp. 106, 117.
54. "Discussion," *PAMPA* 19 (1912): 190–96, 190–93.

was then viewed as a chronic mental disease that developed in adolescence, resisted treatment, and resulted in progressive deterioration over time. Almost all psychiatrists with clinical exposure to the disease were in agreement that an immigrant diagnosed with it suffered from an authentically constitutional illness whose seeds predated landing; in other words, "a constitutional psychopathic state." Such an immigrant was an indisputable candidate for deportation. To have a layperson overrule this diagnosis as "a mere matter of medical opinion" was an egregious insult and a further imposition on state public charity. As one state medical superintendent complained in 1912, psychiatrists "know that *dementia praecox* is a constitutional disease, and yet the alienist is often helpless in such cases provided he cannot obtain specific facts in relation to the patient's history, because of late the department at Washington has been declining to accept 'constitutional psychopathic state' as a cause for the mental disease existing prior to landing in this country." The solution, according to members of the AMPA, was as clear in 1912 as it had been ten years earlier: the eligibility period for deportation should be extended well beyond three years, and the immigrant should be forced to prove that his or her mental illness arose from causes occurring *since* landing.[55] Members concurred that the task of screening immigrants for health reasons was "a purely medical one and, therefore, should be based on medical opinions" alone.[56]

At the 1912 annual meeting the AMPA resolved to do something about the unsatisfactory state of immigration inspection and hastily formed a new, five-person committee. The resulting report urged that only psychiatrically trained physicians be delegated "in sufficient numbers" to perform mental examinations; that there be "adequate facilities for the detention and examination of immigrants in whom insanity or mental defect is suspected"; that those aliens excluded be provided with "safe and humane return to their homes"; that insane aliens be eligible for deportation "within at least three years after landing"; that deportations take place "unless it shall be shown conclusively that such insanity or mental defect has resulted from causes arising since the landing of said aliens"; that "all questions of fact or opinion involved be governed and decided solely by the teachings of modern psychiatry"; that the fine imposed on transportation companies for bringing mentally ill immigrants

55. James V. May, "Immigration as a Problem in the State Care of the Insane," *PAMPA* 19 (1912): 181–90; "Discussion," ibid., pp. 193–96. For other remarks on the "fertile recruiting ground for dementia praecox" among "young immigrants," see Charles P. Bancroft, "Is There an Increase among the Dementing Psychoses?" *PAMPA* 21 (1914): 287–301, 297.
56. "Discussion," *PAMPA* 19 (1912): 111.

into the United States be at least doubled; and that "the barbarous custom of deporting insane or mentally defective aliens without accompanying nurses or qualified attendants, of his or her own sex and of experience in caring for such cases" be ended immediately. This report, which neatly synthesized the humanitarian, professional, and xenophobic concerns of the AMPA, indicated that psychiatrists would be happy only when the entire decision-making process of admission and deportation of mentally ill aliens was placed squarely in their hands and kept out of the hands of politicians. A motion that it be received, accepted, and adopted was carried.[57]

The next step was a meeting on 16 November 1912 between the AMPA's committee and various psychiatrists, social workers, and health care reformers in New York City. There the AMPA's resolutions were endorsed by, among other groups, the Immigration Committee of the Eugenics Section of the American Breeders' Association, the forerunner of the American Genetics Association and controlled by Prescott Hall and Robert DeCourcy Ward of the IRL. Copies were then sent to the Senate Committee on Immigration, the House Committee on Immigration and Naturalization, and—on Thomas Burgess's suggestion—the Canadian government.[58] This AMPA activism did help to generate congressional interest in the mental health dimensions of immigration. State health officials from Massachusetts and Rhode Island all agreed that the regulations governing deportation had to be changed. Belying the charge that psychiatrists were worried mainly about immigrants from southern and eastern Europe, one of them cited the example of "the beer-drinking German" as the kind of alien who managed to get into the country and who soon became a drain on the public purse. National prejudices notwithstanding, the immediate challenge was to convince Congress of the need for reform.[59]

The NCMH also supported the AMPA's stance—hardly surprising, as it had hired Thomas Salmon that year. Salmon was considered by then to be the foremost national psychiatrist with expertise on immigration. In 1915 he would be appointed medical director of the NCMH and served in that capacity until 1922, except for a two-year hiatus between 1917 and 1919 when he was on leave with the U.S. Army. Thanks primarily to him, the NCMH was gradually to extend its scope beyond the study of institutionalized mental patients to encompass the social con-

57. *PAMPA* 19 (1912): 105–12. A copy of the document can be found in WAW, box 8.
58. AFMH, Thomas Salmon Papers, box 1, folder 6.
59. *Hearings before the Committee on Immigration and Naturalization, House of Representatives, 4, 7, 8 May 1912*, pp. 125, 168–73, 221–24; p. 224.

ditions presumed responsible for psychological disease. Convinced that there was only a tiny gap between mental health and mental illness, Salmon thought psychiatrists had an important public health role to play outside the confines of the mental hospital. He was a militant convert to the notion that psychiatrists' expertise lay not just in the diagnosis and treatment of hospitalized persons but also in the study and management of issues that shaped the emotional health of U.S. citizens.[60]

Shortly after joining the NCMH, Salmon was instrumental in pressuring its executive committee to pass a resolution urging Congress to ensure that mental examinations of immigrants were conducted only by clinically trained psychiatrists. Salmon's public views on immigration, a mixture of humanitarianism, professional partisanship, and uncritical and ill-informed opinions about national tendencies toward mental illness, closely mirrored those of psychiatrists generally. Like C. K. Clarke, he had a talent for getting into trouble with vested financial, bureaucratic, and political interests. While working for the New York State Commission in Lunacy in 1911 he had been censured for his efforts to improve conditions on board for immigrants returned to their native lands. He had also tried to end the practice of simply dumping deported aliens at the foreign ports where they had embarked, often without alerting their families or friends. At the same time, Salmon was little different from most psychiatrists on the subject of immigration and the national rate of mental and nervous disease. Immigration, he would declare in 1913, "provides the material for a vast experiment in eugenics." Quoting race theorists such as Houston Stewart Chamberlain and Prescott Hall, Salmon argued that "race" had a "paramount" influence on character, health, and disease.[61] He too believed there were fundamental biologic and cultural discrepancies between the "old" and "new" immigrants; that certain national groups of immigrants were more predisposed to insanity than others; and that there was "a tremendously undue prevalence of mental diseases in the foreign-born population."[62]

60. Grob, *Mental Illness and American Society*, pp. 160–63; Dain, *Clifford W. Beers*, pp. 168–71.
61. "Discussion by Dr. Thomas W. Salmon," *New York State Hospitals Bulletin* 3 (1910): 131–35, 134. As Samuel B. Thielman points out, the term *race* had, for Salmon, a somewhat different meaning than it has for us today. Salmon and his contemporaries used the word loosely to denote physical, mental, behavioral, and cultural distinctions between ethnic groups, differences that were supposedly shaped by biologic inheritance and could be transmitted from one generation to the next. This definition of race fell out of favor by the mid-twentieth century. See Samuel B. Thielman, "Psychiatry and Social Values: The American Psychiatric Association and Immigration Restriction, 1880–1930," *Psychiatry* 48 (1985): 299–310, 301 n. See also George W. Stocking, "Race," in *Dictionary of the History of Science*, ed. W. F. Bynum, E. J. Browne, and Roy Porter (Princeton: Princeton University Press, 1981), pp. 356–57.
62. "Discussion by Dr. Thomas W. Salmon," p. 134. See also Thomas W. Salmon, "The

Yet Salmon was quite capable of saying in literally the very next moment that "no man can say positively to-day what the disproportion [between insanity rates in the native- and foreign-born populations] actually is nor answer the question whether the 'new immigration' is more harmful in this respect than the old."[63] On another occasion he conceded that there was a "lack of accurate information as to the prevalence of insanity among the foreign-born population" of New York State, "especially with reference to nativity, race, age, occupation, forms of mental diseases, recoverability and many other factors which have a direct bearing upon the eligibility of immigrants."[64] Salmon believed heredity was not necessarily the most powerful influence on immigrants' susceptibility to insanity; environmental factors, such as "the evils of overcrowding," the stress of making a living in a new land, and separation from kith and kin made it "small cause for wonder if it is found that excessive ratios of insanity prevail among the new immigrant races under such conditions."[65] This was probably one reason he rejected Charles Davenport's proposal to select immigrants on the basis of their heredity, at least until more should be known about the mechanism of inheritance.[66] Nor did

Relation of Immigration to the Prevalence of Insanity," *AJI* 64 (1907–8): 53–71; "Memorandum regarding the Admission and Deportation of Alien Patients and Others not Entitled to Treatment in New York State Hospitals," *New York State Hospitals Bulletin* 4 (1911): 151–56; "Discussion," ibid. 5 (1912): 148–53; "Immigration and the Mixture of Races in Relation to the Mental Health of the Nation," in White and Jelliffe, *Modern Treatment*, 1:241, 243–76, esp. p. 258; and "Immigration and the Prevention of Insanity," *Boston Medical and Surgical Journal* 169 (1913): 297–301. For Salmon's references to immigration as "a problem of eugenics and public health," see Salmon to Frederick Peterson, 14 November 1912, AFMH, Salmon Papers, box 1, folder 6.

63. "Discussion by Salmon," p. 134. Salmon still felt much the same way in 1917 when he told the Rockefeller Foundation that he did "not think that it is quite correct to assume that any larger proportion of cases of *dementia praecox* come to us through immigration than through the other route by which our population is recruited." AFMH, Thomas Salmon Papers, box 2, folder 2.

64. Thomas W. Salmon, "Insanity and the Immigration Law," *New York State Hospitals Bulletin* 4 (1911): 396. In 1913 Salmon anyhow conceded that psychiatrists' recommendations about immigration did not depend on the theory that immigrants were disproportionately represented among the nation's insane. Thomas W. Salmon, "Immigration and the Prevention of Insanity," AFMH, Salmon Papers, box 1, folder 8.

65. Salmon, "Immigration and the Mixture of Races," p. 270. In 1912 Salmon cited the great "stress" immigrants had to endure and argued that this factor rendered "the assumption that immigrants have a special susceptibility to mental disease quite unnecessary in explaining the great prevalence of insanity among them." Salmon, "Some Medical Phases of Immigration."

66. Salmon, "Immigration and the Prevention of Insanity," Salmon Papers. Barbara Sicherman, "The Quest for Mental Health in America, 1880–1917" (Ph.D. diss., Columbia University, 1967), p. 348 n. See also Thomas W. Salmon, "Mental Hygiene," in *Preventive Medicine and Hygiene*, ed. Milton J. Rosenau (New York: D. Appleton, 1917), p. 337, for Salmon's cautionary comments about "making sweeping rules against the marriage of those who have had mental troubles either themselves or in their families" when so little was known about heredity.

he provide nativists and racists with grounds for their fears of miscegenation. Intermarriage between Jewish immigrants and US-born men and
women was actually a good thing, he said in 1913. Finally, he dismissed
the idea that the selection of immigrants from the standpoint of health
could be effectively achieved with "arbitrary restriction of immigration"
by such means as a literacy test. His position was that of most psychiatrists: if immigrants were to be excluded for mental health reasons, it
had to be on an *individual* basis; "It would be a confession of the inadequacy of the resources of modern psychiatry if we were obliged to restrict immigration arbitrarily," Salmon wrote. In fact he was not terribly
interested in sweeping changes to the laws. "The most pressing need,"
he argued, "is not for better immigration laws but for facilities for enforcing those which we have."[67]

In other words, Salmon's views were far from systematic or consistent,
except when it came to psychiatrists' hegemony over medical inspection
of aliens. Like other psychiatrists, he mainly wanted this field free of any
influence extraneous to pure psychiatry, especially pressure brought to
bear on politicians by steamship companies. To him psychiatrists were
locked in a struggle with "the interests" that often poisoned the health
of countless innocent men, women, and children, including immigrants;
it was a battle in defense of humane values and sentiments. As he wrote
in 1913,

> The exclusion of insane and mentally defective immigrants is a question of
> public health. It is not a political question, it is only incidentally an eco-
> nomic question, but it affects the welfare of coming generations of Amer-
> icans as deeply as any question before the people of this country today. The
> interests of the capital invested in foreign steamship companies should have
> just as much weight with Congress in the solution of this question as the
> interests of the capital invested in the manufacture of fire arms should have
> in the protection of song birds.[68]

Salmon plainly imagined himself occupying the ground outside the cor-
ridors of power and influence. For both selfless and selfish reasons, he
and other psychiatrists desperately wanted to be allowed in.

Despite Salmon's evasiveness about the effects of heredity on immigrants' rates of insanity, his lack of concern about miscegenation, his

67. Salmon, "Immigration and the Mixture of Races," pp. 267, 277–78, 284. See also Salmon,
"Immigration and the Prevention of Insanity," Salmon Papers.
68. Salmon, "Immigration and the Prevention of Insanity," p. 301. See also Salmon, "Immigration and the Mixture of Races," pp. 257–58.

qualifications about the reliability of statistics describing immigrants' propensity for mental illness, his lukewarm attitude toward substantive reform of immigration laws, and his rejection of "arbitrary" means of restriction, Hall and the IRL tried nevertheless to convey the impression that psychiatrists were their steadfast allies in the struggle to secure a literacy test. This emphatically was not Salmon's view; nor was it the AMPA's. Its 1913 Committee on Immigration had been successful in getting legislators to include four of its six 1912 recommendations in an immigration bill that both houses of Congress passed in early 1913. President Taft vetoed the bill in February. Just before he did so, however, he held a public hearing, and the AMPA's committee attended. Taft told the committee that he regretted vetoing the bill and expressed admiration for the AMPA recommendations. The committee stressed to Taft that it was interested "only in better protection against the admission of insane and mentally defective immigrants and not in any policy of general restriction." One year later, the AMPA stated it supported only immigration legislation that included its recommendations and *not* "an illiteracy clause" that was likely to be vetoed by the new president, Woodrow Wilson. Not only did the AMPA dislike the professional implications for psychiatry of a literacy test, but it could sense that its own provisions would be defeated if combined with such a feature.[69] Taft's personal endorsement of the AMPA position and his simultaneous opposition to a literacy test confirms the subtle yet important distinction between psychiatrists and the IRL on immigration.

The IRL pretended not to notice the distinction, and it found some of the medical literature on immigrants useful to its own eugenic theories.[70] It continued vigorously lobbying Congress both to persuade legislators of the unity of the IRL and psychiatrists and to revitalize the campaign for a literacy test after the Taft veto. Hall argued for the efficacy of a literacy screening test, cited New York State data to highlight the "threat" from immigration, and tried to expand the common ground between the IRL and psychiatrists by adding the term *constitutional psychopathic inferiority* to the list of excludable conditions. Hall favored this term for reasons he shared with psychiatrists: the use of this diagnosis would suggest that an alien's mental condition was chronic and hereditary, thus due to causes existing *before* landing. Immigrants, their

69. "Report of Committee on Immigration," *AJI* 70 (1913): 231–32; "Report of Committee on Immigration," *AJI* 71 (1914): 206–8. See also Hutchinson, *Legislative History*, pp. 153–55, 160–63.
70. Barbara M. Solomon, *Ancestors and Immigrants: A Changing New England Tradition* (Cambridge: Harvard University Press, 1956), pp. 149–50.

friends and families, and immigrant organizations would therefore find it much harder to overturn medical decisions to deport. But for all his effort, Hall could not paper over the differences. A literacy test, as he himself admitted, largely obviated the need for psychiatric inspection and medical diagnostic expertise. He also came extremely close to blaming medical inspectors themselves for the "laxness" at entry sites, hinting that they were susceptible to pressure from immigrant organizations such as the Jewish Immigrant Aid Society.[71] In short, Hall proved why psychiatrists distrusted restriction by literacy tests or any other general principle: asserting a need for such guidelines implied that medical inspectors were not doing or could not do their job.

In the meantime, Salmon and other psychiatrists kept up the pressure for reform and enforcement. First and foremost was the addition of "constitutional psychopathic inferiority" to the list of excludable classes: a new bill before Congress in 1914 included an amendment doing just that for the first time. A brief flurry of congressional debate erupted on 10 December. Some senators were suspicious of assurances that psychiatrists using the term truly knew what they were talking about. These senators were reluctant to endorse the amendment simply because psychiatrists supported it, a stance Salmon was bound to interpret as an insult to his professionalism and expertise. Five days later a letter from Salmon was read in the U.S. Senate stressing the importance of the amendment to the current legislation. Salmon claimed the amendment enjoyed the approval of the NCMH, AMPA, New York Psychiatric Society, National Association for the Study of Epilepsy, Mental Hygiene Committee of the New York State Charities' Aid Association, and a number of eminent physicians and state charity officials. He emphasized that "constitutional psychopathic inferiority" had a precise diagnostic usefulness for psychiatrists working in the field of immigration. "A competent medical examination can detect many cases of constitutional psychopathic inferiority," he concluded.[72]

To Salmon's chagrin his efforts were unsuccessful. The amendment was referred back to committee for further consideration in late December. Salmon defined the term as "a congenital defect in the emotional or volitional fields of mental activity which results in inability to make proper adjustments to the environment," an explanation that could mean

71. Prescott F. Hall, "The Recent History of Immigration and Immigration Restriction," *Hearings before the Committee on Immigration and Naturalization, House of Representatives, 6 December 1913*, 63d Cong., 2d sess., 1913, pp. 18–26.
72. U.S. Senate, *Congressional Record*, 63d Cong., 3d sess., 10 December 1914, 52:82–83; ibid., 15 December 1914, 52:206–7, 216.

a lot of things or very little at all. Some senators may have been uneasy about the amendment precisely because they thought it was all too clear what Salmon had in mind. As more than one senator declared, constitutional psychopathic inferiority referred to "a hereditary taint" and thus could be used to exclude or deport aliens mistaken as degenerate. This would account for the fact that in 1916 a senator from New York, a state with many immigrant voters, would make an unsuccessful attempt to remove the amendment when it appeared in a new immigration bill.[73] For his part Salmon did little to discourage the association between constitutional psychopathic inferiority and hereditary degeneracy in immigrants. Anxious for congressional approval, he stressed how the diagnosis particularly applied to social deviants, such as criminals, "vagrants," prostitutes, drug addicts, and alcoholics, groups that one senator claimed imposed "a tremendous burden on the taxpayers of the States."[74] The entire exercise became moot in January 1915 when President Wilson vetoed the bill, his chief reason being all too familiar: the bill contained a clause calling for a literacy test. As the psychiatrist Stewart Paton learned in a 22 January 1915 interview with the president himself, Wilson, like Taft, had no disagreement with the psychiatric provisions and amendments.[75]

Paton (1865–1942), a neuropathologist with a faculty appointment in psychiatry at Johns Hopkins, was a much-respected researcher involved in cutting-edge studies on the microscopic anatomy of the brain. He had been hired by Edward Brush in 1899 to direct a new laboratory at the Sheppard and Enoch Pratt Hospital, where C. B. Farrar was his first trainee. Like Clarke, Paton was convinced that what psychiatry needed most were psychiatric clinics, facilities where clinical training, laboratory medicine, and genuinely remedial treatment of the mentally ill could be located under one roof. Accordingly he campaigned tirelessly for what ultimately became the Henry Phipps Psychiatric Clinic at Johns Hopkins, opened in 1908.[76]

73. Ibid., 64th Cong., 1st sess., 27 March 1916, 53:4951–52.
74. U.S. Senate, *Congressional Record*, 63d Cong., 3d sess., 15 December 1914, 52:224. See also Hutchinson, *Legislative History*, pp. 162–65, 414–15.
75. Paton had appeared before Wilson on Salmon's urging. See AFMH, Thomas Salmon Papers, box 2, folder 1. For Paton's report to the president stressing that the NCMH did not defend the "illiteracy test," see *Boston Medical and Surgical Journal* 172 (1915): 313–15.
76. Arthur P. Noyes, "History of Psychiatry: Dr. Stewart Paton," APA, MS, pp. 299–300. See also Edward Shorter, "C. B. Farrar: A Life," in "TPH: Histories and Memories of the Toronto Psychiatric Hospital," ed. Edward Shorter, QSMHC, Unpublished MSS, pp. 96–98. For Paton's career in the eugenics movement, see Barry Alan Mehler, "A History of the American Eugenics Society, 1921–1940" (Ph.D. diss., University of Illinois at Urbana-Champaign, 1988), pp. 176–77, 412–13.

Paton complained that there was too much "glib talk about the problems of heredity," too little concrete knowledge about the distinctions between environmental and hereditary causes of insanity, and too much attention among psychiatrists paid to "the so-called signs of degeneracy." Nonetheless he was a militant eugenicist. His reservations about hereditarianism did not keep him from advocating measures such as "castration" or institutional segregation for mental defectives.[77] He was a member of the AES and the ERO and a defender of eugenic immigration restriction. Paton asserted that in immigration "we are dealing with one of the great biological problems which fundamentally affect not only the future of this country but the future of the race." As he stated in 1915, "It is in eliminating the insane and mentally defective from the great tide which flows through Ellis Island that the most practical and humane field for the control of insanity and feeblemindedness in this country is to be found." For him these eugenic goals could be reached by following psychiatrists' standard recommendations since the early years of the century. Paton's comments reflected psychiatrists' conviction that the mental health problems posed by immigration—eugenic or otherwise—could best be solved by enabling physicians to do their jobs better as medical inspectors.[78]

But by 1915, Paton's eugenic approach to immigration was becoming increasingly outdated in psychiatric circles, thanks to new statistical evidence that sweeping negative eugenic measures were ineffective in reducing the hereditary components of mental illness. That some of this evidence came from studies conducted by Aaron J. Rosanoff (1878–1943) of the Kings Park State Hospital (N.Y.) was news worth reporting. Rosanoff was a researcher who worked closely with Charles Davenport's ERO. A Jewish immigrant himself, Rosanoff demonstrated that his ancestry and active membership in the eugenics movement were not incompatible. Initially he favored the theory that certain individuals inherited a "neuropathic constitution" that predisposed them to a host of mental and neurological disorders. From his studies of family histories he concluded that a neuropathic constitution was a recessive trait that conformed to Mendel's laws of genetics. But, perhaps because of his own immigrant background, Rosanoff gave no encouragement to restrictionists who wanted to go beyond the AMPA's modest reforms. After examining the data on the relationship between immigration and insanity,

77. Stewart Paton, *Psychiatry: A Text-Book for Students and Physicians* (Philadelphia: Lippincott, 1905), pp. 147–48, 178–86.
78. *Hearings before the Committee on Immigration and Naturalization, House of Representatives*, 21 *January 1915*, 64th Cong., 1st sess., 1915, pp. 26–28.

he decided that whatever it cost the states to take care of insane aliens was far less than the wealth generated by the foreign born. Rosanoff's position was, then, fairly typical among psychiatrists. Though he urged greater vigilance in screening and deporting "insane and otherwise mentally defective immigrants," he confessed that there was no statistical reason for a literacy test.[79] His comments were perfectly consistent with the overall guiding principle espoused by U.S. psychiatrists: prohibition on the basis of medical diagnosis rather than single factors like literacy or national background.[80] Rosanoff's attitude also demonstrated that heterodox views were possible even within the mainstream eugenics movement.

Their reservations about a literacy test notwithstanding, in 1917 psychiatrists finally got what they had been demanding for roughly fifteen years. Only then did literacy test restrictionists manage to garner enough congressional support to override Woodrow Wilson's second presidential veto. Besides doubling the head tax to eight dollars, the 1917 law excluded adult aliens who could not read a short passage in English or some other language or dialect. This test applied neither to immigrants fleeing religious persecution nor to illiterate relatives of literate immigrants' immediate families. Psychiatrists considered the 1917 act, with its literacy test clause, far from perfect; but it was, nonetheless, a milestone in the history of psychiatry because it extended the eligibility period for deportation to five years and included "constitutional psychopathic inferiority," as well as "vagrancy" and "chronic alcoholism," as grounds for exclusion and—by implication—deportation. Never happy that the fate of their own amendments had depended on the legislative fate of the literacy test, psychiatrists could still take satisfaction at the culmi-

79. A. J. Rosanoff, "Some Neglected Phases of Immigration in Relation to Insanity," *AJI* 72 (1915): 45–58. See also A. J. Rosanoff and Gertrude L. Cannon, "Preliminary Report of a Study of Heredity in Insanity in the Light of the Mendelian Laws," *New York State Hospitals Bulletin* 4 (1911): 112–20. For biographical data on Rosanoff, see Barry Alan Mehler, "A History of the American Eugenics Society, 1921–1940" (Ph.D. diss., University of Illinois at Urbana-Champaign, 1988), pp. 65, 419–20. Mehler writes that Rosanoff, born in Russia in 1878, "was almost certainly a Jew by birth." This did not keep him from being a student of Ernst Rüdin, a notable German "race hygienist" who did much to pave the way for Nazi eugenics in the 1930s. Mehler, ibid., p. 65 n. See also Robert Proctor, *Racial Hygiene: Medicine under the Nazis* (Cambridge: Harvard University Press, 1988), pp. 17, 26, 40, 95, 112, 212, 292, 341 n. 24, 345 n. 60; Stefan Kühl, *The Nazi Connection: Eugenics, American Racism, and German National Socialism* (New York: Oxford University Press, 1994), pp. 20, 21–22, 24, 30, 33–34, 50, 85, 94, 102; and Sheila Faith Weiss, "The Race Hygiene Movement in Germany, 1904–45," in *The Wellborn Science: Eugenics in Germany, France, Brazil, and Russia*, ed. Mark B. Adams (New York: Oxford University Press, 1990), pp. 8–68.
80. For Salmon's 1916 views on the literacy test, see Salmon to Ben Appleby, 7 April 1916, AFMH, Thomas Salmon Papers, box 2, folder 2.

nation of their many years of dramatizing the health dangers of unregulated immigration. It looked as if the nation was finally listening to them, as if an important victory for psychiatry had been won. The battle to secure the personnel, facilities, and resources to inspect immigrants appeared to be over. It seemed as if the country were preparing responsibly for the anticipated deluge of newcomers once the European war should end.[81]

But proof of how little psychiatric opinion had in common with public opinion was the fact that as psychiatrists congratulated themselves, the country was becoming steadily more xenophobic and nativist. Whereas most psychiatrists optimistically viewed the act as the end of their collective effort to influence federal policy, the restrictionists perceived it as a beachhead from which to launch further attempts to reduce the flow of immigrants. Up to then, many groups had, like the AMPA, favored regulation as a method of selecting desirable immigrants,[82] but the bill marked a change of emphasis toward outright exclusion.

Nativists, heady with victory, began positioning themselves for the next battle. Like many Americans, they favored a quota system. Growing support for a national quota system had a great deal to do with the effects of the world war on U.S. life. The war was a watershed in the history of American nativism.[83] Its deadly and protracted nature, with the mobilization of entire nations in a quest for total victory, caused many Americans to become deeply conscious of their own and other citizens' national roots. This tendency was exacerbated by swelling anti-German and anti-Irish sentiment, especially after the United States entered the war in April 1917. These xenophobic phenomena temporarily made life easier for those immigrant national groups that had earlier faced nativist prejudices, but the stress on "Americanization" that accompanied the war effort translated into mounting conformist pressure to prove patriotism and loyalty to the country's values, symbols, and institutions. The Americanization movement remained vigorous into the postwar period and led

81. For one psychiatrist's view of the 1917 legislation, see Charles G. Wagner, "Presidential Address: Recent Trends in Psychiatry," *AJI* 74 (1917): 1–14, esp. 8. For another interpretation, see Spencer Dawes, "The New Immigration Law," New York State Charities Aid Association *News* 5 (1917): 10–11. Although Dawes applauded the new provisions of the law pertaining to medical inspection and deportation, he alleged that foreign governments had been tutoring immigrants to enable them to pass a language test, thereby rendering the literacy test ineffective as a principle of exclusion.

82. Hutchinson, *Legislative History*, pp. 166–67. Indeed, there is some evidence to suggest that congressional approval of the literacy test was so formidable precisely because it was seen as a more moderate alternative to the increasingly popular idea of a quota system based on nationality.

83. Jones, *American Immigration*, p. 270.

to further efforts to enforce national homogeneity. With Germany defeated, Americanization also helped to shift public attention toward the presence of foreigners in radical organizations. In the Red Scare of 1919–20 thousands of immigrants with socialist sympathies were deported, many to Bolshevik Russia itself.

Even with the abatement of the Red Scare, suspicion of foreigners, Europe, and Old World loyalties lingered on. The collapse of Wilsonian idealism along with the U.S. rejection of the League of Nations reflected the profoundly isolationist mood of the country. As the United States turned its back on Europe, its citizens projected their fears and hatreds onto the supposed enemy within. Anti-Catholic and anti-Semitic nativism peaked in the 1920s, fostering the view that immigration was an overwhelming liability. This was a striking change from the prewar national mood, which at worst was conflicted.[84] One symptom of 1920s intolerance was the revival of the Ku Klux Klan, which reached a membership of roughly two and a half million by 1923. Interest in the writings of authors such as William Z. Ripley and Madison Grant also began to pick up. Grant's *The Passing of the Great Race in America* (1916) became a virtual manifesto for the restrictionists who had assumed leadership of the cause after the decline of the IRL. Grant, IRL member and preeminent eugenicist, argued that American culture and institutions would never be able to assimilate the many arriving immigrants. Choosing a racial standard for determining undesirability, he specifically warned about Polish Jews, who, he alleged, wore Americans' clothes, adopted their language, used their names, stole their women, and secretly rejected their values. The main consequence of immigration, he concluded, would be the end of the white race of America.[85]

Grant's views had crystallized into a kind of consensus among eugenically inclined restrictionists by the early 1920s. Indeed the AES took over leadership of the U.S. restrictionist cause almost as soon as it was formed in 1921, succeeding where the IRL had failed. It managed to make biology a salient theme of the national debate over immigration, alongside economics. A major step in this direction occurred in 1919 when Representative Albert Johnson of Washington was appointed chair of the House Immigration Committee. He solicited the advice of important eugenicists such as Grant, Kenneth Roberts, and Lothrop Stoddard. He was also mainly responsible for having Harry Laughlin

84. Kenneth M. Ludmerer, *Genetics and American Society: A Historical Appraisal* (Baltimore: Johns Hopkins University Press, 1972), p. 98.
85. Jones, *American Immigration*, pp. 270–77; Solomon, *Ancestors and Immigrants*, pp. 195–209; Higham, *Strangers in the Land*, pp. 264–99.

appointed as "expert eugenics agent" of the House Committee on Immigration and Naturalization. Johnson proceeded to lobby hard for what ultimately became the 1921 Immigration Act. With the war over, immigration had begun to pick up again, unemployment was high, and a depression had set in. Thanks to these circumstances and Johnson's power and influence, the 1921 act imposed 3 percent quotas on each national group based on its representation in the 1910 census.

But because of pronounced opposition from the transportation companies and industry, the 1921 act proved to be only a temporary measure. The eugenicists, fearing that this national origins test might not last long, mobilized quickly to introduce new legislation. Their efforts were rewarded by the 1924 Immigration Act, which lowered the 1921 quotas to 2 percent based on the 1890 census. The 1924 act remained in effect until 1929 when an upper limit of 150,000 immigrants per year was introduced, each nationality being awarded a quota in proportion to its contribution to the existing American white population. Johnson, Grant, and their followers were jubilant because the new legislation penalized southern and eastern European immigrants most heavily. They considered the 1924 act their greatest victory. Antirestrictionists, for their part, had few illusions about what was driving much of the restrictionist movement. As the president of the American Jewish Committee of New York City had told Johnson's committee in 1922, there were "among the people who are opposed to immigration and who desire to close the doors, some who entertain the erroneous idea that the Jews who come from Eastern Europe are all tainted with the taint of Bolshevism."[86] This and similar complaints failed to sway congressional opinion, and the 1924 act ending three centuries of open immigration remained the law of the land until 1965 when the national origins test was scrapped.[87]

In the meantime, what was the reaction of U.S. psychiatrists? Curiously, there was little. For one thing, there had been no mass movement to join the AES in its campaign for immigration restriction by national origins. Though a handful of psychiatrists—Paton, Rosanoff, Adolf Meyer, Henry Goddard, and Walter Fernald—were AES members or on its advisory council, only Paton was still a fervent eugenicist by the end of the war. Rosanoff never shared the anti-immigrant views of AES

86. *Hearings before the Committee on Immigration and Naturalization, House of Representatives*, 26 *January 1922*. 67th Cong., 3d sess., 1922, p. 325.
87. For the AES's campaign to secure immigration legislation between 1921 and 1924, see Mehler, "American Eugenics Society," pp. 180–217, esp. p. 185. See also Higham, *Strangers in the Land*, pp. 300–324; Ludmerer, *Genetics and American Society*, pp. 95–113; and Jones, *American Immigration*, pp. 276–77.

leaders. Goddard and Fernald had retracted most of their eugenic theories about the feebleminded by the early 1920s, so their support was lukewarm at best. Meyer had become extremely dubious about the ways eugenicists were trying to translate their ideas into practice. In 1923 he received a report on selective immigration from the Eugenics Committee of the United States of America, an organization campaigning furiously for the national quotas bill. Politely but firmly Meyer criticized the committee for "giving the appearance of scientific support to matters which after all are just a little bit too frankly human and not strict science."[88] Meyer was as uneasy about the political implications of this legislation as he had been about those pertaining to involuntary sterilization laws. In sum, psychiatrists constituted neither a doctrinaire nor a sizable bloc in the AES, and those who did join had little to do with the AES campaign for a national quotas bill. They tended to disagree with what the organization's leaders were doing and saying, and though they rarely objected openly to its policies, their silence should not be construed as consent.

Noticeably absent from AES membership rolls was Thomas Salmon. He, after all, sometimes used the word *eugenics* to describe his own studies of immigration. Why then did he not join? The likely answer is that he employed the term *eugenics* only as a rhetorical device to promote the occupational and humanitarian interests of psychiatry. With his less than literal usage, he showed that although many U.S. professionals and community leaders deployed the vocabulary of eugenics, there was considerable diversity of opinion about what eugenics stood for and what people hoped it would accomplish. Though patently convinced of some eugenic ideas, Salmon cautiously kept the movement at arm's length, whether embodied in the IRL or the AES—and all the more so after the war. Salmon was affected sharply by his war experience overseas, during which he organized neuropsychiatric units for the army and navy. In 1922, having left the NCMH and accepted a position as professor of psychiatry at Columbia University College of Physicians and Surgeons, his interests quickly shifted to medical education for psychiatrists.[89]

88. Irving Fisher to Adolf Meyer, 19 and 24 November 1923, with "Report of the Committee on Selective Immigration of the Eugenics Committee of the United States of America," and Meyer to Fisher, 22 November 1923, AMCMA, ser. II. Cited in Grob, *Mental Illness and American Society*, p. 171.

89. For Salmon's changing interests after the war, see Salmon to Walter B. James, 9 April 1919, and Frederick Tilney to Salmon, 5 April 1919, AFMH, Thomas Salmon Papers, box 2, folder 5. Further evidence that Salmon's interest in immigration might not have been as profound as it seemed was his presidential address to the APA in 1924. Though it was a potentially grand opportunity to broadcast his and psychiatry's achievements in eugenics and

As striking as Salmon's disengagement from the eugenics movement is the fact that the question of medical inspection of immigrants had a negligible impact on Johnson and his committee's deliberations. Despite Johnson's self-professed interest in the subject, the topic rarely arose in the hearings. A survey of witnesses reveals that no psychiatrists testified, either individually or as representatives of psychiatric organizations, with the one exception of Spencer L. Dawes, special commissioner of the Alien Insane in New York. Since the prewar years Dawes had been urging the federal government to assume financial responsibility for insane immigrants as a way of relieving New York State. On 6 February 1922 he appeared before Johnson's committee, but as he told the APA two years later, he had largely wasted his time. Like other public health officials, he was in a difficult position when he called for improvements to the medical inspection system. The more he highlighted the deficiencies of this system, the more he drew potentially critical attention to the performance and credentials of the inspection officers.[90]

According to Dawes, neither the 1924 act nor the 1917 and 1921 laws had solved the principal problems—especially in New York State. Since the quota bill of 1921 had been in effect, he contended, the number of deportable insane aliens in New York State institutions had actually risen. In addition, New York State was bristling over Washington's failure to honor a promise to reimburse the state almost $17 million for its proportional costs of housing the country's insane immigrants. New York State's leading public charity organization decided to form a special committee on immigration with Salmon as a member. Its report on the Johnson bill supported Governor Al Smith's efforts to get Washington to pay up. It also urged that Johnson include other provisions dealing with the regulation of mentally ill aliens, including the inspection of immigrants before embarkation. But Johnson ultimately ignored all but one of the committee's recommendations, leaving psychiatrists and state charity officials bitter and disappointed.[91]

---

immigration, Salmon said not a word about either subject. Thomas W. Salmon, "Presidential Address," *AJP* 4 (1924): 1–11.

90. *Hearings before the Committee on Immigration and Naturalization, House of Representatives, 6 February 1922,* 67th Cong., 2d sess., 1922, pp. 608–19. Dawes was reassured by Johnson that the topic of medical inspection had arisen "several times" during the hearings. As had been the case with the IRL, nativist restrictionists tended to exploit data supplied by New York State officials, not because they accepted their recommendations but because they felt that either a literacy test or a national origins law would eliminate the problem of mentally ill aliens.

91. Homer Folks to Everett Elwood, 11 March 1924; George A. Hastings to David A. Reed, 21 April 1924; C. Floyd Haviland to Hastings, 12 June 1924; and Spencer Dawes to Hastings, 20 June 1924, AFMH, Thomas Salmon Papers, box 4, folder 5. Referring to the Johnson

Even in the wake of the Johnson bill, "political pressure upon the department [of Labor] by Representatives and Senators and other influential political personages, mainly from the cities filled with the foreign born" continued to be a major problem, according to Dawes. Accusing Congress of "criminal negligence" at the 1924 APA annual meeting, he lamented that there were still too few medical inspectors at Ellis Island. He added that when immigrants were detained either for deportation or exclusion, politicians beholden to "the shipping rings" and "many so-called philanthropic societies" intervened to prevent the enforcement of the laws. In other words, the 1924 legislation had changed nothing much; "the quota [bill], a purely arbitrary arrangement for limiting the number of immigrants" fell far short, Dawes said, of what he had hoped Congress would do.[92]

Dawes's comments elicited similar ones from APA psychiatrists. Salmon agreed that the AMPA's efforts over the years to bring its concerns to the attention of presidents and congressional committees had had "very little effect, probably none at all." His complaint in 1924 was the same as it had been fifteeen years earlier: the advice of psychiatrists is "neither welcomed nor at any time employed." Some of the language employed by Dawes and his fellow APA psychiatrists sounded suspiciously like that of Johnson and the eugenicists; so much so, that one psychiatrist warned his colleagues: "If we join an unscientific clamour on behalf of so-called Nordic races we shall be ridiculed." But Dawes himself hastily stated, "It is not a question of the Nordic races. It is not a question of Italy or any other country. I think we should forget all that, because this is a country composed of all kinds of races." Psychiatrists may well have had little sympathy for the notion of America as the "melting pot of the world,"[93] but their alarm over immigration had long since emphasized the exclusion of insane individuals, not races or nationalities. They were also well aware that much of the national debate was monopolized by nativist bigots little interested in medical science. That psychiatrists were a disgruntled lot *after* 1924 confirms that their aims in lobbying for changes to immigration legislation were not synonymous with those of the IRL, AES, and Johnson's congressional allies.

---

bill's controversial national quotas, Salmon said they had "no particular bearing on the question of the alien insane." "Minutes: Meeting of Special Committee on Immigration Legislation as to the Alien Insane" and Salmon's "Proposed Report of the Sub-Committee on Alien Insane, 11 April 1924," ibid.

92. Spencer L. Dawes, "Immigration and the Problem of the Alien Insane," and "Discussion," *AJP* 4 (1925): 449–70; 449, 451.

93. Ibid., 455, 462, 465–66, 467, 469.

Thus in one important respect the attitudes of U.S. and Canadian psychiatrists were remarkably similar. Although circumstances differed somewhat, psychiatrists north and south of the forty-ninth parallel agreed that the real danger to both nations was the political forces that compromised the efficient operation of the law. Psychiatrists certainly must share some of the responsibility for creating a xenophobic cultural atmosphere during an age of mass immigration, although few Americans listened seriously and carefully to what psychiatrists were saying anyway. The only people willing to listen were nativist restrictionists, for whose ideas psychiatrists had limited sympathy. Therefore, though there was near unanimity among U.S. psychiatrists about immigration—indeed more agreement than on the issue of eugenic sterilization—psychiatrists were not the most powerful eugenic lobby, and their theories were not based chiefly on nativist, xenophobic considerations.[94] Clearly many of their eugenic reasons for opposing unrestricted immigration were intellectually flawed, but that did not make them unique. Nor should it lead historians to ignore fundamental distinctions when and where they existed. Most psychiatrists had little interest in quotas or other arbitrary devices for restricting immigration. What they sought was greater professional autonomy, augmented respect for medical opinions, improved working conditions and facilities, and reforms that dismantled legal obstacles to the deportation of dependent aliens. Psychiatrists' flirtation with eugenic immigration inspection demonstrated that within the fabric of eugenics there were several different strands and threads. Ultimately eugenics was imprecise enough to unite under its banner quite a diversity of opinions, creating a motley, loosely coordinated movement encompassing assorted goals and motives.

94. One historian has gone so far as to claim that "psychiatrists ranked among the moderate forces on restriction." See Sicherman, "Quest for Mental Health," p. 359.

CONCLUSION: REFLECTIONS ON
THE HISTORY OF EUGENICS

By the Second World War the eugenic impulse in U.S. and Canadian psychiatry was largely spent. As immigration gradually ceased to be contentious in the interwar period, psychiatrists' calls for tougher medical inspection of immigrants failed to find a receptive audience and quickly shrank to a whisper. By the time new controversies over immigration arose in the 1960s the old eugenic context had disappeared, replaced by a climate inhospitable to national-origin quotas, racial discrimination provisions, or alarmist predictions about the public health menace posed by newcomers.

The erosion of faith in eugenics also guaranteed that, though sterilization laws already on the books would continue to operate, they would do so haphazardly. In the post-1945 period there was virtually no chance of further asexualization legislation. Knowledge of Nazi atrocities reinforced the trend among social scientists to cease linking intelligence with race and to stress the influence of nurture and environment over nature, biology, heredity, and instinct.[1] But eugenics did not die out entirely.

---

1. See Carl N. Degler, *In Search of Human Nature: The Decline and Revival of Darwinism in American Social Thought* (New York: Oxford University Press, 1991), esp. pp. 59–211.

Numerous voluntary and involuntary sterilizations, eugenic or otherwise, continued to be performed off the record. Eugenicists, worried that revulsion at the barbarism of the Holocaust would discredit their own enterprise, frantically tried to cover the tracks that led back and forth between America and Nazi Europe. Their damage control fell short of success. Though public opinion has remained stubbornly sympathetic toward proposals for forcible sterilization of repeat offenders or long-term welfare beneficiaries, eugenics has had an exceedingly difficult time shaking the stigma of Hitlerian science.

That eugenics in Canada and the United States had a comparatively easier time of it before the Nazi era is thanks in no small measure to the efforts of G. Alder Blumer, C. K. Clarke, and other psychiatrists. Twentieth-century psychiatrists in both countries played a far from negligible role in the dissemination and popularization of eugenics. They not only participated in creating a moral and cultural climate that nurtured an interest in eugenics but pressured policy makers to introduce laws governing marriage, reproduction, immigration, and the custodial segregation of the mentally handicapped. These contributions came at a time when debates over eugenics at all levels of government were hotly contested and could have gone either way. Expert opinion was critical in these debates and deliberations. By endorsing eugenic ideas some psychiatrists conveyed the inaccurate impression that the study and practice of eugenics was based on sound scientific principles. The examples of Clarke, William Partlow, Clare Hincks, and Frederick Winslow Hatch show just how considerable psychiatrists' influence often was. Incontestably the history of eugenics would have been different without them.

Nonetheless, the nature of psychiatrists' thinking about eugenics was much more complex than this historical fact might suggest. Most psychiatrists subscribed to theories about eugenics that could be variously described as ambivalent, imprecise, inconsistent, or heterodox. They often recommended eugenic measures for noneugenic reasons. Some psychiatrists promoted sterilization and immigration restriction for reasons that had nothing to do with heredity, confirming that eugenics did not necessarily privilege solely genetic interpretations of human nature. They exploited the frequently sensationalist vocabulary of eugenics to convince legislators that public health reforms were long overdue. But with few exceptions, psychiatrists felt little intellectual loyalty to eugenics. The correspondence of pivotal figures such as Blumer, Clarke, Adolf Meyer, William White, and Thomas Salmon shows that their minds were only intermittently focused on strictly eugenic matters. Eugenics was simply not a central concern for most of them. Interest tended to be shallow, opportunistic, and sporadic, depending less on genuine conviction than on relevance to shifting professional circumstances—thus the sundry opinions among psychiatrists about what eugenics was, what it authorized, and what it stood for. Psychiatrists' eugenic views had just enough in common to help sustain a movement that surely needed elite sanction to survive. But it is no less true that their eugenic views lacked rigor and consensus.

These qualities of psychiatrists' thoughts about eugenics were shaped, as I have argued, by the circumstances of practicing mental medicine between the 1880s and the Second World War. Psychiatrists' real concerns were clinical, administrative, therapeutic, and occupational and hinged primarily on their troubled relations with the state as a source of funding, credentialing, resources, and policy. Most psychiatrists promoted reform of state and provincial systems of mental health care, especially institutional care of the mentally ill, only to discover that wider collaboration between psychiatry and government brought loss of independence and influence over state policy making. As state and provincial charity bureaucracies grew, psychiatrists found themselves accountable to cost-conscious officials who, frustrated over federal policy in important fields such as immigration, preached the need for deportation, literacy tests, and involuntary sterilization. Psychiatrists laboring in state hospitals had little choice but to tailor their ideas to those of more powerful civil servants and politicians, a sober reminder of the all-too-human propensity to follow intellectual fashion when it is in one's own interests to do so. It was no coincidence that once large numbers of psychiatrists were finally in a position to cut their ties to "the enduring asylum" after the Second World War their enthusiasm for eugenics swiftly evaporated.

The attraction of eugenics was not, however, restricted to psychiatrists mired in state and provincial hospitals for the mentally handicapped. The rhetoric and theory of eugenics had a two-dimensional appeal. Besides providing a reassuring explanation for the occupational difficulties faced by state hospital psychiatrists, it spoke convincingly to psychiatrists who longed to practice medicine outside the asylum, as the examples of Clarke, Hincks, and Salmon show. By stressing the importance of prevention and the need for refined medical diagnosis, eugenics was an excuse to desert the asylum as the primary locus of psychiatric practice. Eugenics encouraged psychiatrists—especially those of Hincks's and Salmon's generation—to promote the utility of their self-professed expertise in mental illness in the struggle to improve public mental health.

Psychiatrists' attitudes toward eugenics were also shaped by a subtle psychological sensitivity about their professional identity. Prolonged service in state and provincial hospitals was a dispiriting experience. Most of the nineteenth-century psychiatrists had thought of themselves as pious, humanitarian, and medically expert stewards of the insane, dispensing medicine and moral advice to the innocent victims of a cruel affliction within the walls of the asylum, the institution that symbolized the profession's social status and authority. Psychiatrists then watched with dismay as late nineteenth-century, encroaching state bureaucratization steadily whittled away at the already tenuous distinctions between the asylum and less reputable public institutions such as prisons and reformatories. State hospital psychiatrists worried they were in danger of becoming virtual prison wardens, responsible for the maintenance and rehabilitation of patients who were defined more often in terms of their dangerousness to society than their medical condition.

Blumer's transfer from state to private hospital psychiatry gave him the opportunity to recast his own professional identity in ways that married the most appealing elements of nineteenth-century asylum psychiatry and twentieth-century scientific medicine. In his new job as Butler Hospital's medical superintendent, he figuratively took both a step backward and a step forward: he rediscovered the pleasures and privileges of being a "gentleman" alienist while investing himself with the mantle of progressive clinical and laboratory medicine. What mattered most was his revived sense of professional self-esteem, which rested on his *image* as the confident embodiment of learned and charitable authority. As a colleague told him, by moving to Butler, Blumer rose "from a system of complicated estimates to a higher estimation of yourself."[2] To Blumer and other psychiatrists this change was synonymous with the resumption of genuine medicine. Mere liberation from the asylum was not enough. Others, like Clarke, realized that recapturing their original enthusiasm for psychiatry was not as simple as leaving a state or provincial asylum service. Clarke's bold battle to extend the scope of psychiatry beyond the walls of the asylum simply put him once again in confrontation with government. Blumer blazed a path that Clarke and other psychiatrists longed to follow, so the decline of his interest in eugenics after transferring to Providence speaks volumes about the emotional as well as intellectual reasons why psychiatrists were attracted to the eugenic message. In other words, it is impossible to account for psychiatrists' shifting views of eugenics without seeing them primarily as products of a critical transitional era in the history of mental medicine when psychiatrists'

2. Selden H. Talcott to Blumer, 8 July 1899, BP, box 29.

highly fragile professional identity was being buffeted by momentous trends in society, politics, and culture.[3]

Progressivism, one such trend, made it easier for psychiatrists to talk about leaving the asylum and joining the eugenic crusade to reduce the incidence of mental and physical diseases. Progressivism stressed the need for Americans to take back the nation from the corrupt, self-interested, and inefficient groups that purportedly dominated governments at all levels. Progressives believed that these groups had to be replaced by reliable and scientifically educated public servants who would then use their expertise and civic virtue to study, publicize, and solve social problems. The progressive goal was a reform movement designed to force governments to fulfil their duty to national welfare and security, and no issue loomed larger in the eyes of progressives than immigration. Psychiatrists such as Clarke and Salmon were committed to the progressive task of alerting federal government to the need to reform immigration laws. They and their peers who emphasized the "menace of the feebleminded" discovered that their views were all the more resonant in a political culture that authorized scientifically inspired state intervention as a solution to social problems.

By stressing that psychiatrists could be more useful, progressivism also guaranteed that in their capacity as stewards of the mentally ill they could hardly avoid the debates over eugenics. The mentally ill constituted the largest category of state dependants on public charity. Because of the widespread belief in the biomedical nature of mental illness and the prevailing view that preventive measures could make serious inroads into the incidence of disease, state and provincial hospital psychiatrists were catapulted into the ranks of the eugenics movement whether they wanted to be or not. Under fierce pressure from governments to be more utilitarian, accountable, and cost effective, psychiatrists leaned toward eugenic initiatives to signal their willingness to change, modernize, and streamline services. In eugenic immigration they discovered an issue of far-reaching fiscal importance: letting mentally ill aliens into the country simply ran up states' charity bills. To psychiatrists, sterilization programs and the medical inspection of immigrants seemed important and scientifically sensible pillars of social policy.

But progressivism was double edged. Just as a sense of frantic desper-

3. For an account of the way many of these same issues bore on the history of eighteenth-century German medicine, see Thomas Broman, "Rethinking Professionalization: Theory, Practice, and Professional Ideology in Eighteenth-Century German Medicine," *Journal of Modern History* 67 (1995): 835–72.

ation and pessimism lurked below its optimistic surface, so psychiatrists were drawn toward eugenics because of a deep-seated and gloomy frustration at the growing realization that their therapeutics were "a pile of rubbish," as one psychiatrist said in 1907.[4] Eugenics—like most aspects of public health—implicitly raised the prospect of remedial psychiatry's obsolescence. Thus psychiatrists could never be dogmatic converts to eugenics without eventually drawing attention to their inadequacies in the field of treatment. This intrinsically subversive element from the perspective of organized medicine, qualified psychiatric support for eugenics. Eugenic statements definitely served certain purposes within certain settings for certain constituencies, but they were bound to mean less and less to a medical specialty keen on proving its therapeutic competence and establishing its credentials as a legitimate branch of organized medicine. Once events in the 1940s conveyed the impression that psychiatrists had the therapeutic means to *cure* disease, eugenics lost its allure.

Thus, when it came to eugenics, psychiatrists were singularly conflicted. They could be found both among the worst of the eugenicists and the best of the anti-eugenicists. They must bear some blame and can take some credit. As a group they made up a fairly distinctive constituency whose relations with eugenicists from outside the profession were often uneasy. As the career of C. K. Clarke demonstrated, stresses and strains over eugenic issues within the profession bely any notion of a seamless organizational web of physicians, politicians, and bureaucrats united in a hegemonic effort to penalize immigrants and the handicapped.[5]

The significance of this conclusion lies in its congruence with what other historians of eugenics are saying. The more scholars explore the history of eugenics in different national, professional, and institutional settings, the more they learn that international eugenics resists any reductive explanation.[6] The standard political interpretation that eugenics

4. Charles G. Hill, "How Can We Best Advance the Study of Psychiatry?" *AJI* 64 (1907): 6.
5. For examples of this thesis, see Zlata Godler, "Doctors and the New Immigrants," *Canadian Ethnic Studies* 9 (1977): 6–17; and Angus McLaren, *Our Own Master Race: Eugenics in Canada, 1885–1945* (Toronto: McClelland and Stewart, 1990), esp. pp. 66–67.
6. Robert A. Nye, "The Rise and Fall of the Eugenics Empire: Recent Perspectives on the Impact of Biomedical Thought in Modern Society," *Historical Journal* 36 (1993): 687–700; Mark B. Adams, "Eugenics in the History of Science" and "Toward a Comparative History of Eugenics," in *The Wellborn Science: Eugenics in Germany, France, Brazil, and Russia*, ed. Mark B. Adams (New York: Oxford University Press, 1990), pp. 3–7, 217–31.

was a ruling-class, reactionary, or conservative phenomenon is no longer tenable.[7] National comparisons like mine indicate that eugenics both respected and crossed national borders, taking various shapes. It followed no particular ideological blueprint. It meant different things to different people in different settings. Racial, gender, and class prejudices were rarely absent, but eugenics was—and is—far more complex than simply a pseudoscientific excuse for indulging these biases. Historically it was a theory whose many elements crystallized into a volatile intellectual compound that united constituencies with often dramatically dissimilar agendas and interests. Its inclusive and pluralist resonance perhaps stands out most graphically in light of the considerable eugenicism of early twentieth-century women's groups, especially in Canada, many of which currently are considered protofeminist. That eugenics may even have enjoyed an authentically populist backing in some countries undermines the customary notion that it was a pet theory of the elite, knowledge-broking professions. No less intriguing is the possibility that eugenics thrived notably in countries like Canada and Germany with significant statist medical traditions. Essentialist interpretations of eugenics only obscure the complexity and colorful variety that characterized the international eugenics movement.[8]

It is hardly surprising that a "new eugenics" should enjoy some popularity in the wake of current changes in attitudes toward human nature as well as stunning new developments in reproductive technology. Beginning in the 1960s scholars began to reexamine what passed for received wisdom in the social sciences, looking once more to biology to

7. As Sheila Weiss has shrewdly noted, if anything united German race hygienists (eugenicists) of different political persuasions it was their antipathy toward what they thought were the dysgenic consequences of corporate capitalism. Sheila Faith Weiss, "The Race Hygiene Movement in Germany, 1904–1945," in Adams, *Wellborn Science*, pp. 9–10. This observation also applies to U.S.-Canadian eugenicists.

8. Richard Cleminson, "Eugenics by Name or Nature? The Spanish Anarchist Sex Reform of the 1930s," *History of European Ideas* 18 (1994): 729–40. For an account that disputes distinctions between German racist and non-racist eugenics, see Robert Proctor, *Racial Hygiene: Medicine under the Nazis* (Cambridge: Harvard University Press, 1988), pp. 20–30. For other scholars who have challenged the theory that eugenics was the exclusive property of a reactionary and racist political Right, see Loren R. Graham, "Science and Values: The Eugenics Movement in Germany and Russia in the 1920s," *American Historical Review* 82 (1977): 1133–64; Diane Paul, "Eugenics and the Left," *Journal of the History of Ideas* 45 (1984): 567–90; Paul Weindling, *Health, Race, and German Politics Between National Unification and Nazism, 1870–1945* (Cambridge: Cambridge University Press, 1989); and Weiss, "Race Hygiene Movement in Germany," pp. 8–68. See also the chapters by Mark Adams, William Schneider, and Nancy Leys Stepan in Adams, *Wellborn Science*.

explain human nature.[9] Some observers see this as a felicitous development; others have their doubts. Disturbing trends in public opinion suggest that opposition to involuntary sterilization is not as strong as many
would believe. The popularity of tubal ligation and vasectomy as family
planning alternatives probably has undermined resistance to the notion
of mandatory asexualization.[10] As Daniel Kevles and others have warned,
the futile struggles of experts today to resolve the thorny ethical and
moral problems raised by genetic science and reproductive engineering
are not promising signs for the future.[11] The popularity of a book such
as *The Bell Curve* may likewise signal a revival of eugenics and scientifically authorized racial prejudice. And some of what is being said about
immigration has a familiar, progressive-era ring to it.[12]

Yet it remains to be seen whether these phenomena will ever resus-
citate a public toleration of eugenics like that of the early twentieth century. Unquestionably, by highlighting the disturbing ties between
eugenics and Third Reich atrocities scholars have helped to stimulate
debate about medical ethics and morality. The theory that eugenics is
the exclusive intellectual property of rabid Nazis may, however, cloud
rather than clarify the issues and the terms of reference ruling current
discussions of eugenics.[13] Numerous constituencies today demonstrate a
commendable vigilance about eugenics and its policy implications, and
there has been a diffuse collapse of confidence in traditional statist, tech-
nocratic approaches to the problems of education, welfare, and health
care. A return to the managerial, coercive, and discriminatory eugenic
laws of the early 1900s would encounter fierce opposition. If there is in
fact a "return of eugenics" it will probably be because of the critical
inability of the American public to see the authentic similarities between
the discourse of early twentieth-century eugenicists and that of contem-

9. Degler, *In Search of Human Nature*, esp. pp. 216, 329.
10. Philip R. Reilly, *The Surgical Solution: A History of Involuntary Sterilization in the United
States* (Baltimore: Johns Hopkins University Press, 1991), pp. 148–65.
11. Daniel J. Kevles, *In the Name of Eugenics: Genetics and the Uses of Human Heredity* (New
York: Knopf, 1985), esp. pp. 291–301.
12. See, e.g., Ben J. Wattenberg and Karl Zinsmeister, "The Case for More Immigration,"
Commentary, April 1990, pp. 19–25. "It is clear enough," the authors write, "that recent
policies have not always produced the optimal immigrant stream. Deportation of undesirable
individuals could be greatly speeded, and careful selection of future citizens is well within
national prerogatives. American immigration, after all, is one of the world's great buyer's
markets—many fine candidates are lined up for each spot—and we need only specify more
carefully what we are looking for" (p. 23). See also Michael Lind, "Huddled Excesses," *New
Republic*, 1 April 1996, p. 6.
13. Weiss, "Race Hygiene Movement in Germany," p. 9.

porary medical ethicists grappling with the questions raised by euthanasia, fetal tissue research, and artificial insemination. The taste for the eugenic policies of an earlier time may have diminished, but the core spirit of eugenics is hardly crushed. Even among those who warn that eugenics is a dangerous weapon in the hands of powerful ruling groups there is a worrisome, neoprogressive faith in collectivist solutions to intimate moral problems, as well as the belief, shared with eugenicists, that human nature can be changed through social engineering. This faith helped to mobilize consent for eugenics in the first place. Were the new eugenics to become the old eugenics, it would be a sad commentary on the way ideology has eclipsed historical understanding and overshadowed moral common sense as the twentieth century draws to a close.

INDEX

London, Jack, 74
Longue Pointe (Quebec) asylum, 15
Lunbeck, Elizabeth, 57

MacDonald, Carlos, 39, 45–47, 51–54, 56,
    104–5, 211
Macklin, Madge Thurlow, 183
MacMurchy, Helen, ix, 135, 137, 162–67,
    169
  and sterilization, 164–65
malarial shock therapy, 22
Mann, Horace, 5
marriage laws:
  in the United States, 75–76, 100
  See also eugenics; immigration;
    sterilization laws
Maudsley, Henry, 81–83, 86, 88, 94, 176
McGhie, B. T., 188
McGovern, Francis E., 126
McLaren, Angus, 188
medicine, U.S., in the nineteenth
    century, 4–5, 7
mental hospitals:
  Canadian origins of, 14–17
  U.S. origins of, 5–7
Metcalf, William, 25–26, 27
Meyer, Adolf, 2, 53, 64–65, 105, 110, 233
  and eugenics, 113–14, 131, 227–28
Meyers, D. Campbell, 159–60
Meyerson, Abraham, 114
  and eugenics, 114–15, 131, 188
Mitchell, C. D., 129–30
Mitchell, S. Weir, 27
Montreal Medico–Chirurgical Society, 15
moral treatment, 6–7
Morel, Bénédict–Augustin, 72–73, 82
Morris, Frank, 74
Morton, Levi, 47
Murray, Charles, viii

National Association of Manufacturers, 208
National Committee for Mental Hygiene,
    19, 112, 134, 169, 170, 199, 228
  and eugenics, 127–29
  and immigration, 216, 221
National Conference of Charities and
    Corrections, 44
Neurasthenia, 62–63
neurology, 10–13
New Deal, x, 130
New Westminster (British Columbia)
    asylum, 143
New York State asylum for incurables
    (Willard), 40
New York State Board of Alienists, 213
New York State Board of Charities, 13

New York State Care Act of 1890, 39–40
New York State Charities Aid Association,
    55
New York State Commission in Lunacy,
    13, 38–39, 41–42, 44–49, 192, 217
New York State mental health care:
  history of, 37–49
  and women physicians, 42–43
New York State Pathological Institute, 51–
    54, 106
Nordau, Max, 74

Ochsner, A. J., 77
Odell, Benjamin, 55–56
Ontario, history of mental health care in,
    16–19
Ontario Conservative Party, 30
Ontario Liberal Party, 17
Ontario Medical Act, 186
Ontario Medical Association, 186
Ontario Provincial Board of Health, 136,
    145
Osler, William, 184

Packard, Elizabeth, 10
Pagé, J. D., 156
Partlow, William, ix,
  and eugenics, 117–19, 121, 233
Paton, Stewart, 128, 222–23, 227–28
Pearson, Karl, xi, 78
Pennsylvania Hospital for the Insane, 4
Pilcher, Hoyt, 76–77
Pinel, Philippe, 6
Potts, Charles, 211
Pratt, Foster, 195
Progressivism, x, 236
  and eugenics, 124–31
  in New York State, 37–38
  and U.S. immigration, 197–98, 202–3,
    205
Provincial Association for the Care of the
    Feeble–Minded, 166–67
psychasthenia, 64–65
psychiatry:
  attacks on, 10–13
  in Ontario, 25
  and World War I, 111–13, 191–92
psychosurgery, 22
public health, in Canada, 134–36
Public Health Service (U.S.), 201–2, 205

Ray, Isaac, 50
Reeves, Henry, 39
Régis, Emmanuel, 64
Reilly, Philip, 78